INTERPERSONAL RELATIONSHIPS IN EDUCATION

ADVANCES IN LEARNING ENVIRONMENTS RESEARCH
Volume 3

Series Editors

Barry J. Fraser
Curtin University of Technology

Jeffrey P. Dorman
Australian Catholic University

Editorial Board

Perry den Brok, *Eindoven University of Technology, The Netherlands*
Shwu-yong Huang, *National Taiwan University, Taiwan*
Bruce Johnson, *University of Arizona, USA*
Celia Johnson, *Bradley University, USA*
Rosalyn Anstine Templeton, *Marshall University, USA*
Bruce Waldrip, *University of Southern Queensland, Australia*

Scope

The historical beginnings of the field of learning environments go back approximately 40 years. A milestone in the development of this field was the establishment in 1984 of the American Educational Research Association (AERA) Special Interest Group (SIG) on Learning Environments, which continues to thrive today as one of AERA's most international and successful SIGs. A second milestone in the learning environments field was the birth in 1998 of *Learning Environments Research: An International Journal* (LER), which fills an important and unique niche.

The next logical step in the evolution of the field of learning environments is the initiation of this book series, *Advances in Learning Environments Research,* to complement the work of the AERA SIG and LER. This book series provides a forum for the publication of book-length manuscripts that enable topics to be covered at a depth and breadth not permitted within the scope of either a conference paper or a journal article.

The *Advances in Learning Environments Research* series is intended to be broad, covering either authored books or edited volumes, and either original research reports or reviews of bodies of past research. A diversity of theoretical frameworks and research methods, including use of multimethods, is encouraged. In addition to school and university learning environments, the scope of this book series encompasses lifelong learning environments, information technology learning environments, and various out-of-school 'informal' learning environments (museums, environmental centres, etc.).

Interpersonal Relationships in Education
An Overview of Contemporary Research

Edited by

Theo Wubbels
Utrecht University, The Netherlands

Perry den Brok
Eindhoven University of Technology, The Netherlands

Jan van Tartwijk
Utrecht University, The Netherlands

and

Jack Levy
University of Massachusetts, USA

SENSE PUBLISHERS
ROTTERDAM / BOSTON / TAIPEI

A C.I.P. record for this book is available from the Library of Congress.

ISBN 978-94-6091-937-4 (paperback)
ISBN 978-94-6091-938-1 (hardback)
ISBN 978-94-6091-939-8 (e-book)

Published by: Sense Publishers,
P.O. Box 21858, 3001 AW Rotterdam, The Netherlands
https://www.sensepublishers.com/

Printed on acid-free paper

TABLE OF CONTENTS

TEACHER ORIENTED

ACKNOWLEDGEMENTS

We would like to thank the following persons for reviewing draft versions of the contributions to this book:

Roel Bosker, University of Groningen, The Netherlands
Mieke Brekelmans, Utrecht University, The Netherlands
Darrell Fisher, Curtin University, Perth, Australia
Jerome Freiberg, University of Houston, United States
Helma Koomen, University of Amsterdam, The Netherlands
Leonidas Kyriakides, University of Cyprus, Cyprus
Paulien Meijer, Utrecht University, The Netherlands
Marie-Christine Opdenakker, University of Groningen, The Netherlands

The production of the book would not have been possible without the careful copy editing and organization of the final publishing by Madelon Pieper.

THEO WUBBELS, PERRY DEN BROK,
JAN VAN TARTWIJK AND JACK LEVY

1. INTRODUCTION TO: INTERPERSONAL RELATIONSHIPS IN EDUCATION

CONTENTS OF THE BOOK

This book is the third volume in a series reporting on advances in learning environments research. While the first two volumes dealt with 'outcomes-focused learning environments and its determinants and effects' (Aldridge & Fraser, 2008) and 'applications of Rasch measurement in learning environments research' (Cavanagh & Waugh, 2011), the present volume entirely focuses on the interpersonal aspect of the learning environment.

In 2010 on April 28-29, over 90 researchers and teacher educators from more than ten countries gathered in Boulder, Colorado, for the first *International Conference on Interpersonal Relationships in Education: ICIRE 2010*. Through keynote addresses by Jerome Freiberg (University of Houston), Kathryn Wentzel (University of Maryland at College Park), Walter Doyle (University of Arizona) and Theo Wubbels (Utrecht University), two roundtable, two poster, and six paper sessions, the participants exchanged research results and discussed the conference theme.

The invitation for the conference described the theme as follows:

Clearly, a positive teacher-student relationship strongly contributes to student learning. Educators, parents and students understand that problematic relationships can be detrimental to student outcomes and development. Productive learning environments are characterized by supportive and warm interactions throughout the class: teacher-student and student-student. Similarly, teacher learning thrives when principals facilitate accommodating and safe school cultures. A variety of research perspectives help explain how these constructive learning environment relationships can be developed and sustained. Contributions have come from educational and social psychology, teacher and school effectiveness research, and communication and language studies, among other fields. Recently, developments such as dynamic system theories have added often-spectacular directions to the topic. While the importance of interpersonal relationships in education has been appreciated for decades, research in this field is still young, with an increasing number of studies appearing in journals and books. Therefore, it is an appropriate time to celebrate, evaluate and advance these efforts through a conference that focuses on the state of the field and avenues for future research.

The *ICIRE 2010* participants approached the conference theme from several different perspectives. This book includes a number of the conference presentations that demonstrate the breadth and depth of the contributions. The chapters are organized in three sections:

1. Those that primarily focus on individual students and how peers or teachers treat them;
2. Those in which relationships at the school level are central; and
3. Those that focus on the role of the teacher. Most of these chapters are based on teachers' or students' perceptions of teacher actions or teacher-students' relationships in class.

The first section begins with the keynote presentation by Kathryn Wentzel. The chapter focuses on student motivation and engagement for learning, with the teacher-student relationship as its precursor. Wentzel integrates many different theoretical perspectives and provides examples from empirical studies of adolescents' relationships with their teachers. The chapters by Spilt and Koomen, and Roorda, Koomen and Oort are closely connected. Both report on observational studies of interactions between kindergarten teachers and their students. Spilt and Koomen investigated teacher perceptions of teacher-student relationships, observed interactions for disruptive children and analyzed associations between the two. Roorda, Koomen and Oort, discuss whether observed interactions between teacher and children can be predicted from teachers' perceptions of the relationship. Finally, McGee reports on a study of teacher perceptions of bullying in elementary schools. As frequently noted, a teacher's role in and reaction to bullying has important implications for her/his relationship with students, especially at the primary level.

The second section examines relations at the school level, mostly among teachers and between teachers and principals. The chapter by Moolenaar, Daly and Sleegers examines relationships among teachers and how the interconnected patterns of associations affect school resource allocation. Price reports on a study on the relationships of principals and teachers and how positive attitudes can upgrade school climate. The next chapter by Georgiou and Kyriakides could have been placed in either the second or third sections, since it examines the impact of principal-teacher relationships as well as teacher-students relationships on student outcomes.

As noted, the last section of the book focuses primarily on teachers and their role in providing learning opportunities for students. Most of the chapters approach this theme by investigating teachers' or students' perceptions of teacher actions or teacher-students' relationships. The section opens with a chapter by Doyle and Rosemartin, based on Walter Doyle's keynote address. The authors analyze how curriculum influences instructional strategies in the context of teacher-student interpersonal relationships. They begin with the longstanding observation that many curriculum innovations are not implemented in the classroom, an occurrence that highlights the essential role of the teacher. The next chapter, by Riley, Watt, Richardson and De Alwis, explores relationships between beginning teacher background variables such as unconscious motives, self-efficacy, role stress and teachers' burnout and their self reported use of aggressive techniques to cope with student disruptive behaviour. The section continues with a study by Fricke, Van Ackeren, Kauertz and Fisher on students' perceptions of their teachers' classroom management strategies. They investigate the relationship between K-12 students' perceptions and their interest and achievement in physics. The last three chapters focus on the use of the Questionnaire on Teacher Interaction (QTI) for measuring teacher-students' relationships. The QTI has served as a valid measure of teacher-student relationships for over two decades, and has been effectively utilized in over 20 countries. Telli and Den Brok report on the adaptation of the questionnaire to the Turkish language and context. The authors adapted the instrument across a wide student age range - from primary to higher education. Next, Maulana, Opdenakker, Den Brok and Bosker describe how the QTI was used to investigate the development of the teacher-student relationship in students' first year of secondary education. Examination of this context is particularly important since the transition from primary to secondary school can significantly affect students' perceptions of the learning environment. The final chapter by Wubbels, Brekelmans, Den Brok, Levy, Mainhard and Van Tartwijk, focuses on the theory, assumptions and conceptualization behind the original version of the Model for Interpersonal Teacher Behaviour and the QTI. After reflecting on some problematic issues of previous work, the authors analyze research on moment-to-moment interactions and teacher-students' relationships. They conclude with an outline of future developments in the field.

THEORETICAL PERSPECTIVES

As mentioned, this book reflects the many theoretical perspectives that have informed the study of interpersonal relationships in education. They include a developmental psychological view featuring (among others) models of attachment, as well as a perspective from general interpersonal theory and explanations from dynamic systems, social networks, school effectiveness, school and class climate, and class management. These conceptual frameworks are briefly described below.

Developmental Psychological Theory

In the opening chapter, Wentzel views the affective quality of teacher-student relationships as the central and critical motivator of student adjustment (Pianta, Hamre, & Stuhlman, 2003). The developmental psychological perspective is also presented in chapters by Roorda et al., Spilt and Koomen and McGee. As Wentzel notes, models that guide the study of child and adolescent development are derived from analyses of parent-child relationships that are thought to be experienced through the lens of mental representations developed over time with respect to specific experiences (Bowlby, 1969; Laible & Thompson, 2007). Early representations of relationships with caregivers theoretically provide the foundation for interactions with people outside the family context, with the quality of parent-child relationships (i.e., levels of warmth and security) often predicting the quality of subsequent peer and teacher associations in early and middle childhood (Wentzel & Looney, 2007). The basic tenets of attachment theory (Bowlby, 1969; Bretherton, 1987) reflect this notion.

Other perspectives that have contributed to this literature describe teacher-student relationships along specific dimensions and provisions, as specified by models of parent-child interactions (e.g., Baumrind, 1971). In greater detail Wentzel (2004) described how teacher-student interactions along these dimensions can promote student motivation and subsequent performance. Derived from theoretical perspectives on person-environment fit and personal goal setting (e.g., Bronfenbrenner, 1989; Eccles & Midgley, 1989), she argues that school-related competence is achieved to the extent that students are able to accomplish goals that have personal as well as social value, in a manner that supports continued psychological and emotional well-being (Wentzel, this volume).

Interpersonal Theory

The research reported in several chapters (Roorda et al., Georgiou and Kyriakides, Telli and Den Brok, Maulana et al., Wubbels et al.) is founded on general interpersonal theory, often embedded in a systems approach to communication (Watzlawick, Beavin, & Jackson, 1967). Interpersonal theory originally offered a conceptual framework to describe and predict dyadic interactions between individuals (Kiesler, 1996; Sadler & Woody, 2003). The chapters cited above extend this model to teacher-class relationships. According to interpersonal theory (Leary, 1957), interactions can be described according to two dimensions: Control and Affiliation (see the Wubbels et al. chapter for a discussion of these terms). Control represents the degree of influence that one person applies to the partner in the interaction, with dominance at one end of the dimension and submissiveness at the other. Affiliation describes the degree of emotional immediacy, warmth, and support in the interaction, and ranges from friendliness to hostility (Gurtman, 2001; Kiesler, 1996). These dimensions are considered to be orthogonal (Sadler & Woody, 2003).

Roorda et al. (this volume) state that a central concept in interpersonal theory is the complementarity principle (Carson, 1969; Kiesler, 1983). Complementarity can be used to predict people's reactions to the behaviours of their partner in the communication. For the Affiliation dimension complementary behaviours would include reactions that are similar – friendly behaviour is answered with friendly behaviour, anger with anger. The opposite would be expected on the Control dimension – dominance might be met with submissiveness or vice-versa. For example, a person might be talking (high Control), while the companion responds by listening (low Control; Dryer & Horowitz, 1997; Sadler & Woody, 2003; Tracey, 1994; 2004; Wubbels et al., this volume). While complementarity is theorized to be the most probabilistic pattern, it is quite possible for partners to respond in a variety of ways (Estroff & Nowicki, 1992; Tiedens & Jimenez, 2003; Tracey, 2005).

Dynamic Systems Theory

A recent theoretical framework known as Dynamic Systems Theory, is employed in the work of Wubbels et al. (this volume), among others. Teacher-students' relationships can be understood in terms of the general interpretations that students and teachers attach to their interactions with each other. However, the exact moment-to-moment, individual interpretations that together produce generalized meaning remain unknown. Dynamic Systems Theory (e.g., Thelen & Smith, 1994) can help analyze the relationship between these levels by connecting two separate time scales: a micro-social or moment-to-moment scale (i.e., teacher-students interaction) and a macro-social or outcome scale (i.e., the teacher-students' relationship). The theory aims to understand the changing patterns of moment-to-moment interactions in relation to changes in outcome patterns. For example, Bronfenbrenner and Morris's (1998) bio-ecological theory posits that the micro-social scale is the primary engine of development and outcomes (e.g., teacher-students' relationships). Thus, these individual interactions may be regarded as the building blocks of patterns of interaction within a social system (Hollenstein, 2007). Self-stabilizing feedback, such as the self-fulfilling prophecy, is the mechanism by which moment-to-moment processes determine macro-level outcomes. In turn, macro-level factors can respond to and restrict moment-to-moment interactions, thus serving both as outcomes (of previous processes) and as constraints (for subsequent processes). In terms of dynamic systems theory, the challenge for future research is to learn which type of moment-to-moment interactions lead to profitable teacher-students relationships.

Linked to both the developmental psychological perspective and dynamic systems theory, the Developmental Systems Model of Teacher-Child Relationships (Pianta, Hamré, & Stuhlman, 2003) attempts to describe the teacher's observable interactive behaviour. It supports the research featured in the Roorda et al., and Spilt and Koomen chapters. This perspective considers interactive behaviours as one of the key components of affective relationships between teachers and children (Roorda et al., this volume). It consists of four relationship components: features of individuals (developmental history and biological factors), representational models of teacher and child (perceptions and emotions), information exchange processes (interactive behaviours), and external influences. These factors influence each other in dynamic, reciprocal ways.

Social Network Theory

Social network theory highlights the manner in which the underlying patterns of relationships among teachers shape professional communities and affect educational improvement (Moolenaar et al., this volume). The chapters by Moolenaar et al. and Price feature this concept. In educational research social network theory and analysis help explain how relationships among teachers in social networks can support or constrain their learning, instructional practice, and approach to change (Daly & Finnigan, 2010; McCormick, Fox, Carmichael, & Procter, 2010; Moolenaar, 2010). Social network theory builds on the notion that social resources such as information, knowledge, and expertise are exchanged through informal networks of actors in a system. Social network theory focuses on both the individual actors and the social relationships connecting them (Wasserman & Galaskiewicz, 1994), and several network features and mechanisms highlight a distinctive facet of the interaction between individuals. Together these offer a nuanced understanding of social structure as they explain the flow of resources among individuals and its implications for individual behaviour, opinions, and preferences (Moolenaar et al., this volume). For example, these networks can facilitate or inhibit access to social capital (Lin, 2001). Network visualizations and characteristics such as density and centrality aid scholars in illuminating how social networks in schools are shaped and changed to achieve individual and organizational goals. As a result, applying social network theory to the study of teachers' interpersonal relationships makes the social fabric of schools and their influence more tangible (Moolenaar et al., this volume).

Price (this volume) proposes faculty networks as the central mechanisms that bind schools together in terms of structure and organizational culture (Bidwell & Yasumoto, 1999; Meyer & Rowan 1977; Ogawa & Bossert, 1995). Through relationships, principals and teachers develop and evolve a school culture out of relational trust, shared values and norms, diffuse work roles, and common experiences (Bryk & Driscoll, 1988; Bryk et al., 2010). Thus, the network's membership produces a structural interdependence that has attitudinal ripple effects throughout the building (Price, this volume). For example, principals' interactions with their staff are found to be central variables associated with these outcomes (Hoy & Henderson, 1983; Leithwood & Jantzi, 1990; Ogawa & Bossert, 1995).

School Effectiveness Theory and School and Class Climate

The chapters by Price, and Georgiou and Kyriakides (among others) are rooted in the school effectiveness tradition. Creemers and Kyriakides (2008) developed a dynamic model of educational effectiveness. This perspective defines the dynamic relations between the multiple factors associated with teacher effectiveness. It includes eight factors describing teachers' instructional role that are associated with student outcomes: *orientation, structuring, questioning, teaching-modelling, applications, management of time, teacher role in making the classroom a learning environment, and classroom assessment* (Georgiou and Kyriakides, this volume). Due to their influence on classroom-environment and teaching practice, school-level factors are expected to have both direct and indirect effects on student achievement, though an indirect impact is in greater evidence. Educational effectiveness research has shown that aspects at the classroom level have a more significant relationship with educational outcomes than those at the school level (e.g., Kyriakides, Creemers, Antoniou, & Demetriou, 2000; Teddlie & Reynolds, 2000).

Closely connected to school effectiveness theory are the school and class climate and environment conceptualizations included in the Price, Georgiou and Kyriakides, and Wubbels et al. chapters. These models originated in early teacher effectiveness studies and research on the interaction between people and their environment (Moos, 1979; Walberg, 1979). Over the past thirty years, classroom environment research has shown the quality of the classroom environment in schools to be a significant determinant of student learning (Dorman, 2003; Fraser, 1994). School effectiveness and climate research solidly identified the variables associated with successful schools: shared values and norms, openness of governance, and trusting relationships (Price, this volume).

Classroom Management Theories

Theories on classroom management are discussed in the Wentzel, Doyle and Rosemartin, Fricke et al., Riley at al., and Wubbels et al. chapters. They present a wide variety of views on the nature of classroom management, including a range of effectiveness aspects (Fricke et al., this volume). Anderson, Evertson, and Emmer (1980) contend that classroom management is too complex a construct to account adequately for all dimensions. Duke (1979, p. xii) describes classroom management as the "provisions and procedures necessary to establish and maintain an environment in which instruction and learning can occur". Doyle (1986) focuses on the guidance of student behaviour: "Classroom management refers to the actions and strategies teachers use to solve the problem of order in classrooms" (Doyle, 1986, p. 397). According to Fricke et al. (this volume) the efficient management of a class includes reactive, preventive and proactive elements (Helmke, 2009). Based on these parameters, they identify discipline, rule clarity, and prevention of disruptions as the three main constructs of classroom management.

The ecological approach to classroom management originated from the seminal work of Gump (1969), Kounin (1970) and Doyle (2006) and emphasizes how to create a classroom ecology that invites student cooperation rather than disruption. Doyle and Rosemart (in this volume) argue that classrooms are multidimensional activity settings or ecologies in which teachers must establish, orchestrate, and sustain events that elicit student collaboration over long periods of time and across challenging daily, weekly, monthly, and seasonal variations. These events are jointly constituted by a teacher and her or his students and contain, at their core, action vectors that draw participants to learning and maintain order. Seatwork, for example, is a familiar event in which students typically work individually on well-structured assignments or worksheets that sustain their involvement. A class discussion, on the other hand, is a more complex action system involving bidding for turns, multiple speakers whose contributions may or may not address the central topic, and unpredictable sequences and directions (Doyle & Rosemartin, this volume). We also know that the ability and willingness of students to engage in classroom tasks affects classroom stability. "When familiar work is being done, the flow of classroom activity is typically quite smooth and well ordered. Tasks are initiated easily and quickly, work involvement and productivity are typically high, and most students are able to complete tasks successfully" (Doyle, 1988, p. 174).

Classroom management can be seen from the perspective of individual students or from the class as an entity (Fricke et al., this volume). From the student's standpoint it specifies expectations, clarifies duties, and establishes possibilities in a specific situation. Fricke et al. (this volume) state that at the class level management is aimed at giving all students the boundary conditions for learning-oriented interaction. This is a necessary prerequisite for ensuring time-on-task, which is again closely related to students' knowledge gains. Also, according to theories about the development of interest, learning-related interactions and the individually-perceived quality of classroom management can evoke and foster topic-related interest.

When, however, students misbehave, teachers have a responsibility to manage the situations as they arise and employ strategies to reduce disruptions over time. In doing so they must manage their own emotional reactions to students, which in turn affects their own classroom behaviour (Riley et al., this volume). Student misbehaviour may provoke an aggressive teacher response (Sava, 2002) that can take many forms, from overt acts such as yelling, to more subtle, even covert behaviours, such as not rewarding or acknowledging students' pro-social behaviours. Three types of aggressive conduct are distinguished: deliberately embarrassing students, using sarcasm to discredit, and yelling angrily (Riley et al., this volume).

INSTRUMENTS

Given the breadth of theoretical perspectives it is no surprise that a number of instruments have been employed to investigate the various interactions and relationships discussed in these chapters. The tools range from questionnaires that have been specifically developed to measure relationships or interactions, to excerpts or results from existing broader instruments with the same purpose. Although the use of existing instruments limits the number and type of variables that can be investigated, it presents a clear resource advantage to developing new measures since data can be collected or reused more efficiently. As noted, a number of our authors (Price, Wentzel, and Spilt & Koomen) utilized this approach. The following is a brief discussion of instruments that were specifically developed to measure teacher-student relationships and interactions.

Student-Teacher Relationship Scale

Roorda et al., and Spilt and Koomen employed the Student-Teacher Relationship Scale (STRS; Pianta, 2001), which was derived from the Developmental Systems Model. The STRS measures teacher perceptions of her/his relationship with a child and includes three dimensions: closeness, conflict, and dependency. Closeness measures the degree of affection, warmth, and open communication in the teacher-child relationship. Conflict describes the extent of negativity, anger, and discordance. Dependency refers to the degree of clinginess, overreliance, and possessiveness of the child in the relationship.

Questionnaire on Teacher Interaction (QTI)

Several chapters (Georgiou & Kyriakides, Telli & Den Brok, Maulana et al.) utilized the Questionnaire on Teacher Interaction (QTI), which is based on Interpersonal Theory (Wubbels et al., this volume). The QTI measures the perceptions of teachers and students of teacher-students relationships according to a two-dimensional model first described by Leary. In addition to the two dimensions – Control and Affiliation – the instrument assesses the following eight teacher behaviour types based on dimensional ratings: Steering, Friendly, Understanding, Accommodating, Uncertain, Dissatisfied, Reprimanding, and Enforcing. The QTI items are divided into eight scales that correspond to the eight behaviour types. (Wubbels et al., 1985; 2006). Also in this volume, Georgiou and Kyriakides describe the use of a similar instrument – the Questionnaire on Principal Interaction (Kremer-Hayon & Wubbels, 1993) – to assess relationships between principals and teachers.

Students' Perceptions of Classroom Management

The Students' Perceptions of Their Teacher's Classroom Management (SPCM) by Fricke et al. is a newly developed instrument reported in this volume. It consists of three scales, with five or six items in each: (1) discipline (how disruptive perceive the students their lessons and how often has the teacher to remind students to work quietly), (2) rule clarity (did the teacher set up a system of rules and rituals, and know, understand, and adhere students to these), and (3) prevention of disruptions (is the teacher "omnipresent" and is he or she able to notice and prevent disruptive behaviour, even when being busy with individual students).

Observational Measures

In studies reported in two chapters – Mainhard, Brekelmans and Wubbels (2011, reported in the Wubbels et al. chapter) and Roorda et al. – similar observational measures were utilized that are based on Interpersonal Theory. Roorda et al. analyzed videotaped teacher behaviours towards a child by having them rated independently by different groups of observers. They viewed five-second episodes, using two six-point scales for Teacher Affiliation and Teacher Control (Thijs, Koomen, Roorda, & Ten Hagen, 2011). Teacher Affiliation ranged from *very low* (1) "is repulsive, morose, or unfriendly to the child" to *very high* (6) "is strongly positive, clearly supportive, companionable, or warm, both verbally and nonverbally". Teacher Control varied from *very low* (1) "shows a passive attitude towards the child, and does not try to influence his/her behaviour at all" to *very high* (6) "tries to have a strong influence on the child, has (or takes) complete control over the situation without acknowledging and permitting any independent contribution from the child".

The Mainhard et al. (2011) study coded teacher behaviour in a similar manner and also rated class behaviour in real-time following an event-sampling procedure. They employed five-point scales that extended from dependent to independent (Control) and hostile to friendly (Affiliation) for both teacher and class.

CONCLUSION

As can be seen, combining and integrating various theoretical perspectives greatly enriches the study of interpersonal relationships in education. The combination of developmental and interpersonal models in the Roorda et al. chapter is a good example. By developing an observational measure based on interpersonal theory and combining it with a developmental systems instrument that assessed teacher-student relationships, the authors were able to describe novel associations between teacher-student relationships and actual teacher-child interactions. Price demonstrated how a merger of social network and school climate and effectiveness can enhance the prediction of principal-teacher relationships and attitudes. The Wubbels et al. chapter illustrates the benefits of linking dynamic systems and interpersonal theory to unravel the effects of moment-to-moment interactions on the long-term development of teacher-students' relationships. Finally, it is important to recognize Georgiou and Kyriakides' integration of school effectiveness and interpersonal theories, which resulted in a clear demonstration of the importance of interpersonal relations to educational effectiveness.

The combination and integration of different theoretical perspectives might support future progress and developments in the study of interpersonal relationships in education. The following section presents some examples.

A central problem in the study of interpersonal relationships in education is the question of causality versus reciprocity. Do interactions influence a relationship or vice versa? Are student attitudes caused by teacher-student relationships, or do they help determine them? As Wentzel notes:

> *From a theoretical perspective, advances in understanding teacher-student relationships require additional consideration of causal mechanisms and pathways of influence. The predominant approach to the study of teacher-student relationships is to assume a causal connection such that the nature and quality of relationships and interactions influence student outcomes. A consideration of alternative pathways, however, would add critical and important insights to the discussion of these relationships. For instance, models that address the potential impact of children's motivation and engagement on teachers' behaviour, and that identify motivational processes that lead to receptive as opposed to rejecting or neglectful behaviour on the part of teachers need to be developed to inform this area of research.*

For example, one might assume from the Riley, et al. chapter that disruptive student behaviour causes emotional feelings that lead teachers to respond aggressively. However, it is quite possible that aggressive teacher behaviours have caused students to disrupt lessons. It is attractive but dangerous to quickly resolve this quandary by assuming reciprocal associations. Dynamic systems theory has begun to provide a framework as well as statistical analytic tools that might ultimately disentangle the causal links between these and other variables (e.g., Mainhard et al., 2011).

Dynamic systems theory might also help to determine the strength of mechanisms relating attitudes, motivation and interpersonal relationships for students of different ages. A micro level examination might describe the relationship between these variables at one age, while the macro level analysis would focus on different ages. As Wentzel (this volume) states, establishing such associations is essential for understanding developmental changes in the importance of teacher-student relationships. Similarly, dynamic systems theory might inform our understanding of the cumulative effects that repeated positive relationships with many teachers have on students, especially with regard to a student's sense of school community and belongingness. As Wentzel (this volume) states: "The extent to which these more global beliefs develop out of interactions and relationships with single or multiple teachers, and reflect a student's ongoing history of relationships or a single but salient recent relationship are important remaining questions to address in this area of work".

Interpersonal and dynamic systems theory might further illuminate the importance of the social network context. Moolenaar notes that "… in a social network, individuals are embedded within dyadic relationships, and dyadic relationships are embedded in larger sub-groups of three, four, or more actors that eventually shape a social network. Even a social network itself is embedded in a larger social structure, for instance an organization, a community, or a country". Interpersonal theory provides an excellent framework to describe dyadic relationships that can then be depicted on all structural levels. When researchers combine this interpersonal approach with dynamic systems and social network theories, it becomes possible to map the development of network structures on the micro and macro level.

On the other hand, the developmental perspective should increase the understanding of researchers who follow interpersonal, social network, school effectiveness and/or classroom management models. The developmental perspective has highlighted four relationship components: features of individuals (developmental history and biological factors), representational models of teacher and child (perceptions and emotions), information exchange processes (interactive behaviours), and external influences. These components influence each other in dynamic, reciprocal ways (Wentzel, this volume). In many studies, features of individuals and the processes of information exchange do not receive as much attention as required.

A final challenge for both developmental and interpersonal theorists is the difference in dimensions that describe relationships embodied in these two perspectives. Whereas interpersonal theory identifies two dimensions – variously known as Control and Affiliation or Warmth and Influence – developmental researchers often use three: Closeness, Conflict and Dependency. In this instance the two theoretical frameworks are clearly at odds and this issue must be resolved in order to progress.

REFERENCES

Aldridge, J. M. & Fraser, B. J. (2008). *Outcomes-focussed learning environments: Determinants and effects.* Rotterdam, The Netherlands: Sense Publishers.

Anderson, L. M., Evertson, C. M., & Emmer, E. T. (1980). Dimensions in classroom management derived from recent research. *Journal of Curriculum Studies, 12*(4), 343-356.

Baumrind, D. (1971). Current patterns of parental authority. *Developmental Psychology Monograph, 4,* (1, Pt. 2).

Bidwell, C. E. & Yasumoto, J. Y. (1999). The collegial focus: Teaching fields, collegial relationships, and instructional practice in American high schools. *Sociology of Education, 72,* 234-256.

Bowlby, J. (1969). Attachment and loss. *Attachment*, vol. 1. New York: Basic Books.

Bretherton, I. (1987). New perspectives on attachment relations: Security, communication and internal working models. In J. Osofsky (Ed.), *Handbook of infant development* (pp. 1061-1100). New York: John Wiley.

Bronfenbrenner, U. (1989). Ecological systems theory. In R. Vasta (Ed.), *Annals of child development* (Vol. 6, pp. 187-250). Greenwich, CT: JAI.

Bronfenbrenner, U. & Morris, P. A. (1998). The ecology of developmental processes. In W. Damon (Series Ed.) & R. M. Lerner (Vol. Ed.), *Handbook of child psychology: Vol. 1. Theoretical models of human development* (5th ed., pp. 993-1028). New York: Wiley

Bryk, A. S. & Driscoll M. (1988). *The high school as community: Contextual influences and consequences for students and teachers.* Madison: University of Wisconsin, National Center on Effective Secondary Schools.

Bryk, A. S., Sebring, P. B., Allensworth, E., Luppescu, S., & Easton, J. Q. (2010). *Organizing schools for improvement: Lessons from Chicago.* Chicago: The University of Chicago Press.

Carson, R. C. (1969). *Interaction concepts of personality.* Chicago: Aline.

Cavanagh, R. F. & Waugh, R. F. (Eds.) (2011). *Applications of Rasch measurement in learning environments research.* Rotterdam, The Netherlands: Sense Publishers.

Creemers, B. P. M. & Kyriakides, L. (2008). *The dynamics of educational effectiveness: A contribution to policy, practice and theory in contemporary schools.* London/New York: Routledge.

Daly, A. J. & Finnigan, K. (2010). A bridge between worlds: Understanding network structure to understand change strategy. *Journal of Educational Change, 11*, 111-138.

Dorman, J. P. (2003). Cross national validation of the What Is Happening in This Class questionnaire using confirmatory factor analysis. *Learning Environments Research, 6*, 231-245.

Doyle, W. (1986). Classroom Organization and Management. In C. M. Wittrock (Ed.), *Handbook of research on teaching*, third edition (pp. 392-431). New York: Macmillan Publishing.

Doyle, W. (1988). Work in mathematics classes: The context of students' thinking during instruction. *Educational Psychologist, 23*, 167-180.

Doyle, W. (2006). Ecological approaches to classroom management. In C. Evertson & C. Weinstein (Eds.), *Handbook of classroom management: Research, practice, and contemporary issues* (pp. 97-125). New York: Erlbaum.

Dryer, D. C. & Horowitz, L. M. (1997). When do opposites attract? Interpersonal complementarity versus similarity. *Journal of Personality and Social Psychology, 72*, 592-603.

Duke, D. L. (Ed.) (1979). Editor's preface. In D. L. Duke (Ed.), *Classroom management* (78th Yearbook of the National Society for the Study of Education, Part 2). Chicago: University of Chicago Press.

Eccles, J. S. & Midgley, C. (1989). Stage-environment fit: Developmentally appropriate classrooms for young adolescents. In C. Ames & R. Ames (Eds.), *Research on motivation in education*, vol. 3 (pp. 139-186). New York: Academic Press.

Estroff, S. D. & Nowicki, S. (1992). Interpersonal complementarity, gender of interactants, and performance on word puzzles. *Personality and Social Psychology Bulletin, 18*, 351-356.

Fraser, B. J. (1994). Research on classroom and school climate. In D. Gabel (Ed.), *Handbook of research on science teaching and learning* (pp. 493-541). New York: Macmillan.

Gump, P. V. (1969). Intra-setting analysis: The third grade classroom as a special but instructive case. In E. Williams & H. Rausch (Eds.), *Naturalistic viewpoints in psychological research* (pp. 200-220). New York: Holt, Rinehart & Winston.

Gurtman, M. B. (2001). Interpersonal complementarity: Integrating interpersonal measurement with interpersonal models. *Journal of Counseling Psychology, 48*(1), 97-110.

Helmke, A. (2009). *Unterrichtsqulität und Lehrerprofessionalität. Diagnose, Evaluation und Verbesserung des Unterrichts* [Quality of instruction and teacher profession. Diagnostic, evaluation and improvement of instruction]. Seelze: Knallmeyer.

Hollenstein, T. (2007). State space grids: Analyzing dynamics across development. *International Journal of Behavioral Development, 31*(4), 384-396.

Hoy, W. K. & Henderson, J. E. (1983). Principal authenticity, school climate, and pupil-control orientation. *Alberta Journal of Educational Research, 29*, 123-130.

Kiesler, D. J. (1983). The 1982 Interpersonal Circle: A taxonomy for complementarity in human transactions. *Psychological Review, 90*, 185-214.

Kiesler, D. J. (1996). *Contemporary interpersonal theory and research: Personality, psychopathology, and psychotherapy*. Oxford, England: Wiley.

Kounin, J. S. (1970). *Discipline and group management in classrooms*. New York: Holt, Rinehart and Winston.

Kremer-Hayon, L. & Wubbels, Th. (1993). Principals' interpersonal behavior and teachers' satisfaction. In T. Wubbels & J. Levy (Eds.), *Do you know what you look like?* (pp. 113-122). London: Falmer Press.

Kyriakides, L. B., Creemers, P. M., Antoniou, P., & Demetriou, D. (2010). A synthesis of studies searching for the school factors: Implications for theory and research. *British Educational Research Journal, 36*(5), 807-830.

Laible, D. & Thompson, R. A. (2007). Early socialization: A relationship perspective. In J. Grusec & P. Hastings (Eds.), *Handbook of social development* (pp. 181-207). New York, NY: Guilford.

Leary, T. (1957). *An interpersonal diagnosis of personality*. New York: Ronald Press Company.

Leithwood, K. & Jantzi, D. (1990, June). *Transformational leadership: How principals can help reform school cultures*. Paper presented at the Annual Meeting of the Canadian Association for Curriculum Studies, Victoria.

Lin, N. (2001). *Social capital: A theory of social structure and action*. New York, NY: Cambridge University Press.

Mainhard, T., Brekelmans, M., & Wubbels, Th. (2011). Coercive and supportive teacher behaviour: Associations with the social climate within and across classroom lessons. *Learning and Instruction, 21*, 345-354.

McCormick, R., Fox, A., Carmichael, P., & Procter, R. (2010). Researching and understanding educational networks. *New Perspectives on Learning and Instruction.* London, UK: Routledge.

Meyer, J. W. & Rowan, B. (1977). Institutionalized organizations – Formal-structure as myth and ceremony. *American Journal of Sociology, 83*, 340-363.

Moolenaar, N. M. (2010). *Ties with potential: Nature, antecedents, and consequences of social networks in school teams.* Unpublished doctoral dissertation. University of Amsterdam, The Netherlands.

Moos, R. H. (1979). *Evaluating educational environments: procedures, measures, findings and policy implications.* San Francisco: Jossey-Bass.

Ogawa, R. T. & Bossert, S. T. (1995). Leadership as an organizational quality. *Educational Administration Quarterly, 31*, 224-243.

Pianta, R. C. (2001). *Student-teacher relationship scale.* Professional manual. Lutz, Florida: Psychological Assessment Resources.

Pianta, R. C., Hamre, B., & Stuhlman, M. (2003). Relationships between teachers and children. In W. M. Reynolds & G. E. Miller (Eds.), *Handbook of psychology: Educational psychology,* vol. 7. (pp. 199-234). Hoboken, NJ, US: John Wiley & Sons.

Sadler, P. & Woody, E. (2003). Is Who You Are Who You're Talking to? Interpersonal Style and Complementarity in Mixed-Sex Interactions. *Journal of Personality and Social Psychology, 84*(1), 80-96.

Sava, F. A. (2002). Causes and effects of teacher conflict-inducing attitudes towards pupils: A path analysis model. *Teaching and Teacher Education, 18*, 1007-1021.

Teddlie, C. & Reynolds, D. (2000). *The international handbook of school effectiveness research.* London/New York: Falmer Press.

Thelen, E. & Smith, L. B. (1994). *A dynamic system approach to the development of cognition and action.* Cambridge, MA: Bradford/MIT Press.

Thijs, J., Koomen, H. M. Y., Roorda, D., & Ten Hagen, J. (2011). Explaining teacher-student interactions in early childhood: An interpersonal theoretical approach. *Journal of Applied Developmental Psychology, 32*(1), 34-43.

Tiedens, L. Z. & Jimenez, M. C. (2003). Assimilation for affiliation and contrast for control: Complementary self-construals. *Journal of Personality and Social Psychology, 85*(6), 1049-1061.

Tracey, T. J. (1994). An examination of complementarity of interpersonal behavior. *Journal of Personality and Social Psychology, 67*, 864-878.

Tracey, T. J. G. (2004). Levels of interpersonal complementarity: A simplex representation. *Personality and Social Psychology Bulletin, 30*, 1211-1225.

Tracey, T. J. G. (2005). Interpersonal rigidity and complementarity. *Journal of Research in Personality, 39*, 592-614.

Walberg, H. J. (1979). *Educational environments and effects: Evaluation, policy, and productivity.* Berkely: McCutchan.

Wasserman, S. & Galaskiewicz, J. (1994). *Advances in social network analysis: Research in the social and behavioral sciences.* Thousand Oaks, CA: Sage.

Watzlawick, P., Beavin, J. H., & Jackson, D. (1967). *The pragmatics of human communication.* New York: Norton.

Wentzel, K. R. (2004). Understanding classroom competence: The role of social-motivational and self-processes. In R. Kail (Ed.), *Advances in child development and behavior,* vol. 32 (pp 213-241). New York, NY: Elsevier.

Wentzel, K. R. & Looney, L. (2007). Socialization in school settings. In J. Grusec & P. Hastings (Eds.), *Handbook of social development* (pp. 382-403). New York, NY: Guilford.

Wubbels, T., Créton, H. A., & Hooymayers, H. P. (1985, March-April). *Discipline problems of beginning teachers, interactional teacher behavior mapped out.* Paper presented at the annual meeting of the American Educational Research Association, Chicago (ERIC document 260040).

Wubbels, T., Brekelmans, M., Den Brok, P., & Van Tartwijk, J. (2006). An interpersonal perspective on classroom management in secondary classrooms in the Netherlands. In C. Evertson & C. S. Weinstein (Eds.), *Handbook of classroom management: Research, practice and contemporary issues* (pp. 1161-1191). New York: Lawrence Erlbaum Associates.

STUDENT ORIENTED

KATHRYN R. WENTZEL

2. TEACHER-STUDENT RELATIONSHIPS AND ADOLESCENT COMPETENCE AT SCHOOL

INTRODUCTION

There is growing consensus that the nature and quality of children's relationships with their teachers play a critical and central role in motivating and engaging students to learn (Wentzel, 2009). Effective teachers are typically described as those who develop relationships with students that are emotionally close, safe, and trusting, who provide access to instrumental help, and who foster a more general ethos of community and caring in classrooms. These relationship qualities are believed to support the development of students' motivational orientations for social and academic outcomes, aspects of motivation related to emotional well-being and a positive sense of self, and levels of engagement in positive social and academic activities. They also provide a context for communicating positive and high expectations for performance and for teaching students what they need to know to become knowledgeable and productive citizens.

Despite this consensus, there is much yet to learn about the nature of teacher-student relationships and their significance for motivating students to excel academically and behave appropriately. At the most general level, the conceptual underpinnings of work in this area tend to suffer from lack of clarity and specificity. For example, it is not always clear what scholars mean when they talk about 'relationships' between teachers and students. Similarly, motivational constructs are often vague and ill-defined (see Murphy & Alexander, 2000). In addition, explanatory models that provide insights into the mechanisms whereby teacher-student relationships have a meaningful impact on student outcomes are rare.

In light of these issues, this chapter highlights various perspectives on teacher-student relationships and motivation, including definitions of constructs and theoretical perspectives that guide current work in this area. A specific model of teacher-student relationships that focuses on relationship provisions in the form of emotional warmth and expectations for goal pursuit is presented, and suggestions for future directions for theory and research are offered.

T. Wubbels et al. (eds.), Interpersonal Relationships in Education, 19–36.

DEFINITIONS AND CONCEPTUAL MODELS

Defining Teacher-Student Relationships

In the developmental literature, relationships are typically defined as enduring connections between two individuals, uniquely characterized by degrees of continuity, shared history, and interdependent interactions across settings and activities (Collins & Repinski, 1994; Hinde, 1997). In addition, definitions are frequently extended to include the qualities of a relationship, as evidenced by levels of trust, intimacy, and sharing; the presence of positive affect, closeness, and affective tone; and the content and quality of communication (Collins & Repinski, 1994; Laible & Thompson, 2007). Along each of these dimensions, relationships can evoke positive as well as negative experiences. Finally, relationships are often thought of in terms of their influence and what they provide the individual. In this regard, researchers have focused on the benefits of various relationship provisions such as emotional well-being, a sense of cohesion and connectedness, instrumental help, a secure base, and a sense of identity for promoting positive developmental outcomes (Bukowski & Hoza, 1989).

From a developmental perspective, relationships are believed to be experienced through the lens of mental representations developed over time and with respect to specific experiences (Bowlby, 1969; Laible & Thompson, 2007). Mental representations that associate relationships with a personal sense of power and agency, predictability and safety, useful resources, and reciprocity are believed to be optimal for the internalization of social influence (see Kuczynski & Parkin, 2007). These representations also provide stability and continuity to relationships over time. In this regard, early representations of relationships with caregivers are believed to provide the foundation for developing relationships outside the family context, with the quality of parent-child relationships (i.e., levels of warmth and security) often predicting the quality of peer and teacher relationships in early and middle childhood (see Wentzel & Looney, 2007).

Although stability and continuity are viewed as hallmarks of relationships, they also are viewed as dynamic; relationships undergo predictable changes as a function of development and the changing needs of the individual. For example, over the course of adolescence, children's relationships with parents improve with respect to overall positive regard and reciprocity; in early and middle adolescence, relationships with parents are marked by heightened negative affect and conflict; and adolescents experience discontinuities in the frequency and meaning of interactions with parents and the availability of resources from them (Collins & Repinski, 1994). Similarly, relationships with peers change with age. Whereas younger adolescents tend to form relationships within peer crowds and cliques, older adolescents tend to focus on relationships with a more limited number of friends (Brown, Mory, & Kinney, 1994). As children move through adolescence, they also view relationships with peers as the most important sources of intimacy, nurturance, companionship, and admiration (Lempers & Clark-Lempers, 1992).

Of particular interest for the current chapter are adolescent's relationships with teachers. Although less is known about these relationships relative to those with parents and peers, teacher-student relationships are typically defined with respect to emotional support as perceived by the student and examined with respect to their impact on student outcomes. There are several issues, however, that make this literature problematic. First, although there is general recognition that by adolescence, students have a well-formed mental schema of their relationships with teachers, perceptions of teacher support most often reflect relationships with teachers in general, rather than with one specific teacher (cf., Wentzel, 1991). Therefore, findings typically do not reflect the nature of a dyadic relationship or its unique influence on school-related outcomes.

Of additional importance is that when school-aged children rate the importance of their relationships with teachers, mothers, fathers, siblings, and friends, they typically report being very satisfied with their relationships with their teachers. However, on affective dimensions such as intimacy, nurturance, and admiration, teachers are routinely ranked by children as the least likely source of support when compared to parents and peers (Furman & Buhrmester, 1985; Lempers & Clark-Lempers, 1992; Reid, Landesman, Treder, & Jaccard, 1989; see also Darling, Hamilton, & Niego, 1994). Rather, they tend to rank teachers as most important for providing instrumental aid and informational guidance (Lempers & Clark-Lempers, 1992). Therefore, the literature provides fairly clear support for including provisions of instrumental help as a dimension of teacher-student relationships that is important to students at all ages, but calls into question the relative role of teachers' emotional support in most students' lives. Finally, few researchers have examined the dynamic qualities of teacher-adolescent relationships and the potential for them to change in quality and function over time.

Defining Motivation at School

Whereas conceptualizations of teacher-student relationships are often simplistic, definitions of motivation are numerous and often highly nuanced. However, motivation is typically defined as a set of interrelated beliefs that direct behaviour, and researchers typically focus on these beliefs in relation to academic tasks and activities (see Wentzel & Wigfield, 2009). Motivational beliefs most commonly studied are personal goals, values associated with goals, beliefs about ability, and beliefs about causality and control. Personal goals determine why students do what they do. The content of goals (e.g., Ford, 1992) directs efforts toward specific outcomes (e.g., to learn algebra), and goal standards (e.g., Bandura, 1986) define acceptable levels of accomplishment (e.g., to learn enough algebra to pass the exam). Values associated with goals reflect the costs and benefits of goal accomplishment, the importance and long-term utility of goal achievement, and the intrinsic pleasure of engaging in goal-directed behaviour (Eccles, 2005). Students' beliefs about their abilities (e.g., "I am able to learn math") also appear to influence what they choose to do and why they persist at certain activities and not others

(Schunk & Pajares, 2009). The stronger a student's beliefs about personal efficacy and competence, the more likely they are to engage in goal pursuit. Finally, beliefs about autonomy and control (e.g., "I am learning algebra because it is my choice") provide students with a lens for interpreting past events and with a basis for developing expectations for the future. More specifically, they represent reasons for why they succeed or fail and therefore, for engaging in or refraining from future goal pursuit (e.g., Graham & Williams, 2009).

Although less common in discussions of motivation, students also are motivated by social concerns that emanate from social interactions and contextual cues (see Ford, 1992; Wentzel, 2004). Of direct relevance to interpersonal relationships are beliefs about belongingness and emotional connectedness to others, that is, feeling like one is a valued and integral member of a social group (Connell & Wellborn, 1991). From this perspective, engagement in a socially-valued activity is more likely to occur if students believe that others care about them and want them to engage. As described in subsequent sections, much work has linked these beliefs to a range of social and academic outcomes. In addition, moral and social obligations, based on the extent to which students believe they are *supposed* to engage in an activity, can have a powerful influence on behaviour. As a central aspect of instrumental help, communications about what is expected from students academically and socially should play a central role in motivating students' achievement-specific outcomes and therefore, in defining the contribution of teacher-student relationships to student accomplishments. However, the role of expectations in motivating student outcomes, especially as they apply to specific teacher-student relationships, is not well understood.

Explanatory Models

Given the various constructs associated with relationships and motivation, why then, might students' relationships with teachers be associated with or even influence their motivation to engage in positive school-related outcomes? The prevailing theoretical models that guide work in this area are derived from work on parent-child relationships and typically adopt a causal approach, with the affective quality of teacher-student relationships viewed as the central and critical motivator of student adjustment (e.g., Pianta, Hamre, & Stuhlman, 2003). The basic tenets of attachment theory (Bowlby, 1969; Bretherton, 1987) reflect this notion. Other perspectives that have contributed to this literature describe teacher-student relationships along specific dimensions and provisions (Wentzel, 2004), as specified by models of parent-child interactions (e.g., Baumrind, 1971). In the following sections, each of these approaches will be described.

Attachment theory perspectives. Attachment theory has provided the strongest impetus for work on teachers' relationships with young children. According to this perspective, the dyadic relationship between a child and caregiver (usually the mother) is a system in which children experience various levels of positive affect and responsiveness to their basic needs, with predictable and sensitive responses being associated with secure attachments, and more arbitrary and insensitive responses leading to insecure attachments (see Bowlby, 1969). Theorists hypothesize qualitatively different outcomes associated with secure and insecure attachment systems. Secure relationships are believed to foster children's curiosity and exploration of the environment, positive coping skills, and a mental representation of one's self as being worthy of love and of others as being trustworthy. In contrast, insecure attachments are believed to result in either wary or inappropriately risky exploratory behaviour, difficulty in regulating stress in new settings, and negative self-concepts. A basic tenet of attachment theory is that the primary attachment relationship results in children's mental representations of self and others, which are then used as a basis to interpret and judge the underlying intentions, reliability, and trustworthiness of others' actions in new relationships (Bretherton, 1987). Depending on the nature of primary attachments, children will expect to experience new relationships with respect to positive affect and trust, by conflict and rejection, or as anxiety-producing, overly-dependent or enmeshed.

Although teacher-student relationships are not typically viewed as primary attachment relationships, attachment theory principles imply that they would be fairly concordant with the quality of parent-child attachments. Therefore, attachment theory has been used as a framework for generating predictions concerning children's relationships with their teachers, especially during the preschool and elementary school years. Hypothesizing connections between secure attachments and children's motivation for school-related activities is fairly straightforward. A positive sense of self, curiosity and willingness to explore, and trust in others can be viewed as central precursors to children's beliefs about emotional connectedness with others, efficacy to learn and interact socially with others, personal control, and intrinsic interest in classroom activities (e.g., Harter, 1978; Raider-Roth, 2005). To the extent that student-teacher attachments are positive, researchers assume that these same outcomes associated with secure parent-child attachments should occur in association with teacher-student relationships.

In line with attachment theory principles, evidence from correlational studies confirms that secure and close relationships with teachers are related positively to young children's motivation toward school and associated cognitive and social competencies. In work on young children, teacher-student relationships typically are assessed by asking teachers about the affective quality of their relationships with students and relating their responses to academic outcomes such as school readiness and test scores, and social competencies such as prosocial and antisocial forms of behaviour and peer relationships (e.g., Howes & Hamilton, 1993; Peisner-Feinberg et al., 2001; Pianta, Nimetz, & Bennett, 1997). Motivational outcomes have been studied less frequently, although teacher-student relationships marked by emotional closeness have been related positively to students' reports of school liking (Birch & Ladd, 1997) and students' identification with teachers' values and positive social self-concept (Davis, 2001); affectively negative relationships have been related to student anxiety and depression (Murray & Greenberg, 2000). In general, however, these relations have been fairly weak and appear to differ as a function of measurement and design strategies, and specific outcomes being predicted (see Wentzel, 2009).

Dimensions of teacher-student relationships. An additional approach has been to consider relationships as serving a broader range of functions that contribute to students' competence at school. This approach has been used primarily to study relationships in middle childhood and adolescence. For the most part, scholars adopting this approach have focused on teachers as socialization agents who create interpersonal contexts that influence levels and quality of student motivation and engagement (see Connell & Wellborn, 1991; Wentzel, 2004). Although the affective tone of teacher-student interactions is a central focus of discussion, these perspectives propose that the contribution of teachers' relationships with students should be defined in terms of multiple dimensions that combine with emotional support to motivate students to engage in the social and academic life of the classroom.

Similar to those described in models of effective parenting and parenting styles (e.g., Baumrind, 1971; Darling & Steinberg, 1993), these dimensions reflect levels of concern with a student's emotional and physical well-being, predictability and structure, and instrumental resources. These dimensions are believed to reflect necessary interpersonal resources that support a child's pursuit of social and academic goals that are valued by others. When applied to the social worlds of the classroom, these dimensions are reflected in opportunities for learning as reflected in teachers' communications of rules and expectations for behaviour and performance, provisions of instrumental help, and opportunities for emotional support and interpersonal connectedness.

Support for this perspective is found in students' and teachers' qualitative descriptions of caring and supportive teachers, and from studies relating multiple dimensions of support to student outcomes. Qualitative approaches have identified multiple types of teacher support by asking students and teachers what a supportive or caring teacher is like (see Hoy & Weinstein, 2006). For example, when asked to characterize teachers who care, middle school students describe teachers who demonstrate democratic and egalitarian communication styles designed to elicit student participation and input, who develop expectations for student behaviour and performance in light of individual differences and abilities, who model a 'caring' attitude and interest in their instruction and interpersonal dealings with students, and who provide constructive rather than harsh and critical feedback (Wentzel, 1998). Moreover, students who perceive their teachers as providing high levels of these multiple supports also tend to pursue appropriate social and academic classroom goals more frequently than students who do not (Wentzel, 2002).

Others have documented differences in middle school students' characterizations of supportive teachers as a function of student ability, with students from high ability tracks valuing teachers who challenge them, encourage class participation, and who express educational goals similar to theirs. In contrast, students from low ability tracks tend to value teachers who treat them with kindness, who are fair, explain subject matter clearly, and maintain control in the classroom (Daniels & Arapostathis, 2005). Ethnographic studies document that academically successful inner-city ethnic minority adolescents value instrumental help from teachers but also warmth and acceptance coupled with high academic expectations (Smokowski, Reynolds, & Bezrucko, 2000). Racially mixed groups of middle school students highlight the importance of teachers who are responsive to individual differences and needs, who provide students with autonomy and choice (Oldfather, 1993), who show interest in students as individuals, help with academics, encourage students to work up to their potential, and who teach well and make subject matter interesting (Hayes, Ryan, & Zseller, 1994).

Additional evidence concerning provisions associated with teacher-student relationships is provided in studies where multiple dimensions of supports have been assessed simultaneously. This work has documented differential effects as a function of dimension and the outcome being studied (see Wentzel, 2009 for a review). For example, Wentzel and her colleagues (Wentzel, Battle, Russell, & Looney, 2010) documented unique relations of teachers' provisions of clear expectations, classroom safety, instrumental help, and emotional support to students' interest in class and efforts to behave appropriately. Skinner and Belmont (1993) also documented significant relations between teachers' provisions of involvement and structure (e.g., clear expectations, instrumental help) and students' engagement in class. Finally, researchers also have documented significant main effects of structure and emotional support from teachers on positive behaviour at school (Gregory, Cornell, Fan, Sheras, Shih, & Huang, 2010; Gregory & Weinstein, 2004).

INTEGRATION AND EXTENSION OF THEORETICAL PERSPECTIVES

Wentzel (2004) has described more specifically how teacher-student interactions along these dimensions can promote student motivation and subsequent performance. Derived from theoretical perspectives on person-environment fit and personal goal setting (e.g., Bronfenbrenner, 1989; Eccles & Midgley, 1989), she argues that school-related competence is achieved to the extent that students are able to accomplish goals that have personal as well as social value, in a manner that supports continued psychological and emotional well-being. More specifically, Bronfenbrenner (1989) argues that competence can only be understood in terms of context-specific effectiveness, being a product of personal attributes such as goals, values, self-regulatory skills, and cognitive abilities, and of ways in which these attributes contribute to meeting situational requirements and demands. Bronfenbrenner further suggests that competence is facilitated by contextual supports that provide opportunities for the growth and development of these personal attributes as well as for learning what is expected by the social group.

Therefore, students' ability to accomplish their goals is contingent on opportunities and affordances of the school context that allow them to pursue their multiple goals. Moreover, Wentzel argues that students will come to value and subsequently pursue academic and social goals valued by teachers when they perceive their interactions and relationships with them as providing clear expectations concerning goals that should be achieved; as facilitating the achievement of their goals by providing help, advice, and instruction; as being safe and responsive to their goal strivings; and as being emotionally supportive and nurturing (see also Ford, 1992).

In line with attachment theory and work by Darling and Steinberg (1993), Wentzel also assigns a unique role to the emotional climate of relationships such that teachers are believed to have the strongest motivational impact on students if they provide instrumental resources within a context of warmth and emotional support. In this view, the roles of relationship warmth and communication of expectations and values in motivating students are unique but interrelated. With respect to their unique contribution, it is well-documented that warmth and expectations each have direct, main effects on adolescents' social and academic functioning at school. Research has yielded the most consistent findings in support of a link between emotional support from teachers and classroom goal pursuit. With respect to social outcomes, Wentzel's work in this area has documented significant, positive relations between middle school students' perceptions of emotional support from teachers and pursuit of goals to be prosocial and socially responsible (e.g., Wentzel, 1991, 1994, 1997, 1998, 2002). In these studies, emotional support was assessed from the perspective of teachers and peers, including teacher reports of preference for students and classmate reports of teachers as being supportive and caring. In addition, although much of this work has examined concurrent relations between social support and goal pursuit, longitudinal studies have provided evidence that perceived support from teachers predicts student goal pursuit across the middle school years (Wentzel, 1997, 2003). Finally, perceived emotional support from teachers has been related to academic aspects of student motivation, including pursuit of goals to learn (Wentzel, 2002), effort (i.e., a behavioural manifestation of academic goal pursuit; Wentzel, 1997), and mastery goal orientations toward learning (Wentzel, 1998, 2002).

Although research has just begun, students' perceptions of teachers' expectations for social behaviour and academic performance also have been related to social goal pursuit as well as academic goal pursuit (Wentzel et al., 2010). However, it is reasonable to assume that the degree to which students pursue goals valued by teachers is dependent on whether teachers communicate clearly and consistently their values and expectations concerning classroom behaviour and performance. Clarity of communications and consistency of classroom management practices early in the academic year tend to predict positive academic and social outcomes in elementary and secondary level classrooms throughout the year (see Gettinger & Kohler, 2006). Beyond communicating values and expectations for behaviour and achievement at the classroom level, teachers also convey expectations about ability and performance to individual students. As part of ongoing interpersonal interactions, these communications have the potential to influence a student's beliefs about her own ability and goals to achieve academically (Weinstein, 2002). Of particular note is that teachers who communicate high expectations for individual students can bring about positive changes in academic accomplishments. However, the direct impact of these expectations on student motivation has been examined infrequently (see Jussim, Robustelli, & Cain, 2009).

Of additional interest, however, is the possibility that warmth and expectations might influence motivation and engagement not only in additive fashion but also as interactive effects. Indeed, Darling and Steinberg (1993) argued that the effectiveness of domain-specific parenting practices will be determined in part, by the overall warmth and emotional climate of the parent-adolescent relationship. Applied to the classroom, this notion suggests that communication of specific expectations for social and academic outcomes should be more predictive of motivation and engagement outcomes if they are communicated within the context of an emotionally caring relationship. Although recognition of Darling and Steinberg's model is widespread, few researchers have examined their hypotheses concerning the interactive influence of a teacher-student relationship's emotional climate and expectations for social and academic outcomes on motivation. Findings are suggestive, however, in that adolescents' tend to perceive parental expectations more accurately when parental warmth and responsiveness is high (Knafo & Schwartz, 2003), emotionally secure relationships with teachers are related to students' identification with teachers' values (Davis, 2001), and parental warmth moderates the effects of parental monitoring on academic achievement (Spera, 2006).

In her ongoing program of research, Wentzel has also begun to examine these issues. Preliminary evidence of the main effects as well as interactive effects of teachers' emotional caring and expectations on adolescents' social and academic outcomes are described in the following section.

Evidence of the Interactive Influence of Emotional Support and Expectations from Teachers on Motivation

Research on the interactive role of perceived emotional support and expectations from teachers in motivating adolescent's social and academic competence at school has begun to yield support for Darling and Steinberg's model. In particular, results support the notion that teacher expectations for academic outcomes are most effective when communicated within a context of emotional warmth and caring; these findings reflect students' perceptions of a single teacher and the degree to which they are motivated to achieve academic and social outcomes in that particular teacher's class. To illustrate, in a sample of 254 middle and high school students (70% European American) from a suburban middle-class school district, perceived expectations from teachers for academic performance predicted mastery goal pursuit only under conditions of high and medium levels of perceived emotional support (Wentzel & Looney, 2007), see Figure 1. In a second sample of 595 fifth and sixth graders (92% Mexican American) from a low income school district, similar results were obtained in that perceived academic expectations from teachers predicted academic effort most strongly under conditions of high emotional support provided by teachers (Wentzel, Russell, & Baker, 2011), see Figure 1.

As part of this work, the domain-specificity of teacher influence also was examined. Of interest in this regard was whether the interactive model was robust across academic and social domains and whether the model was applicable to peer relationships as well as to adolescents' relationships with teachers. In both sets of analyses predicting academic aspects of motivation, teachers' emotional support x expectations for academic performance interaction terms were significant predictors of motivation and engagement while controlling for the potentially confounding role of perceived emotional support and expectations for academic performance from peers. The peer variables were non-significant predictors. Therefore, dimensions of teacher-student relationships appeared to have primary influence in the academic domain.

Wentzel and her colleagues also have examined the role of teacher emotional support and expectations in predicting adolescents' social goal pursuit, while also including perceived emotional supports and expectations for social behaviour from peers in the model. In this case, the role of the teacher-student relationship in predicting social motivation was negligible, whereas the interactive model was robust for peer relationships. To illustrate, in a sample of 358 sixth, seventh, and eighth graders (75% European American, 22% African American) from a suburban middle school, peer expectations predicted pursuit of goals to be responsible (e.g., to follow rules, keep commitments) only under conditions of high and medium levels of emotional support (based on data from Wentzel et al., 2010), see Figure 2. In a second sample (Wentzel et al., 2011), perceived expectations for social behaviour predicted pursuit of goals to be prosocial (to help, cooperate, and share), but only under conditions of low and medium levels of emotional support, see Figure 2. Although this latter finding is counter-intuitive, it likely reflects the fact that positive peer relationships are founded on prosocial forms of behaviour (e.g., Wentzel & Erdley, 1993), and that students with low levels of support who are seeking higher levels of acceptance and emotional support from peers will be more motivated to display such behaviour.

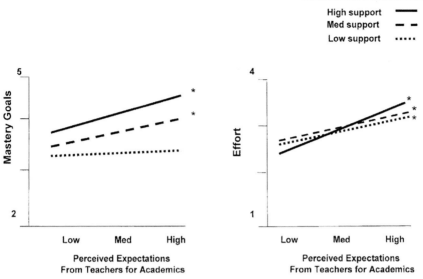

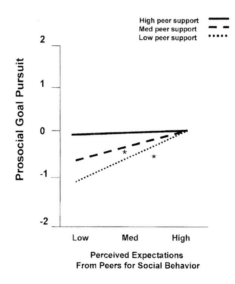

Figure 1. Interactions of emotional support and expectations as predictors of academic engagement.

Figure 2. Interactions of emotional support and expectations for social behaviour as predictors of social goal pursuit.

CONCLUSIONS AND FUTURE DIRECTIONS

In this chapter, literature on the nature of relationships and motivation as it relates to the influence of teacher-student relationships in adolescence has been reviewed. A model of teacher-student relationships that focuses on relationship provisions in the form of emotional support and expectations for behaviour also was described. Finally, evidence supporting the moderating role of emotional support on associations between teacher's expectations for performance and motivational outcome (i.e., goal pursuit and engagement) was presented. Although these initial findings have the potential to move the field forward, important issues remain unresolved. These methodological and theoretical challenges are described in the following section.

Methodological Challenges

Some of the most challenging issues that limit conclusions concerning the importance of teacher-student relationships are found in research designs. For the most part, conclusions are based on correlational data; studies of change in student outcomes as a result of changes in relationships with teachers are rare. However, limited evidence suggests that when teachers are taught to provide students with warmth and support, clear expectations for behaviour, and developmentally appropriate autonomy, their students tend to develop a stronger sense of community, increase displays of socially competent behaviour, and show academic gains (e.g., Schaps, Battistich, & Solomon, 1997; see also, Kuijpers, Houtveen, & Wubbels, 2010). Many comprehensive school reform models also incorporate an explicit focus on teacher-student relationships as a strategy for improving student engagement and learning (Stipek, 2004), although few of these efforts have documented the unique impact of teacher-student relationships on student motivation and academic improvements. Therefore, future work needs to establish causal connections by assessing change in student outcomes as a function of changing perceptions of teachers from one year to the next (Wentzel, Williams, & Tomback, 2005), documenting changes in students' perceptions and outcomes as they experience different teachers and classrooms, or by designing interventions to change the quality of support from a particular teacher (see Pianta et al., 2003).

An additional issue with respect to research design concerns the unit of analysis and whether dimensions of support are assessed at the level of the individual student, classroom, or school (Fraser & Fisher, 1982). Studies relating individual students' perceptions of supports to their social and academic accomplishments yield important information about the psychological impact of social support. For the most part, however, researchers that focus on individual differences typically disregard the fact that teacher or classroom effects might also explain student outcomes (cf., Den Brok, Brekelmans, & Wubbels, 2004). For instance, class size has been related significantly and negatively to teachers' provisions of emotional support (Mashburn, Hamre, Downer, & Pianta, 2006; Pianta et al., 2003).

Emotional support from teachers also appears to account for only a small amount of variance in observed climate in elementary classrooms (Pianta et al., 1997). Therefore, studies could profit from an examination of between-classroom effects by gathering information on a larger number of classrooms and a greater range of classroom characteristics. More complex designs that take into consideration the nested quality of teacher supports at the level of student, classroom, and school are needed in this regard.

The moderating influence of students' and teachers' sex, race, and other background characteristics on the impact of teacher-student relationships also requires further examination. Indeed, research indicates that personal characteristics might enhance or detract from a student's tendency to establish supportive relationships with teachers and therefore, benefit from them. For example, in the elementary-school years, relations between close and secure teacher-student relationships and student adjustment tend to be stronger for ethnic minority and at-risk students than for Caucasian students (see Wentzel, 2009). Relatedness with teachers also tends to be associated with student outcomes more strongly for special education students than for regular students, and more for boys than for girls. Similarly, relations between perceived emotional support from teachers and student adjustment are moderated by SES and race such that students from lower SES backgrounds (Dornbusch, Erickson, Laird, & Wong, 2001), and members of minority groups (Certo, Cauley, & Chafin, 2003; Crosnoe, Johnson, & Elder, 2004; Den Brok, Van Tartwijk, Wubbels, & Veldman, 2010) tend to benefit more from close relationships with teachers than do other students.

Finally, relatedness with teachers appears to differ as a function of students' age, with more elementary grade students reporting optimal or adequate relationships than middle school students (Lynch & Cicchetti, 1997). School-level factors such as safety, racial homogeneity, SES of the student body (Crosnoe et al., 2004), and composition of instructional teams (Murdock & Miller, 2003) also appear to moderate relations between perceived teacher support and student outcomes. Most of these studies have focused on fairly objective outcomes such as grades, test scores, or delinquent and aggressive forms of behaviour. The moderating impact of these characteristics on motivational processes is not well-understood.

Theoretical Challenges

From a theoretical perspective, advances in understanding teacher-student relationships requires additional consideration of causal mechanisms and pathways of influence. The predominant approach to the study of teacher-student relationships is to assume a causal connection such that the nature and quality of relationships and interactions influence student outcomes. A consideration of alternative pathways, however, would add critical and important insights to the discussion of these relationships. For instance, models that address the potential impact of children's motivation and engagement on teachers' behaviour, and that identify motivational processes that lead to receptive as opposed to rejecting or neglectful behaviour on the part of teachers need to be developed to inform this area of research.

Assuming that teacher-student relationships have a causal influence on student adjustment, greater understanding of what it is that develops or is changed on the part of students as a function of their relationships and interactions with teachers also is necessary. As noted in this chapter, teacher-student relationships have been related positively to a range of motivational outcomes such as students' goal pursuit, beliefs about competence and control, effort and persistence, and self-regulatory strategies. These findings, however, tell us little about how and why these relationships impact students' accomplishments at school. Therefore, an important remaining theoretical challenge is to articulate the various pathways and mechanisms by which teacher-student relationships have influence. To illustrate this latter point, relations between perceived emotional support from teachers and achievement appear to be mediated by students' mastery goal orientations and self-efficacy (Patrick, Ryan, & Kaplan, 2007), and their social goal pursuit tends to mediate relations between perceived teacher supports and students' prosocial behaviour (Wentzel, 2002). Continued work in this area is essential if we are to understand fully the role of motivation in explaining the unique impact of teacher-student relationships on students' social and academic competencies at school.

Developmental issues require additional attention as well. For example, determining the strength of these mechanisms for students of different ages is essential for understanding developmental changes in the importance of teacher-student relationships. Also important for understanding 'what develops' is a focus on the cumulative effects of having positive relationships with many teachers over time, and their contribution to a student's sense of school community and belongingness. School belongingness measures assess in part, students' perceptions of the quality of relationships with all of their teachers as a group (see Goodenow, 1993; Roeser & Eccles, 1998). The extent to which these more global beliefs develop out of interactions and relationships with single or multiple teachers, and reflect a student's ongoing history of relationships or a single but salient recent relationship are important remaining questions to address in this area of work.

Finally, in this chapter evidence was presented suggesting that models of parenting are generalizable not only to teacher-student relationships but also to peer relationships. Moreover, findings indicate that the impact of relationships on motivation differs as a function of the source of the relationships (teacher vs. peer), but also of the domain of functioning (academic vs. social). Therefore, continued research on the contributions of multiple relationships to student motivation in both academic and social domains is necessary to understanding the multiple social demands and supports that adolescents must coordinate to be successful at school.

REFERENCES

Bandura, A. (1986). *Social foundations of thought and action: A social cognitive theory*. Englewood Cliffs, NJ: Prentice-Hall.

Baumrind, D. (1971). Current patterns of parental authority. *Developmental Psychology Monograph, 4*, (1, Pt.2).

Birch, S. H. & Ladd, G. W. (1997). The teacher-child relationship and children's early school adjustment. *Journal of School Psychology, 35*, 61-79.

Bowlby, J. (1969). Attachment and loss. *Attachment*, vol. 1. New York: Basic Books.

Bretherton, I. (1987). New perspectives on attachment relations: Security, communication and internal working models. In J. Osofsky (Ed.), *Handbook of infant development* (pp. 1061-1100). New York: John Wiley.

Bronfenbrenner, U. (1989). Ecological systems theory. In R. Vasta (Ed.), *Annals of child development* (vol. 6, pp. 187-250). Greenwich, CT: JAI.

Brown, B. B., Mory, M. S., & Kinney, D. (1994). Casting adolescent crowds in a relational perspective: Caricature, channel, and context. In R. Montemayor, G. R. Adams, & T. P. Gullotta (Eds.), *Personal relationships during adolescence* (pp. 123-167). Newbury Park, CA: Sage.

Bukowski, W. M. & Hoza, B. (1989). Popularity and friendship: Issues in theory, measurement, and outcome. In T. J. Berndt & G. W. Ladd (Eds.), *Peer relationships in child development* (pp. 15-45). New York: Wiley & Sons.

Certo, J. L., Cauley, K. M., & Chafin, C. (2003). Students' perspectives on their high school experience. *Adolescence, 38*, 705-724.

Collins, W. A. & Repinski, D. J. (1994). Relationships during adolescence: Continuity and change in interpersonal perspective. In R. Montemayor, G. Adams, & T. Gullotta (Eds.), *Personal relationships during adolescence* (pp. 7-36). Thousand Oaks, CA: Sage.

Connell, J. P. & Wellborn, J. G. (1991). Competence, autonomy, and relatedness: A motivational analysis of self-system processes. In M. R. Gunnar & L. A. Sroufe (Eds.), *Self processes and development: The Minnesota symposia on child development* (vol. 23, pp. 43-78). Hillsdale, NJ: Erlbaum.

Crosnoe, R., Johnson, M. K., & Elder, G. H., Jr. (2004). Intergenerational bonding in school: The behavioral and contextual correlates of student-teacher relationships. *Sociology of Education, 77*, 60-81.

Daniels, E. & Arapostathis, M. (2005). What do they really want? Student voices and motivation research. *Urban Education, 40*, 34-59.

Darling, N., Hamilton, S. F., & Niego, S. (1994). Adolescents' relations with adults outside the family. In R. Montemayor, G. Adams, & T. Gullotta (Eds.), *Personal relationships during adolescence* (pp. 216-235). Thousand Oaks, CA: Sage.

Darling, N. & Steinberg, L. (1993). Parenting style as context – An integrative model. *Psychological Bulletin, 113*, 487-496.

Davis, H. A. (2001). The quality and impact of relationships between elementary school students and teachers. *Contemporary Educational Psychology, 26*, 421-453.

Den Brok, P., Brekelmans, M., & Wubbels, T. (2004). Interpersonal teacher behaviour and student outcomes. *School Effectiveness and School Improvement, 15*, 407-442.

Den Brok, P., Van Tartwijk, J., Wubbels, T., & Veldman, I. (2010). The differential effect of the teacher-student interpersonal relationship on student outcomes for students with different ethnic backgrounds. *British Journal of Educational Psychology, 80*, 199-221.

Dornbusch, S. M., Erickson, K. G., Laird, J., & Wong, C. A. (2001). The relation of family and school attachment to adolescent deviance in diverse groups and communities. *Journal of Adolescent Research, 16*, 396-422.

Eccles, J. S. (2005). Subjective task values and the Eccles et al. model of achievement related choices. In A. J. Elliott & C. S. Dweck (Eds.), *Handbook of competence and motivation* (pp. 105-121). New York: Guilford.

Eccles, J. S. & Midgley, C. (1989). Stage-environment fit: Developmentally appropriate classrooms for young adolescents. In C. Ames & R. Ames (Eds.), *Research on motivation in education*, vol. 3 (pp. 139-186). New York: Academic Press.

Ford, M. E. (1992). *Motivating humans: Goals, emotions, and personal agency beliefs.* Newbury Park, CA: Sage.

Fraser, B. J. & Fisher, D. L. (1982). Predicting students' outcomes from their perceptions of classroom psychosocial environment. *American Educational Research Journal, 19*, 498-518.

Furman, W. & Buhrmester, D. (1985). Children's perceptions of the personal relationships in their social networks. *Developmental Psychology, 21*, 1016-1024.

Gettinger, M. & Kohler, K. M. (2006). Process-outcome approaches to classroom management and effective teaching. In C. Evertson & C. Weinstein (Eds.), *Handbook of classroom management – Research, practice, and contemporary issues* (pp. 73-96). Mahwah, NJ: Erlbaum.

Goodenow, C. (1993). The psychological sense of school membership among adolescents – Scale development and educational correlates. *Psychology in the Schools, 30*, 79-90.

Graham, S. & Williams, C. (2009). An attributional approach to motivation at school. In K. R. Wentzel & A. Wigfield (Eds.), *Handbook of motivation at school* (pp. 11-34). New York, NY: Taylor Francis.

Gregory, A., Cornell, D., Fan, X. T., Sheras, P., Shih, T. H., & Huang, F. (2010). Authoritative school discipline: High school practices associated with lower bullying and victimization. *Journal of Educational Psychology, 102*, 483-496.

Gregory, A. & Weinstein, R. S. (2004). Connection and regulation at home and in school: Predicting growth in achievement for adolescents. *Journal of Adolescent Research, 19*, 405-427.

Harter, S. (1978). Effectance motivation reconsidered toward a developmental model. *Human Development, 21*, 34-64.

Hayes, C. B., Ryan, A., & Zseller, E. B. (1994). The middle school child's perceptions of caring teachers. *American Journal of Education, 103*, 1-19.

Hinde, R. A. (1997). *Towards understanding relationships.* London: Academic Press.

Howes, C. & Hamilton, C. E. (1993). The changing experience of child care: Changes in teachers and in teacher-child relationships and children's social competence with peers. *Early Childhood Research Quarterly, 8*, 15-32.

Hoy, A. W. & Weinstein, C. S. (2006). Student and teacher perspectives on classroom management. In C. Evertson &. Weinstein (Eds.), *Handbook of classroom management – Research, practice, and contemporary issues* (pg. 181-219). Mahwah, NJ: Erlbaum.

Jussim, L., Robustelli, S., & Cain, T. (2009). Teacher expectations and self-fulfilling prophecies. In K. R. Wentzel & A. Wigfield (Eds.), *Handbook of motivation at school* (pp. 349-380). New York, NY: Taylor Francis.

Knafo, A. & Schwartz, S. H. (2003). Parenting and adolescents' accuracy in perceiving parental values. *Child Development, 74*, 595-611.

Kuczynski, L. & Parkin, M. (2007). Agency and bidirectionality in socialization: Interactions, transactions and relational dialectics. In J. Grusec & P. Hastings (Eds.), *Handbook of social development* (pp. 259-283). New York, NY: Guilford.

Kuijpers, J. M., Houtveen, A. M., & Wubbels, T. (2010). An integrated professional development model for effective teaching. *Teaching and Teacher Education, 26*, 1687-1694.

Laible, D. & Thompson, R. A. (2007). Early socialization: A relationship perspective. In J. Grusec & P. Hastings (Eds.), *Handbook of social development* (pp. 181-207). New York, NY: Guilford.

Lempers, J. D. & Clark-Lempers, D. S. (1992). Young, middle and late adolescents' comparisons of the functional importance of five significant relationships. *Journal of Youth and Adolescence, 21*, 53-96.

Lynch, M. & Cicchetti, D. (1997). Children's relationships with adults and peers: An examination of elementary and junior high school students. *Journal of School Psychology, 35*, 81-99.

Mashburn, A. J., Hamre, B. K., Downer, J. T., & Pianta, R. C. (2006). Teacher and classroom characteristics associated with teachers' ratings of prekindergartners' relationships and behaviors. *Journal of Psychoeducational Assessment, 24*, 367-380.

Murdock, T. B. & Miller, A. (2003). Teachers as sources of middle school students' motivational identity: Variable-centered and person-centered analytic approaches. *Elementary School Journal, 103*, 383-399.

Murphy, P. K. & Alexander, P. A, (2000). A motivated exploration of motivation terminology. *Contemporary Educational Psychology, 25*, 3-53.

Murray, C. & Greenberg, M. T. (2000). Children's relationship with teachers and bonds with school an investigation of patterns and correlates in middle childhood. *Journal of School Psychology, 38*, 423-445.

Oldfather, P. (1993). What students say about motivating experiences in a whole language classroom. *The Reading Teacher, 46*, 672-681.

Patrick, H., Ryan, A. M., & Kaplan, A. (2007). Early adolescents' perceptions of the classroom social environment, motivational beliefs, and engagement. *Journal of Educational Psychology, 99*, 83-98.

Peisner-Feinberg, E. S., Burchinal, M. R., Clifford, R. M., Culkin, M. L., Howes, C., Kagan, S. L., et al. (2001). The relation of preschool child-care quality to children's cognitive and social developmental trajectories through second grade. *Child Development, 72*, 1534-1553.

Pianta, R. C., Hamre, B., & Stuhlman, M. (2003). Relationships between teachers and children. In W. Reynolds & G. Miller (Eds.), *Handbook of psychology, vol. 7: Educational psychology* (pp. 199-234). New York: Wiley.

Pianta, R. C., Nimetz, S. L., & Bennett, E. (1997). Mother-child relationships, teacher-child relationships, and school outcomes in preschool and kindergarten. *Early Childhood Research Quarterly, 12*, 263-280.

Raider-Roth, M. B. (2005). Trusting what you know: Negotiating the relational context of classroom life. *Teachers College Record, 107*, 587-628.

Reid, M., Landesman, S., Treder, R., & Jaccard, J. (1989). "My family and friends": Six-to twelve-year-old children's perceptions of social support. *Child Development, 60*, 896-910.

Roeser, R. W. & Eccles, J. S. (1998). Adolescents' perceptions of middle school: Relation to longitudinal changes in academic and psychological adjustment. *Journal of Research on Adolescence, 8*, 123-158.

Schaps, E., Battistich, V., & Solomon, D. (1997). School as a caring community: A key to character education. In A. Molnar (Ed.), *Ninety-sixth yearbook of the National Society for the Study of Education* (pp. 127-139). Chicago: University of Chicago Press.

Schunk, D. & Pajares, F. (2009). Self-efficacy theory. In K. R. Wentzel & A. Wigfield (Eds.), *Handbook of motivation at school* (pp. 35-54). New York, NY: Taylor Francis.

Skinner, E. A. & Belmont, M. J. (1993). Motivation in the classroom: Reciprocal effects of teacher behavior and student engagement across the school year. *Journal of Educational Psychology, 85*, 571-581.

Smokowski, P. R., Reynolds, A. J., & Bezrucko, N. (2000). Resilience and protective factors in adolescence: An autobiographical perspective from disadvantaged youth. *Journal of School Psychology, 37*, 425-448.

Spera, C. (2006). Adolescents' perceptions of parental goals, practices, and styles in relation to their motivation and achievement. *Journal of Early Adolescence, 26*, 456-490.

Stipek, D. (2004). *Engaging in schools: Fostering high school students' motivation to learn.* Committee on increasing high school students' engagement and motivation to learn. Division of Behavioral and Social Sciences and Education. Washington, DC: National Academy Press.

Weinstein, R. S. (2002). *Reaching higher: The power of expectations in schooling.* Cambridge, MA: Harvard University Press.

Wentzel, K. R. (1991). Relations between social competence and academic achievement in early adolescence. *Child Development, 62*, 1066-1078.

Wentzel, K. R. (1994). Relations of social goal pursuit to social acceptance, classroom behavior, and perceived social support. *Journal of Educational Psychology, 86*, 173-182.

Wentzel, K. R. (1997). Student motivation in middle school: The role of perceived pedagogical caring. *Journal of Educational Psychology, 89*, 411-419.

Wentzel, K. R. (1998). Social support and adjustment in middle school: The role of parents, teachers, and peers. *Journal of Educational Psychology, 90*, 202-209.

Wentzel, K. R. (2002). Are effective teachers like good parents? Interpersonal predictors of school adjustment in early adolescence. *Child Development, 73*, 287-301.

Wentzel, K. R. (2003). School adjustment. In W. Reynolds & G. Miller (Eds.), *Handbook of psychology, vol. 7: Educational psychology* (pp. 235-258). New York: Wiley.

Wentzel, K. R. (2004). Understanding classroom competence: The role of social-motivational and self-processes. In R. Kail (Ed.), *Advances in Child Development and Behavior*, vol. 32 (pp 213-241). New York, NY: Elsevier.

Wentzel, K. R. (2009). Students' relationships with teachers as motivational contexts. In K. Wentzel & A. Wigfield (Eds.), *Handbook of motivation at school* (pp. 301-322). Mahwah, NJ: LEA.

Wentzel, K. R., Battle, A., Russell, S., & Looney, L. (2010). Social supports from teachers and peers as predictors of academic and social motivation. *Contemporary Educational Psychology, 35*, 193-202.

Wentzel, K. R. & Erdley, C. A. (1993). Strategies for making friends: Relations to social behavior and peer acceptance in early adolescence. *Developmental Psychology, 29*, 819-826.

Wentzel, K. R. & Looney, L. (2007). Socialization in school settings. In J. Grusec & P. Hastings (Eds.), *Handbook of social development* (pp. 382-403). New York, NY: Guilford.

Wentzel, K. R., Russell, S., & Baker, S. (2011). Emotional support and expectations from teachers, peers, and parents as predictors of young adolescent academic and social outcomes. Unpublished manuscript, University of Maryland, College Park.

Wentzel, K. R., & Wigfield, A. (2009). *Handbook of motivation at school.* New York, NY: Taylor Francis.

Wentzel, K. R., Williams, A. Y., & Tomback, R. M. (2005, April). *Relations of teacher and peer support to classroom behavior in middle school.* Paper presented at the annual meeting of the American Educational Research Association, Montreal, QC.

JANTINE L. SPILT AND HELMA M.Y. KOOMEN

3. UNDERSTANDING DISCORDANT RELATIONSHIPS BETWEEN TEACHERS AND DISRUPTIVE KINDERGARTEN CHILDREN

An Observational Study of Teachers' Pedagogical Practices

INTRODUCTION

Researchers increasingly consider teacher-child relationships in kindergarten as an important indicator of school readiness that forecasts children's future school success (Ladd, Herald, & Kochel, 2006; Mashburn & Pianta, 2006). Especially teacher-child conflict contributes to future socioemotional difficulties and academic underachievement (Hamre & Pianta, 2001; Ladd & Burgess, 1999) and, importantly, predicts children's adjustment beyond children's behavioural risk status (Ladd & Burgess, 2001; Stipek & Miles, 2008). Externalizing child behaviour is the strongest predictor of teacher-child conflict. Recent longitudinal research indicates a negative cycle of pronounced increases in externalizing behaviour and relational conflict over time that begins, importantly, with externalizing child behaviour (Doumen et al., 2008).

Young children's externalizing behaviour accounts for about more than half of the variance in teacher ratings of conflict (Hamre, Pianta, Downer, & Mashburn, 2008). Nowadays, researchers increasingly attempt to identify teacher characteristics and contextual factors that predict levels of conflict beyond children's problem behaviours. Previous research revealed that teacher variables such as depression, self-efficacy, and provision of emotional support at the classroom level could explain some of the variance in conflict above child behaviour (e.g., Hamre et al., 2008). However, the actual patterns and qualities of child and adult responses to one another appear key processes in dyadic relationship systems more than characteristics of individuals. Dyadic relationships result from a history of daily interactions (Pianta, Hamre, & Stuhlman, 2003). Over time, feedback and information exchange processes between partners form a structure for the interactions between adult and child (Pianta et al., 2003). Thus, through observing the verbal and nonverbal behaviour of individuals in dyadic interaction with each other, information could be revealed that is crucial to understand dyadic relationships, and specifically conflictual relationships between teachers and behaviourally-challenging children.

The dyadic relationship systems model of Pianta and colleagues (2003) emphasizes the bidirectional relations between child characteristics and teacher behaviour. Yet, while research consistently shows that relationship quality is a

T. Wubbels et al. (eds.), Interpersonal Relationships in Education, 37–49.

dyadic construct, most research has examined supportive behaviours from teachers at the classroom level (Buyse, Verschueren, Doumen, Van Damme, & Maes, 2008; La Paro, Rimm Kaufman, & Pianta, 2006). These studies mostly observe teacher behaviour in relation to multiple children to obtain a global indication of socioemotional climate and classroom management of teachers. Observational research of dyadic interactions from a relational perspective is relatively sparse.

The handful of studies available indicate that teachers have more interactions during a school day with children with externalizing problems than with typical children (Coplan & Prakash, 2003). However, the quality of these interactions is generally less favourable. Children with under-controlled behaviour or externalizing problems are more easily aroused, have poorer self-regulatory abilities, more difficulties following directions and instructions, and consequently are more likely to provoke confrontations with teachers than typical children. It is generally acknowledged that teachers should intervene and re-direct in such a way that they foster students' capacity for self-regulation rather than exerting control over children's behaviour to attain compliance. It is often seen, however, that teachers struggle with sensitively responding to children with conduct problems and that they experience heightened levels of conflict, anger, and even helplessness in relationships with young disruptive children (Spilt & Koomen, 2009). Teachers tend to be less responsive to prosocial behaviour of behaviourally-challenging children, provide less positive feedback, and show less attempts to engage children in learning activities (Brophy Herb, Lee, Nievar, & Stollak, 2007; Fry, 1983; McComas, Johnson, & Symons, 2005).

Yet, there is evidence from observational research that when teachers create a positive emotional classroom climate, the risk of conflictual relationships with teachers for behaviourally at-risk children is significantly reduced (Buyse et al., 2008). Similarly, Hamre and Pianta (2005) found that children with multiple risk factors had less conflictual relationships with teachers who demonstrated high levels of support as indicated by observation indices of sensitivity towards multiple children, a positive classroom climate, and adequate management behaviours. Comparable positive moderation effects have not been revealed on closeness (Buyse et al., 2008), but Rimm-Kaufmann and colleagues (2002) did find that socially-bold children displayed more socially competent behaviour when their teachers responded more sensitively to the child's behaviour (i.e., high responsiveness, low overcontrol, and low detachment). Together, these studies indicate a buffering effect of sensitive teacher behaviour on social outcomes for behaviourally at-risk children.

Surprisingly, Buyse and colleagues (2008) did not find that observations of effective classroom management were related to relational quality, nor did these influence the relation between aggression and relational conflict. It is likely, however, that teachers' regulating practices toward a *particular* child with behavioural difficulties contribute more to the quality of the relationship than classroom management because behaviour at the dyadic level is a more proximal factor in the dyadic systems model (Pianta et al., 2003). Therefore, we aimed to observe the quality of teachers' behaviour management in relation to *individual* children.

We hypothesized that the quality of teachers' pedagogical practices buffers kindergarten children with externalizing behaviour against poor teacher-child relationships. Moreover, unlike the studies of Hamre and Pianta (2005) and Rimm-Kaufmann and colleagues (2002) but similar to Buyse and colleagues (2008), and in line with the majority of parenting and educational research (Connell & Wellborn, 1991), we distinguished between teacher sensitivity and behaviour management of teachers. We expected that effective pedagogical practices of kindergarten teachers would moderate (i.e., weaken) the association between externalizing child behaviour and relationship quality, and especially relational conflict (cf. Buyse et al., 2008).

PERSPECTIVES ON GENDER DIFFERENCES

When studying linkages between disruptive behaviour problems and relationship quality, it is important to consider differences between boys and girls. In early education, boys typically have poorer behavioural regulation skills and more externalizing problems than girls and consequently have more conflictual relationships with teachers (Birch & Ladd, 1997; Hamre & Pianta, 2001). Because of this heightened risk of school adjustment problems for boys, it has been contended that boys are more susceptible to environmental influences such as social support from teachers in comparison to girls (Ewing & Taylor, 2009; Hamre & Pianta, 2001). Thus, according to this academic/behavioural risk perspective, teachers' responsiveness may have a stronger influence on the linkage between aggressive behaviour and teacher-child relationship quality for boys than girls.

Alternatively, the gender role socialization perspective asserts that girls are more oriented towards social relationships with others (Ewing & Taylor, 2009; Maccoby, 1998). This perspective predicts that girls are more susceptible to messages of acceptance or rejection that are conveyed in teacher behaviour than boys. Following this reasoning, girls may profit more from high-quality interactions with the teacher than boys, which implicates that teachers' responsiveness may have a stronger influence on the linkage between aggressive behaviour and teacher-child relationship quality for girls in comparison to boys.

So far, research has shown limited support for both perspectives (Baker, 2006; Ewing & Taylor, 2009; Hamre & Pianta, 2001). We therefore stated two competing hypotheses. According to the academic risk perspective, we expected that the quality of teacher practices has a stronger influence on the association between externalizing behaviour and conflict for boys. Conversely, based on the gender role socialization perspective, a stronger effect of the quality of teacher practices on the association between externalizing behaviour and conflict was expected for girls.

PRESENT RESEARCH

In this study we observed the quality of pedagogical practices of kindergarten teachers in interactions with individual children to examine the protective role of sensitive teacher practices for behaviourally at-risk children, and for boys and girls separately. More specifically, we aimed to understand whether actual teacher practices moderate the linkage between externalizing child behaviour and relational conflict. As discussed before, this research was guided by Pianta's model of dyadic adult-child relationships and the notion of information exchange processes as well as research highlighting the importance of teachers' actual responsiveness towards individual children.

As teacher-child interactions are embedded in the classroom context, we observed teachers' pedagogical practices in an arranged but ecologically valid small-group task setting that included four individual children with different behaviour profiles. Children were selected based on teacher ratings of externalizing and internalizing behaviour in order to obtain diversity in children's behavioural characteristics that is representative of regular kindergarten classrooms. To minimize differences across classrooms that are due to probability, structured observations were conducted. Structured observations have proven satisfactory predictive validity in previous research (Zaslow et al., 2006).

METHOD

Sample and Selection

The sample consisted of 48 kindergarten teachers (all female). Teachers completed a behaviour checklist for all children in their class. In every class, children were categorized into four groups: 1) 'average children' with relatively low scores on externalizing and internalizing behaviour; 2) 'inhibited children' with relatively high scores on internalizing but not on externalizing behaviour; 3) 'disruptive children' with relatively high scores on externalizing but not on internalizing behaviour; and 4) 'inhibited-disruptive children' scoring relatively high on both externalizing and internalizing behaviour. Cut-off scores were 1.33 and 1.21 on a scale ranging from 1 to 4 for Internalizing and Externalizing Behaviour, respectively. Those values were based on the median values derived from a large randomly-selected kindergarten sample ($n = 1559$). From each group, one child was randomly selected for participation ($n = 192$, 105 boys). In this way, a sample of children with a variety of behaviour characteristics was selected that is representative of the heterogeneity of behaviour characteristics of children in regular kindergarten classrooms. Also, given this selection procedure, Externalizing Behaviour could be used as a continuous variable. Teachers were not informed about the selection procedure.

Measures and Procedures

The study started in early spring. For selection purposes, teachers completed the Behaviour Questionnaire for Two- to Six-Year-Olds-Modified (BQTSYO-M; Goossens, Dekker, Bruinsma, & De Ruyter, 2000; Thijs, Koomen, De Jong, Van der Leij, & Van Leeuwen, 2004). The BQTSYO-M is a Dutch adaptation of the widely-used Preschool Behaviour Questionnaire (Behar, 1977) that comprises broadband scales for Externalizing (14 items; e.g., 'Bullies other children', 'A busy child') and Internalizing Behaviour (15 items; e.g., 'Shy or timid towards other children', 'Easily upset'). Items are rated on a 4-point scale ranging from 1 (*absolutely not characteristic*) to 4 (*very characteristic*). Previous research has supported the reliability and validity of the scale with Cronbach's alpha's ≥ .81 and .91 for Internalizing and Externalizing Behaviour, respectively (e.g., Thijs & Koomen, 2008).

After completion of the selection procedure, data on relationship quality and teacher practices were collected. Teachers filled out a shortened version of the Dutch adapted Student-Teacher Relationship Scale (Koomen, Verschueren, & Pianta, 2007; Koomen, Verschueren, van Schooten, Jak, & Pianta, 2012; Pianta, 2001) including the subscale Closeness (i.e., the degree of warmth, trust, and open communication, 6 items, $\alpha = .78$) and Conflict (i.e., the degree of discordance, stress, and negativity in the relationship, 8 items, $\alpha = .86$).

Teacher behaviour was observed on two regular school days in the classroom within three weeks (at least one week apart). Video-recordings were made of a natural 15-minute small-group task activity with the teacher and the four selected children (see Thijs & Koomen, 2008 for description of the task activity). During the activity, the four children worked individually on a task and teachers were instructed to provide assistance as they were used to. The same interaction task was administered about two weeks later. Videotapes were coded afterwards by trained coders who were not familiar with the participants to increase reliability. For each child, both episodes were independently rated in a random order for the degree of Teacher Sensitivity (TS) and quality of Behaviour Management (BM). Teacher Sensitivity denotes the provision of comfort, reassurance, and support with respect to a child's academic and socioemotional needs. Quality of Behaviour Management refers to proactive responses to influence a child's behaviour through clear communication of expectations, adequate feedback, and consistent consequences. Global ratings of TS and BM were given on a 7-point scale (1 = low quality, 7 = high quality) using an adaptation of the Classroom Assessment Scoring System for observations of teacher behaviour in dyadic interaction with a particular child (La Paro, Pianta, & Stuhlman, 2002; Verschueren, Van de Water, Buyse, & Doumen, 2006). The average score of the two episodes was used in the analyses. Intraclass Correlations (ICCs) were calculated to assess interrater reliability. ICCs between .75 and 1.00 indicate excellent agreement; ICCs between .60 and .74 indicate good agreement; and ICCs between .40 and .59 are considered fair (Cicchetti et al., 2006). The ICCs for TS and BM were .67 and .72, respectively.

Analyses

Linear regression analyses were conducted for the total sample as well as for boys and girls separately. The predictor variables Teacher Sensitivity, Behaviour Management, and Externalizing Child Behaviour were standardized to ease interpretation. To measure moderation effects, interaction terms were computed by multiplying the standardized predictors. All predictors were simultaneously added to the regression models with relationship quality dimensions as the dependent variables. Non-significant interaction terms were removed from the final models. Simple slopes are presented to visually probe significant interaction effects (see Figures 1 and 2).

Because of the nested structure of the data, we examined the level of between-subject variance. Random intercept models without predictors indicated significant between-subject variance for Closeness (21%, $p < .05$). Therefore, a multilevel regression model (i.e., children nested within classrooms) with a random intercept and fixed slope effects was estimated for Closeness in order to reduce the chance of spurious results. For Conflict, no between-subject variance was found and regular regression analyses were performed.

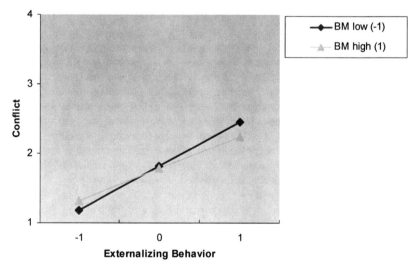

Figure 1. Moderation effect of behaviour management (BM) for boys. Standardized predictor variables are depicted.

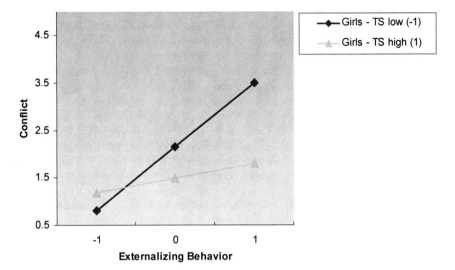

Figure 2. Moderation effect of Teacher Sensitivity (TS) for girls.
Standardized predictor variables are depicted.

RESULTS

Preliminary analyses. Multilevel regression analyses with gender dummy-coded showed that boys received higher scores on Conflict and lower scores on Closeness in comparison to girls ($p < .05$, two-sided). The gender difference with respect to Behaviour Management was marginally significant ($p = .053$, two-sided). Table 1 presents the means, standard deviations and intercorrelations for boys and girls separately.

Moderation effects. The regression coefficients of the final regression models are reported in Table 2. Behaviour Management moderated the link between Externalizing Behaviour and Conflict, such that Externalizing Behaviour was less predictive of Conflict when the quality of Behaviour Management was high (F_{change} $(1,167) = 4.359$, $p < .05$). In addition, when separate analyses were conducted for boys and girls, it was found that Teacher Sensitivity and not Behaviour Management moderated the association between Externalizing Behaviour and Conflict for girls: Externalizing Behaviour appeared less predictive of Conflict when levels of Teacher Sensitivity were high (F_{change} $(1,75) = 12.087$, $p < .01$). The moderation effect of Teacher Sensitivity on the association between Externalizing Behaviour and Conflict for girls is pictured in Figure 2. Under conditions of low Teacher Sensitivity (i.e., 1 standard deviation below the mean), girls with

Externalizing Behaviour (i.e., 1 standard deviation above the mean) had much more conflictual relationships with teachers than under conditions of high Teacher Sensitivity (i.e., 1 standard deviation above the mean). The size of this difference was large (Cohen's $d = 2.58$).

The moderating effect of Behaviour Management was still found for boys though marginally significant (F_{change} (1,87) = 2.727, $p = .10$). Figure 1 depicts the moderation effect of Behaviour Management on the association between Externalizing Behaviour and Conflict for boys. Under conditions of low Behaviour Management (i.e., 1 standard deviation below the mean) the boys with Externalizing Behaviour (i.e., 1 standard deviation above the mean) had significantly more conflictual relationships with teachers than under conditions of high-quality Behaviour Management. The size of this difference was modest (Cohen's $d = 0.23$).

Teacher Sensitivity and Behaviour Management did not moderate the association between Externalizing Behaviour and Closeness.

Table 1. Descriptive statistics and correlations for boys and girls.

	n	M (SD)	2	3	4	5
Boys						
1. Externalizing Behaviour	105	1.55 (.56)	-.38	.68**	-.04	-.20*
2. Closeness	96	4.11 (.68)		-.50**	.02	.16
3. Conflict	96	2.02 (.94)			-.01	-.18[a]
4. Teacher Sensitivity	104	5.02 (.82)				.48**
5. Behaviour Management	104	5.15 (.86)				
Girls						
1. Externalizing Behaviour	87	1.22 (.30)	-.07	.64**	.21*	-.10
2. Closeness	80	4.48 (.62)		-.08	.05	.00
3. Conflict	80	1.49 (.66)			.07	-.11
4. Teacher Sensitivity	87	5.18 (.68)				.54**
5. Behaviour Management	87	5.38 (.68)				

$* p < .05$, $** p < .01$, [a]$p = .06$ (two-tailed)

DISCUSSION

We aimed to understand whether actual pedagogical practices of teachers in dyadic interactions with individual children could reduce the risk for interpersonal conflict that is typically associated with early externalizing behaviour problems. Unlike other studies, we conducted *structured* observations of teachers' sensitivity and quality of behaviour management in interactions with *individual* children. In addition, considering previous research that has hypothesized important gender differences in susceptibility to social influences, we studied the moderating role of pedagogical practices of teachers for boys and girls separately.

Table 2. Final regression models.

	Closeness B (SE)	Conflict B (SE)
Total sample		
Externalizing Behaviour (EB)	-.23 (.05)**	.59 (.05)**
Behaviour Management (BM)	.02 (.06)	-.02 (.05)
Teacher Sensitivity (TS)	.03 (.06)	-.03 (.05)
Interaction EB*BM	-	-.09 (.04)*
Interaction EB*TS	-	-
Boys		
Externalizing Behaviour (EB)	-.23 (.06)**	.55 (.08)**
Behaviour Management (BM)	.05 (.07)	-.01 (.08)
Teacher Sensitivity (TS)	-.01 (.07)	-.02 (.07)
Interaction EB*BM	-	-.09 (.056)
Interaction EB*TS	-	-
Girls		
Externalizing Behaviour (EB)	-.08 (.11)	.83 (.09)**
Behaviour Management (BM)	-.02 (.10)	.04 (.07)
Teacher Sensitivity (TS)	.07 (.10)	-.33 (.11)**
Interaction EB*BM	-	-
Interaction EB*TS	-	-.52 (.15)

$* p < .05$, $** p < .01$, $^{a}p = .10$ (two-tailed). Unstandardized beta's are reported; predictors were standardized. Non-significant interaction terms were removed from the model.

As expected, the association between externalizing behaviour and conflict was most pronounced when teachers demonstrated low responsiveness to children's unique needs (Buyse et al., 2008; Hamre & Pianta, 2005; Rimm-Kaufman et al., 2002). For girls, teacher sensitivity appeared to play an important role. Girls with high levels of externalizing behaviour had significantly less conflictual relationships with their teachers when their teachers responded sensitively to their socioemotional and academic needs. When comparing the predicted group-mean level of conflict with norms for Dutch 5-year old girls, the scores indicate slightly above-average levels of conflict for the high-sensitivity group (Koomen et al., 2007). Importantly, for behaviourally at-risk girls with teachers demonstrating low sensitivity, the degree of conflict points to clinical levels of conflict. No evidence was obtained for the moderating role of the quality of teachers' behaviour management for girls. In line with the gender socialization perspective, these findings suggest that girls in particular are sensitive to teacher behaviours that

45

convey positive messages of care, acceptance, and respect. Teachers who sensitively respond to such needs appear capable of preventing behaviour problems from progressing into conflictual relationships that are characterized by mistrust, negativity, and discordance.

For boys, adequate behaviour management of teachers significantly weakened the association between externalizing behaviour and conflict. The risk of conflictual relationships was slightly reduced for boys with externalizing problems when teachers used proactive strategies to regulate the child's behaviour. In line with the academic risk perspective, it is likely that boys primarily need teachers as an external source of behaviour regulation. Research in kindergarten has shown that boys have less developed self-regulation skills to direct and control their behaviour and attention than girls, though these skills are necessary to facilitate learning processes (Matthews, Ponitz, & Morrison, 2009). Poor behavioural control disrupts classroom routines and could easily lead to conflicts with teachers. The current results signify that proactive behaviour management of teachers through clear communication of expectations, adequate feedback, and consistent consequences could offer boys an external source of regulation that reduces the chance that behavioural difficulties result in misunderstandings and conflicts.

In convergence with other studies on teacher practices, no main effects of teachers' observed practices on teacher-student relationship quality was found (Buyse, Verschueren, & Doumen, 2009; Hamre & Pianta, 2005). Moreover, the quality of teachers' practices was relatively high. The pedagogical practices of teachers seemed on average good enough for typical children to engage in positive relationships with teachers. However, behaviourally-challenging children were at-risk of conflictual relationships under conditions of poor teacher practices, indicating a 'dual risk' of academic failure (Stipek & Miles, 2008).

From a practical perspective, the finding that actual teacher behaviour can reduce the chance of conflictual relationships for behaviourally-challenging children is of high importance. Behaviour problems typically exacerbate relational conflict over time, which in turn undermines children's engagement in learning activities and academic progress (Doumen et al., 2008; Stipek & Miles, 2008). Insight in proximal factors that could ameliorate such negative risk patterns is therefore essential. Previous research already showed that teacher variables such as depression and self-efficacy play a moderating role as well as classroom climate and teachers' pedagogical style (Buyse et al., 2008; Hamre et al., 2008). The current study provides evidence that dyadic interaction processes that are proximal to the teacher-child dyadic system could counteract risks associated with early externalizing behaviour. Importantly, these behaviours of teachers can be influenced. There are promising training programs to help teachers improve their responsiveness in interactions with children (Kinzie et al., 2006; Pianta, Mashburn, Downer, Hamre, & Justice, 2008; Raver et al., 2008; Spilt, Koomen, Thijs, & van der Leij, 2012).

Several remarks about the study can be made. First, in line with the literature, we studied early externalizing behaviour as a predictor of conflict (Doumen et al.,

2008). However, the cross-sectional design of the study precludes causal inferences. Second, teachers reported on both externalizing child behaviour and relationship quality. These associations may have partly reflected same-source, same-method variance. Third, teachers participated voluntary.

It is also noteworthy that the overall sample was not highly at-risk and children exhibited relatively low to moderately mild externalizing problems. Only a minority of the children had more severe behaviour problems. Furthermore, results should be interpreted within the context of a small-group task activity. Unstructured situations provide a different setting to observe the behaviour management of teachers. For instance, free play activities or the transition from one activity to another may provide additional information about the behaviour management of teachers in relation to a target child. Lastly, the dyadic systems model emphasizes the dyadic nature of teacher and child behaviour (Pianta et al., 2003). Therefore, future research could observe both teacher and child behaviour during the same interaction setting in order to obtain a more detailed and in-depth examination of reciprocal behaviour and information exchange processes.

In conclusion, as behaviourally-challenging children are at risk of developing conflictual teacher-child relationships, which increases the chance of academic failure, it is of significance that teachers' actual responsiveness to children's behavioural and socioemotional needs could make a difference. In addition, the study indicates that behaviourally at-risk boys and girls may have different needs that teachers need to be aware of.

REFERENCES

Baker, J. A. (2006). Contributions of teacher-child relationships to positive school adjustment during elementary school. *Journal of School Psychology, 44*(3), 211-229.

Behar, L. B. (1977). The Preschool Behavior Questionnaire. *Journal of Abnormal Child Psychology, 5*(3), 265-275.

Birch, S. H. & Ladd, G. W. (1997). The teacher-child relationship and children's early school adjustment. *Journal of School Psychology, 35*(1), 61-79.

Brophy Herb, H. E., Lee, R. E., Nievar, M. A., & Stollak, G. (2007). Preschoolers' social competence: Relations to family characteristics, teacher behaviors and classroom climate. *Journal of Applied Developmental Psychology, 28*(2), 134-148.

Buyse, E., Verschueren, K., & Doumen, S. (2009). Preschoolers' attachment to mother and risk for adjustment problems in kindergarten: Can teachers make a difference? *Social Development, 20*(1), 33-50.

Buyse, E., Verschueren, K., Doumen, S., Van Damme, J., & Maes, F. (2008). Classroom problem behavior and teacher-child relationships in kindergarten: The moderating role of classroom climate. *Journal of School Psychology, 46*(4), 367-391.

Cicchetti, D., Bronen, R., Spencer, S., Haut, S., Berg, A., Oliver, P., et al. (2006). Rating scales, scales of measurement, issues of reliability: Resolving some critical issues for clinicians and researchers. *Journal of Nervous and Mental Disease, 194*, 557–564.

Connell, J. P. & Wellborn, J. G. (1991). Competence, autonomy, and relatedness: A motivational analysis of self-system processes. In M. R. Gunnar & L. A. Sroufe (Eds.), *Self processes and development* (Vol. 23, pp. 43-77). Hillsdale, NJ: Erlbaum.

Coplan, R. J. & Prakash, K. (2003). Spending time with teacher: Characteristics of preschoolers who frequently elicit versus initiate interactions with teachers. *Early Childhood Research Quarterly, 18*(1), 143-158.

Doumen, S., Verschueren, K., Buyse, E., Germeijs, V., Luyckx, K., & Soenens, B. (2008). Reciprocal relations between teacher-child conflict and aggressive behaviour in kindergarten: A three-wave longitudinal study. *Journal of Clinical Child and Adolescent Psychology, 37*(3), 588-599.

Ewing, A. R. & Taylor, A. R. (2009). The role of child gender and ethnicity in teacher-child relationship quality and children's behavioral adjustment in preschool. *Early Childhood Research Quarterly, 24*(1), 92-105.

Fry, P. S. (1983). Process measures of problem and non-problem children's classroom behaviour: The influence of teacher behaviour variables. *British Journal of Educational Psychology, 53*(1), 79-88.

Goossens, F. A., Dekker, P., Bruinsma, C., & De Ruyter, P. A. (2000). *De gedrags vragenlijst voor peuters en kleuters: Factor structuur, betrouwbaarheid en validiteit.* [Behavior questionnaire for 2- to 6-year-olds: Factor structure, reliability, and validity]. VU University Amsterdam.

Hamre, B. K. & Pianta, R. C. (2001). Early teacher-child relationships and the trajectory of children's school outcomes through eighth grade. *Child Development, 72*(2), 625-638.

Hamre, B. K. & Pianta, R. C. (2005). Can instructional and emotional support in the first-grade classroom make a difference for children at risk of school failure? *Child Development, 76*, 949-967.

Hamre, B. K., Pianta, R. C., Downer, J. T., & Mashburn, A. J. (2008). Teachers' perceptions of conflict with young students: Looking beyond problem behaviors. *Social Development, 17*, 115-136.

Kinzie, M. B., Whitaker, S. D., Neesen, K., Kelley, M., Matera, M., & Pianta, R. C. (2006). Innovative web-based professional development for teachers of at-risk preschool children. *Educational Technology & Society, 9*(4), 194-204.

Koomen, H. M. Y., Verschueren, K., & Pianta, R. C. (2007). *Leerling leerkracht relatie vragenlijst: Handleiding* [Student teacher relationship scale: Manual]. Houten: Bohn Stafleu van Loghum.

Koomen, H. M. Y., Verschueren, K., Van Schooten, E., Jak, S., & Pianta, R. C. (2012). Validating the student-teacher relationship scale: Testing factor structure and measurement invariance across child gender and age in a Dutch sample. *Journal of School Psychology, 50*, 215-234.

La Paro, K. M., Pianta, R. C., & Stuhlman, M. W. (2002). *Classroom Assessment Scoring System (CLASS).* Charlottesville: University of Virginia.

La Paro, K. M., Rimm Kaufman, S. E., & Pianta, R. C. (2006). Kindergarten to 1st grade: Classroom characteristics and the stability and change of children's classroom experiences. *Journal of Research in Childhood Education, 21*(2), 189-202.

Ladd, G. W. & Burgess, K. B. (1999). Charting the relationship trajectories of aggressive, withdrawn, and aggressive/withdrawn children during early grade school. *Child Development, 70*(4), 910-929.

Ladd, G. W. & Burgess, K. B. (2001). Do relational risks and protective factors moderate the linkages between childhood aggression and early psychological and school adjustment? *Child Development, 72*(5), 1579-1601.

Ladd, G. W., Herald, S. L., & Kochel, K. P. (2006). School readiness: Are there social prerequisites? *Early Education and Development, 17*(1), 115-150.

Maccoby, E. E. (1998). *The two sexes: Growing up apart, coming together.* Cambridge, MA: Belknap Press/Harvard University Press.

Mashburn, A. J. & Pianta, R. C. (2006). Social relationships and school readiness. *Early Education and Development, 17*(1), 151-176.

Matthews, J. S., Ponitz, C. C., & Morrison, F. J. (2009). Early gender differences in self-regulation and academic achievement. *Journal of Educational Psychology, 101*(3), 689-704.

McComas, J. J., Johnson, L., & Symons, F. J. (2005). Teacher and peer responsivity to pro-social behaviour of high aggressors in preschool. *Educational Psychology, 25*(2-3), 223-231.

Pianta, R. C. (2001). *Student-teacher relationship scale. Professional manual.* Lutz, Florida: Psychological Assessment Resources.

Pianta, R. C., Hamre, B., & Stuhlman, M. (2003). Relationships between teachers and children. In W. M. Reynolds & G. E. Miller (Eds.), *Handbook of psychology: Educational psychology* (Vol. 7, pp. 199-234). Hoboken, NJ: John Wiley & Sons.

Pianta, R. C., Mashburn, A. J., Downer, J. T., Hamre, B. K., & Justice, L. (2008). Effects of web-mediated professional development resources on teacher-child interactions in pre-kindergarten classrooms. *Early Childhood Research Quarterly, 23*(4), 431-451.

Raver, C. C., Jones, S. M., Li-Grining, C. P., Metzger, M., Champion, K. M., & Sardin, L. (2008). Improving preschool classroom processes: Preliminary findings from a randomized trial implemented in Head Start settings. *Early Childhood Research Quarterly, 23*(1), 10-26.

Rimm-Kaufman, S. E., Early, D. M., Cox, M. J., Saluja, G., Pianta, R. C., Bradley, R. H., et al. (2002). Early behavioral attributes and teachers' sensitivity as predictors of competent behavior in the kindergarten classroom. *Journal of Applied Developmental Psychology, 23*(4), 451-470.

Spilt, J. L. & Koomen, H. M. Y. (2009). Widening the view on teacher-child relationships: Teachers' narratives concerning disruptive versus non-disruptive children. *School Psychology Review, 38*, 86-101.

Spilt, J. L., Koomen, H. M. Y., Thijs, J. T., & Van der Leij, A. (2012). Supporting teachers' relationships with disruptive children: The potential of relationship-focused reflection. *Attachment & Human Development, 14*, 305-318.

Stipek, D. & Miles, S. (2008). Effects of aggression on achievement: Does conflict with the teacher make it worse? *Child Development, 79*(6), 1721-1735.

Thijs, J. T. & Koomen, H. M. Y. (2008). Task-related interactions between kindergarten children and their teachers: The role of emotional security. *Infant and child development, 17*(2), 181-197.

Thijs, J. T., Koomen, H. M. Y., De Jong, P. F., Van der Leij, A., & Van Leeuwen, M. G. P. (2004). Internalizing behaviors among kindergarten children: measuring dimensions of social withdrawal with a checklist. *Journal of Clinical Child and Adolescent Psychology, 33*, 802-812.

Verschueren, K., Van de Water, G., Buyse, E., & Doumen, S. (2006). *Aanpassing van het Classroom Assessment Scoring System-Kindergarten voor meting van de individuele leerkracht-leerling relatie.*[Adaptation of the Classroom Assessment Scoring System-Kindergarten to measure the individual teacher-child relationship].Unpublished manuscript, Centrum voor Schoolpsychologie, K. U. Leuven.

Zaslow, M. J., Weinfield, N. S., Gallagher, M., Hair, E. C., Ogawa, J. R., Egeland, B., et al. (2006). Longitudinal prediction of child outcomes from differing measures of parenting in a low-income sample. *Developmental Psychology, 42*(1), 27-37.

DEBORA L. ROORDA, HELMA M. Y. KOOMEN AND
FRANS J. OORT

4. AN OBSERVATIONAL STUDY OF TEACHERS' AFFILLIATION AND CONTROL BEHAVIOURS TOWARDS KINDERGARTEN CHILDREN[i]

Associations with Teacher-Child Relationship Quality

INTRODUCTION

Previous research has shown that the quality of teacher-child relationships influences a range of children's social and academic outcomes, such as classroom participation (e.g., Ladd, Birch, & Buhs, 1999), academic performance (e.g., Hamre & Pianta, 2001), and peer acceptance (e.g., Henricsson & Rydell, 2006). Most research on teacher-child relationships has used teachers' or students' reports of the global quality of the relationship. Far less is known, however, about the ways in which teachers and children interact with each other in concrete daily situations. The present study addresses the need for observational work that captures how teachers and students interact in real time in authentic classroom settings. Interpersonal theory was used to observe and meticulously analyse teachers' videotaped interactive behaviours towards kindergarten children. This theory offers a conceptual framework to describe and predict dyadic interactions between individuals (Kiesler, 1996; Sadler & Woody, 2003).

Interactive behaviours are considered to be guided by individuals' relationship perceptions, because perceptions work as filters for information about the other's behaviour and are inclined to act as self-fulfilling prophecies (Pianta, Hamre, & Stuhlman, 2003). In the present study, we investigated whether teachers' perceptions about the quality of the relationship with a specific child influenced their actual interactive behaviours towards that child. Teacher-child relationships seem to be especially important for children who are at risk for social and academic maladjustment due to behaviour problems (Hamre & Pianta, 2001). Therefore, we also examined whether teachers interacted differently with children they rated displaying various levels of externalizing and internalizing behaviour.

Interpersonal Theory

According to interpersonal theory (Leary, 1957), interactions can be described on two dimensions: control and affiliation. Control represents the degree of power, dominance and influence in the interaction, with dominance at one end of the dimension, and submissiveness at the other. Affiliation describes the degree of

T. Wubbels et al. (eds.), Interpersonal Relationships in Education, 51–65.

proximity, warmth, and support in the interaction, and ranges from friendliness to hostility (Gurtman, 2001; Kiesler, 1996). These dimensions are considered to be orthogonal (Sadler & Woody, 2003).

A central concept in interpersonal theory is the complementarity principle. This principle can be used to predict people's interactive behaviours based on the behaviours of their interaction partner. The most common conception of complementarity is that of Carson (1969) and Kiesler (1983). According to this approach, interactive behaviours are complementary when they are similar on the affiliation dimension and reciprocal on control (Sadler & Woody, 2003). Thus, friendliness will elicit friendly behaviour, whereas dominance will lead to submissive behaviour and vice versa. Researchers have applied this theory in educational settings, using a questionnaire to measure teachers' interpersonal styles in secondary education (e.g., Wubbels & Brekelmans, 2005). However, these studies are mostly based on aggregates of students' reports of teachers' global interpersonal styles, and not on observations of teachers' interactions with individual students. In the present study, we apply this theory to observations of teachers' dyadic interactions with kindergarten children. Independent observers rated teachers' interpersonal behaviours every five seconds, hereby taking into account the continually changing nature of interactive behaviours. This approach has the added advantage that it provides the opportunity to study reciprocal influences between interaction partners and interventions to break negative interaction cycles in the future.

Developmental Systems Model of Teacher Child Relationships

Pianta and colleagues (2003) present a developmental systems model of teacher-child relationships, which considers interactive behaviours as one of the key components of affective relationships between teachers and children. This model consists of four relationship components: features of individuals (developmental history and biological factors), representational models of teacher and child (perceptions and emotions), information exchange processes (interactive behaviours), and external influences. These components influence each other in dynamic, reciprocal ways. Perceptions and selective attending of teacher and child function as filters for information about the other's behaviour. These filters can limit the nature and form of the information included in feedback processes, and are considered to be influential in guiding behaviours between interaction partners, because perceptions and selective attending are likely to be self-fulfilling. Over time, these feedback and information exchange processes provide a structure for the interactions between teacher and child (Pianta et al., 2003). Although relationship perceptions are considered to guide interactive behaviours, it can also be argued that these influences are in the opposite direction, because relationship perceptions result from a history of daily interactions (Pianta et al., 2003). In the present study, we focus on teachers' interactive behaviours as outcome variable, because interactions were observed at one specific point in time. Therefore, we were not able to investigate how the development of interactive behaviours over time could change relationship perceptions.

Teachers' relationship perceptions are often measured with the Student-Teacher Relationship Scale (STRS; Pianta, 2001). The STRS includes three dimensions: closeness, conflict, and dependency. Closeness measures the degree of affection, warmth, and open communication in the teacher-child relationship. Conflict describes the extent of negativity, anger, and discordance. Dependency refers to the degree of clinginess, overreliance, and possessiveness of the child in the relationship. Accordingly, closeness is looked at as a positive relational factor, supporting children to deal with the requirements in school. Conflict and dependency, on the other hand, are viewed as negative relational factors, hampering and interfering with children's coping with demands they face in school. Especially conflict appears to have a strong influence on children's school functioning (e.g., Hamre & Pianta, 2001).

Child Characteristics and Teachers' Interactive Behaviours

According to the developmental systems model (Pianta et al., 2003), teacher-child relationships are influenced by child characteristics, such as gender and children's behaviours. Previous research based on both teacher reports (e.g., Baker, 2006; Hamre & Pianta, 2001) and independent observations (e.g., Ladd et al., 1999) has found that teachers' relationship perceptions and interactions with children are closer and less conflictual for girls than for boys.

In addition, numerous studies have found that teachers rate their relationships with externalizing children as less favourable than their relationships with normative children, more specifically, less close and more conflictual and dependent (e.g., Doumen et al., 2008; Thijs & Koomen, 2009). Children's disruptive behaviours (i.e., anger, hostility, and aggression) were also negatively associated with observer ratings of teacher sensitivity (Rimm-Kaufman et al., 2002). Likewise, DeMulder, Denham, Schmidt, and Mitchell (2000) showed that teachers' observed interactions with aggressive children were less secure than with normative children. Teachers also frequently reported their relationships with internalizing children as being less close and more dependent than their relationships with average children (e.g., Arbeau, Coplan, & Weeks, 2010; Thijs & Koomen, 2009). Accordingly, teachers' observed interactions with anxious/ withdrawn children were found to be less secure than with normative children (DeMulder et al., 2000). In addition, behavioural observations showed that teachers initiated more interactions towards children they rated as anxious/withdrawn, than towards normative children. They asked more questions, intervened more often, and initiated more interactions with anxious/withdrawn children (Coplan & Prakash, 2003).

PRESENT STUDY

In the present study, we investigated teachers' behaviours during interactions with kindergarten children. We observed teachers' interactive behaviours during a small group task with four behaviourally diverse children. Children were selected based on their scores on internalizing and externalizing behaviours relative to their classmates. We had two main aims. The first aim was to investigate whether teachers' interactive behaviours towards individual kindergarten children could be predicted by their perceptions of the relationships they share with these children. The second aim was to examine the validity of our observation scales for teacher affiliation and control by relating them to children's gender and behaviours. These aims resulted in three research questions: 1) Do teachers' relationship perceptions (i.e., closeness, conflict, and dependency) predict teachers' actual interactive behaviours in the classroom (i.e., affiliation and control)? 2) Are there gender differences in teachers' display of affiliation and control? and 3) Do teachers' ratings of children's externalizing and internalizing behaviours predict the degree of affiliation and control they display towards these children? The expected associations between predictor and outcome variables are presented in Figure 1.

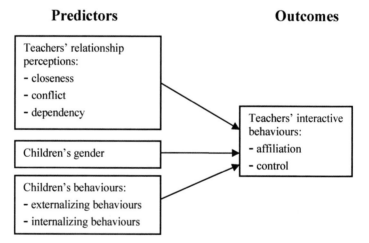

Figure 1. Expected associations between predictor and outcome variables.

As mentioned before, perceptions of teachers are considered to be influential in guiding behaviours between interaction partners (Pianta et al., 2003). With respect to the first research question, we therefore expected that teachers' relationship perceptions, as measured with the STRS, could be used to predict their actual interactive behaviours, which were observed with scales based on interpersonal theory. Because high scores on closeness as well as affiliation represent positive emotions and behaviours, we expected closeness to have a positive influence on teacher affiliation. We hypothesized conflict to have a negative influence on teacher affiliation, because both high scores on conflict and low scores on affiliation represent negative emotions and behaviours. Because dependency is also considered to be a negative dimension of the affective teacher-child relationship (Hamre & Pianta, 2001), we expected dependency to have a negative influence on teacher affiliation. Teacher control focuses solely on power and dominance in the interaction and not on the emotional quality of interactions. Therefore, we expected that teacher control would not be influenced by any of the three relationship dimensions.

The second aim of our study was to investigate the validity of our observation scales. In the present study, we used new observation scales to measure teacher affiliation and control (described below). The validity of these scales for observations in a dyadic setting was supported in a previous study (Thijs, Koomen, Roorda, & Ten Hagen, 2011). In the present study, we slightly adapted the scales for use in a small group setting, without changing their intended meaning. The validity of the scales in this group setting needs further support. According to the model of Pianta and colleagues (2003), interactions between teacher and child are influenced, besides by relationship perceptions, by child characteristics, such as gender and children's behaviours. Therefore, we further investigated the validity of our observation scales by relating them to children's gender and their externalizing and internalizing behaviour (research questions 2 and 3, respectively). Concerning our second research question, we expected that teachers would show more affiliation towards girls than boys (see, Ladd et al., 1999). With regard to our third research question, we hypothesized that teachers would display less affiliation towards children who score high on externalizing behaviour (see DeMulder et al., 2000; Rimm-Kaufman et al., 2002). In addition, we expected teachers to show more control (see Coplan & Prakash, 2003), and less affiliation (see DeMulder et al., 2000) towards children they rated as displaying high levels of internalizing behaviour.

Finally, we expected that teacher affiliation and control would not be related with each other, because these dimensions are considered to be orthogonal (Sadler & Woody, 2003).

METHOD

Sample and Selection

Our sample consisted of 48 teachers (all female) from 48 kindergarten classes of 23 Dutch elementary schools. Four children were selected per teacher ($n = 192$, 105 boys), based on their scores on a Dutch adaptation of the Preschool Behaviour Questionnaire (Behar 1977), which the teacher completed for all children in the classroom. In every classroom, children were categorized in four groups: 1) 'average children' with relatively low scores on both externalizing and internalizing behaviour; 2) 'inhibited children' with relatively high scores on internalizing behaviour but relatively low scores on externalizing behaviour; 3) 'disruptive children' with relatively high scores on externalizing behaviour but relatively low scores on internalizing behaviour; and 4) 'inhibited-disruptive children' with relatively high scores on both externalizing and internalizing behaviour. Cut-off scores were 1.33 for internalizing behaviour and 1.21 for externalizing behaviour on a four-point scale. Those values were based on the median values derived from a large randomly selected kindergarten sample ($n = 1559$). From each group, one child was randomly selected for participation. Because of this selection procedure, the distributions of the scores on internalizing and externalizing behaviour are representative of the variation of behaviours of children in regular kindergarten classrooms.

The present study was part of a larger project, in which teachers completed the STRS three times and observations were conducted at five occasions within nine weeks. In the present paper, we only report results for the first measurement occasion. Due to absences of some children during this occasion, the present sample includes 179 children (95 boys).

Instruments

Children's internalizing and externalizing behaviours. Children's problem behaviours were measured with the Behaviour Questionnaire for Two-to-Six-Year-Olds-Modified (BQTSYO-M; Thijs, Koomen, De Jong, Van der Leij, & Van Leeuwen, 2004). The broadband scales for Internalizing (15 items, e.g., 'Shy or timid towards other children', 'Easily upset') and Externalizing Behaviour (14 items, e.g., 'Bullies other children', 'A busy child') were used. Teachers rated children's behaviours on a 4-point Likert scale, ranging from 1 (*absolutely not characteristic*) to 4 (*very characteristic*). Previous research has reported high internal consistencies (Cronbach's alpha's $\geq$ .81 and .91 for Internalizing and Externalizing Behaviour, respectively) and supported the validity of the scales (Thijs & Koomen, 2009; Thijs, Koomen, & Van der Leij, 2008).

Teachers' relationship perceptions. A shortened version of the Dutch adaptation of the Student-Teacher Relationship Scale (Koomen, Verschueren, Van Schooten, Jak & Pianta, 2010; Pianta, 2001) was used to measure teachers' perceptions of affective relationships with individual children. Cronbach's alpha coefficients were .78, .86, and .75 for Closeness (6 items, e.g., 'I share an affectionate and warm relationship with this child'), Conflict (8 items, e.g., 'This child and I always seem to be struggling with each other'), and Dependency (5 items, e.g., 'This child asks for my help when he/she really does not need help'), respectively. Items were scored on a 5-point scale, ranging from 1 (*not at all applicable*) to 5 (*highly applicable*).

Teachers' interactive behaviours. Videotaped teacher behaviours towards each child were rated independently by different groups of observers in episodes of five seconds on two six-point scales for teacher affiliation and teacher control (Thijs et al., 2011). With Teacher Affiliation ranging from *very low* (1) 'is repulsive, morose, or unfriendly to the child – e.g., shows verbal and nonverbal angry or clearly irritated reactions' to *very high* (6) 'is strongly positive, clearly supportive, companionable, or warm, both verbally and nonverbally – e.g., is truly interested, encouraging, reassuring, or companionable, praises the child, smiles at it, or jokes with it. No ambiguity is observed'. Teacher Control ranged from *very low* (1) 'shows a passive attitude towards the child, and does not try to influence his/her behaviour at all – e.g., does not give clues and lets the child determine the situation' to *very high* (6) 'tries to have a strong influence on the child, has (or takes) complete control over the situation without acknowledging and permitting any independent contribution from the child'. To examine interrater reliability, a random subset of the observations was double coded ($n = 34$; 14% for Teacher Affiliation; $n = 36$; 15% for Teacher Control). ICCs could be interpreted as fair for Teacher Affiliation (all ICCs were .54) and good for Teacher Control (ICCs ranged from .72 to .75; Cicchetti et al., 2006). Observations of teacher behaviours took place during a 15-minute small-group task activity in the classroom with the four selected children. Children had to place different sets of three pictures in a logical chronological order, and tell the corresponding story to the teacher.

Analyses

Hierarchical linear modelling was used for analyzing the longitudinal data, in which the repeated measures (episodes) were considered as nested within children, and children as nested within teachers. Intraclass correlations and deviance tests were used to check whether it was necessary to include random intercept variance on both the child and the teacher level. Compound symmetry appeared to describe the longitudinal structure at the lowest level adequately. Both variances at the child ($\chi^2 (1) = 1229.028$, $p < .001$ for teacher affiliation; $\chi^2(1) = 274.779$, $p < .001$ for teacher control) and teacher level ($\chi^2 (1) = 134.444$, $p < .001$ for teacher affiliation; $\chi^2 (1) = 84.017$, $p < .001$ for teacher control) turned out significant. The intraclass correlations also suggested a three level model: For teacher affiliation, the correlation between two episodes within one teacher was .115, the correlation between two episodes within one child was .134, and the correlation between two children within one teacher was .856. For teacher control, the correlation between two episodes within one teacher was .039, the correlation between two episodes within one child was .046, and the correlation between two children within one teacher was .846. Therefore we used a three level model with variance at episode (87% for teacher affiliation; 95% for teacher control) child (2% for teacher affiliation; 1% for teacher control) and teacher level (11% for teacher affiliation; 4% for teacher control). Standardized regression coefficients are reported. Multilevel analyses were conducted with SPSS Version 17.

RESULTS

Preliminary analyses. Preliminary analyses were conducted by calculating bivariate correlations between the predictor variables (see Table 1). The correlation between externalizing behaviour and conflict was relatively high ($r = .70$). Other significant correlations were found between externalizing behaviour and closeness

($r = -.35$), externalizing behaviour and dependency ($r = -.154$), internalizing behaviour and closeness ($r = -.31$), and closeness and conflict ($r = -.42$).

Table 1. Descriptive statistics and correlations.

	N	M (SD)	2	3	4	5
1.Externalizing beh.	179	1.39 (.49)	-.06	-.35**	.70**	-.15*
2.Internalizing beh.	179	1.40 (.39)		-.31**	-.08	.15
3.Closeness	167	4.26 (.68)			-.42**	.13
4.Conflict	167	1.78 (.87)				.02
5.Dependency	167	2.33 (.81)				
6.Teacher affiliation	11836[a]	4.35 (.66)				
7.Teacher control	12303[a]	3.78 (1.09)				

* $p < 0.05$ ** $p < 0.01$ (two-tailed).
[a] This number refers to the total number of episodes in the analyses.

Multilevel correlations. Through multilevel analyses, we also estimated correlations between teacher affiliation and teacher control for separate levels. Teacher affiliation and control appeared not to be correlated at the episode ($r = .021$, $p = .068$) and child level ($r = .295$, $p = .130$). Unexpectedly, we did find a significant negative correlation at the teacher level ($r = -.589$, $p < .001$).

Table 2. Single predictor models.

	Teacher affiliation		Teacher control	
	β (SE)	p[b]	β (SE)	p[b]
Gender	.044 (.031)	.155	-.035 (.024)	.149
Externalizing behaviour	-.077 (.014)	.000	.008 (.013)	.540
Internalizing behaviour	.049 (.015)	.001	.030 (.012)	.015
Closeness	.005 (.019)	.778	-.027 (.014)	.059
Conflict	-.062 (.016)	.000	.014 (.013)	.282
Dependency	.035 (.019)	.065	.017 (.015)	.246

Standardized beta coefficients are reported.
[b] Probability is associated with Wald Z test.

To answer our research questions, we included several predictors at the child level. Although they are not reported in Tables 2 to 4, the random variances at the different levels (i.e., episode, child, and teacher level) were estimated in all models.

Teachers' relationship perceptions. Separate multilevel analyses with single predictor variables give an indication of their individual effects on the dependent variables (see Table 2). Conflict was the only relationship dimension that had a significant and negative effect on teacher affiliation. Teacher control was not significantly predicted by any of the relationship dimensions. We also included all three relationships dimensions at the same time in the model. In this model (Table

3, Model 1), both conflict and dependency were significant predictors of teacher affiliation. Conflict had a negative influence on teacher affiliation, whereas dependency had a positive effect. Just as in the single predictor models, teacher control was not significantly predicted by any of the relationship dimensions (Table 4, Model 1).

Table 3. Influence of relationship perceptions and child characteristics on teacher affiliation.

	Model 1		Model 2		Model 3	
	β (SE)	p^b	B (SE)	p^b	β (SE)	p^b
Relationship perceptions						
Closeness	-.027 *(.019)*	.147			-.013 *(.021)*	.526
Conflict	-.069 *(.016)*	.000			-.016 *(.023)*	.487
Dependency	.038 *(.018)*	.036			.016 *(.019)*	.379
Child characteristics						
Gender			.013 *(.030)*	.678	.008 *(.033)*	.799
Externalizing behaviour			-.067 *(.016)*	.000	-.058 *(.024)*	.016
Internalizing behaviour			.039 *(.015)*	.009	.032 *(.019)*	.085

Standardized beta coefficients are reported.
[b] Probability is associated with Wald Z test.

Children's gender and behaviours. In the single predictor models, gender did not act as a significant predictor of teacher affiliation and control. However, both externalizing and internalizing behaviours had a significant effect on teacher affiliation. As expected, externalizing behaviour had a negative effect on teacher affiliation. Contrary to our hypothesis, internalizing behaviour had a positive influence on teacher affiliation. Teacher control was only significantly and positively predicted by internalizing behaviour. When all child characteristics were included together in one model (Tables 3 and 4, Model 2), the results were the same as for the single predictor models.

Combined models. Finally, we included all predictor variables together in Model 3 (Tables 3 and 4). For teacher affiliation, the effects of conflict, dependency, and internalizing behaviour were no longer significant. Externalizing behaviour was the only significant predictor of teacher affiliation, and showed a negative effect. Concerning teacher control, the effect of internalizing behaviour was no longer significant.

Table 4. Influence of relationship perceptions and child characteristics on teacher control.

	Model 1		Model 2		Model 3	
	β (SE)	p[b]	B (SE)	p[b]	β (SE)	p[b]
Relationship perceptions						
Closeness	-.027 *(.015)*	.075			-.009 *(.018)*	.601
Conflict	.006 *(.014)*	.671			.010 *(.020)*	.616
Dependency	.021 *(.015)*	.160			.012 *(.016)*	.439
Child characteristics						
Gender			-.016 *(.027)*	.546	-.018 *(.029)*	.525
Externalizing Behaviour			.010 *(.014)*	.449	.003 *(.021)*	.896
Internalizing Behaviour			.030 *(.013)*	.022	.027 *(.016)*	.094

Standardized beta coefficients are reported.
[b] Probability is associated with Wald Z test.

DISCUSSION

Our first research question was whether teachers' observed interactions with kindergarten children could be predicted by their perceptions of the relationships with these children. We expected that teachers' perceptions of closeness in the relationship would have a positive influence, whereas teachers' perceptions of conflict and dependency would have negative effects on teachers' observed affiliation. Furthermore, we hypothesized that teachers' observed control would not be associated with their relationship perceptions. In agreement with expectations, our results showed that only teacher affiliation was significantly predicted by relationship dimensions. As expected, teachers who reported more conflict in their relationship with a particular child, showed less affiliation towards that child. Contrary to our expectations, closeness was not a significant predictor of teacher affiliation. These findings are comparable with those of Stuhlman and Pianta (2001), who found that teachers' mental representations of negative affect in the relationship (as elicited from teachers by the Teacher Relationship Interview) was a significant predictor of teachers' observed interactive behaviours, whereas positive affect was not. Other research revealed that conflict was a stronger predictor of children's school functioning than closeness (e.g., Hamre & Pianta 2001). Our results seem to indicate that conflict is not only a stronger predictor of children's behaviours, but also of teachers' interactive behaviours.

Dependency also had a significant effect on teacher affiliation when included in the model together with closeness and conflict, but this effect was different than expected. In contrast with our hypothesis, the analysis showed that teachers who reported more dependency in their relationship with a particular child, also showed more affiliation towards that child. We expected that dependency would act as a negative dimension of teacher-child relationships, because it was presented as such in the literature (e.g., Hamre & Pianta, 2001). However, in the present study a high level of dependency rather seemed to prompt teachers to provide warmth and support in interactions with children. Presumably, because they notice special needs for their attention. It is important to note that we used a Dutch adaptation of the STRS in the present study, in which the Dependency subscale partly consisted of other items than the original version (Pianta, 2001). Previous research showed that this adapted subscale was substantially more reliable than the original (Koomen et al., 2010). However, it could be that the adapted Dependency subscale records more positive perceptions and feelings of teachers.

Finally, our results showed that teacher control behaviour was not associated with closeness, conflict, or dependency. This finding agrees with our hypothesis that control is not reflective of the affective bond between teacher and child.

Our second aim was to validate the observation scales in a small group situation. Besides the aforementioned relationships, we expected to find associations between child characteristics (i.e., gender, externalizing behaviour, and internalizing behaviour) and teacher affiliation and control, resulting in two research questions (one about gender differences in teachers' interactive behaviours, and the other about the influences of children's externalizing and internalizing behaviours on teachers' interactive behaviours). In addition, we investigated whether teacher affiliation and control could be considered to be orthogonal, as was expected based on the literature (Sadler & Woody, 2003).

Concerning our second research question about gender differences, we expected that teachers would show more affiliation towards girls than boys, because of the findings of Ladd and colleagues (1999) However, neither teacher affiliation nor control was significantly predicted by children's gender. In the present study, teachers' interactive behaviours were rated every five seconds during one measurement occasion, whereas Ladd and colleagues (1999) averaged ratings on three occasions to obtain one emotional tone score for every teacher-child dyad. Perhaps, gender differences are more salient when ratings are more global and based on longer periods of time.

With regard to the third research question about the influences of children's behaviours, we found that both externalizing and internalizing behaviour had a significant influence on teacher affiliation. In line with our hypothesis, teachers displayed less affiliation towards children they considered to be disruptive. In contrast with our expectations, however, teachers showed more affiliation towards children they described as inhibited. Previous research has shown that teachers report more socioemotional support towards inhibited children compared with average children (Thijs, Koomen, & Van der Leij, 2006). Perhaps, teachers display more affiliation and support towards these children, because they are aware of the special pedagogical needs of these children. Teacher control was also significantly associated with children's scores on internalizing behaviour. As expected, teachers showed more control towards children they rated as socially inhibited. Furthermore, teacher affiliation and control were not significantly related at the episode and child level, which is in line with our expectation that the two dimensions would be independent. However, we did find a significant correlation between both dimensions at the teacher level, which seems to indicate that teachers who generally show more control, tend to be less friendly towards their students.

Overall, our results seem to provide some evidence for the validity of our observation scales.

Finally, we investigated whether child characteristics or teachers' relationship perceptions had a stronger influence on teachers' interactive behaviours. For teacher affiliation, the effects of conflict and dependency were no longer significant if child characteristics and relationship dimensions were included together in the model. Only externalizing behaviour remained a significant predictor of teacher affiliation. Teacher control was no longer significantly associated with any of our predictor variables. The findings for teacher affiliation suggest that teachers' actual interactive behaviours are more strongly guided by their perceptions of the problem behaviour of the child, than by their perceptions of the relationship with that child. This makes sense considering that externalizing behaviours of children can be really disturbing in classroom settings. From moment to moment, teachers may be confronted with children's disturbing behaviours and have to decide how they will react on them. Therefore, teachers' perceptions of whether a child displays dysfunctional behaviours may be more influential than teachers' perceptions of the relationship. Another explanation could be that teachers completed the questionnaires about children's externalizing behaviour for (almost) all children in their classroom, whereas they completed the STRS only for the four children included in the observations. It is possible that this focus on four specific children made teachers more aware of their answers on the STRS and consequently more susceptible to social desirability. In comparison, teachers' answers on the behaviour questionnaire could be more valid, and therefore more predictive of teachers' observed interactive behaviours. To be sure about what really happens during teacher-child interactions, more information about the actual interactions is needed. Further research should investigate the influence of children's interactive behaviours on teachers' interactions and vice versa.

Qualifications

A number of qualifications should be made. First, in the present study we treated teachers' interactive behaviours as outcome variables, and relationship perceptions and children's gender and behaviours as predictors. However, the cross-sectional nature of our study does not permit conclusions about causality. It is up to future research to further examine directions of influence by conducting longitudinal and/or experimental studies.

Second, in the present study children's behaviour ratings were solely based on teacher perceptions. Previous research has provided support for the validity of teacher reports of children's social-behaviour functioning and especially of their ratings of externalizing behaviours (Konold & Pianta, 2007). However, to be sure about whether child characteristics or teachers' relationship perceptions are stronger predictors of teachers' interactive behaviours, more objective measures of children's externalizing and internalizing behaviours are needed.

Finally, multilevel models showed that relatively small percentages of the variance were located at the child and teacher level, whereas the largest part of the variance was situated at the episode level for both teacher affiliation and control. Apparently, teachers' interactive behaviours change from moment to moment and are less influenced by teachers' interpersonal style or characteristics of the specific child with whom the teacher interacts. It seems important for future research to examine the relations between moment to moment observations of both teachers' *and* children's interactive behaviours.

In conclusion, these results seem to suggest that our observation scales for teacher affiliation and teacher control are, to some extent, valid, judging from the associations between externalizing behaviour and teacher affiliation, internalizing behaviour and teacher control, and the multilevel correlations on the episode and child level. Furthermore, we did find some evidence that teachers' actual interactive behaviours can be predicted by their relationship perceptions. However, teachers' affiliation towards kindergarten children was more strongly associated with teachers' negative relationship perceptions (conflict) than with their positive relationship perceptions (closeness). This is an alarming finding, because the effects of perceptions on behaviours are considered to be reciprocal and perceptions tend to act as self-fulfilling prophecies (Pianta et al., 2003). Teachers who experience their relationship with a particular child as conflictual tend to behave less warm and supportive towards this child. This could lead to a vicious circle in which negative perceptions and negative behaviours intensify each other. It seems important to intervene in teacher-child relationships that are viewed by the teacher conflictual. In addition, more process studies are needed to learn how teacher-child interactions evolve, and about the reciprocal associations between child characteristics, relationship perceptions, and interactive behaviours.

NOTES

[i] This research was supported by grant 411-03-11 from the Netherlands Organization for Scientific Research assigned to Helma Koomen, and the FMG University of Amsterdam Research Priority Grant Affect Regulation.

REFERENCES

Arbeau, K. A., Coplan, R. J., & Weeks, M. (2010). Shyness, teacher-child relationships, and socio-emotional adjustment in grade 1. *International Journal of Behavioral Development, 34*(3), 259-269.

Baker, J. A. (2006). Contributions of teacher-child relationships to positive school adjustment during elementary school. *Journal of School Psychology, 44,* 211-229.

Behar, L. B. (1977). The Preschool Behaviour Questionnaire. *Journal of Abnormal Child Psychology, 5,* 265-275.

Carson, R. C. (1969). *Interaction concepts of personality.* Chicago: Aline.

Cicchetti, D., Bronen, R., Spencer, S., Haut, S., Berg, A., Oliver, P., et al. (2006). Rating scales, scales of measurement, issues of reliability: Resolving some critical issues for clinicians and researchers. *Journal of Nervous and Mental Disease, 194*(8), 557-564.

Coplan, R. J. & Prakash, K. (2003). Spending time with teacher: Characteristics of preschoolers who frequently elicit versus initiate interactions with teachers. *Early Childhood Research Quarterly, 18*(1), 143-158.

DeMulder, E. K., Denham, S., Schmidt, M., & Mitchell, J. (2000). Q-Sort assessment of attachment security during the preschool years: Links from home to school. *Developmental Psychology, 36*(2), 274-282.

Doumen, S., Verschueren, K., Buyse, E., Germeijs, V., Luyckx, K., & Soenens, B. (2008). Reciprocal relations between teacher-child conflict and aggressive behavior in kindergarten: A three-wave longitudinal study. *Journal of Clinical Child & Adolescent Psychology, 37*(3), 588-599.

Gurtman, M. B. (2001). Interpersonal complementarity: Integrating interpersonal measurement with interpersonal models. *Journal of Counseling Psychology, 48*(1), 97-110.

Hamre, B. K. & Pianta, R. C. (2001). Early teacher-child relationships and the trajectory of children's school outcomes through eighth grade. *Child Development, 72*, 625-638.

Henricsson, L. & Rydell, A.-M. (2006). Children with behaviour problems: The influence of social competence and social relations on problem stability, school achievement and peer acceptance across the first six years of school. *Infant and Child Development, 15*(4), 347-366.

Kiesler, D. J. (1983). The 1982 Interpersonal Circle: A taxonomy for complementarity in human transactions. *Psychological Review, 90*, 185-214.

Kiesler, D. J. (1996). *Contemporary interpersonal theory and research: Personality, psychopathology, and psychotherapy.* Oxford, England: Wiley.

Konold, T. R. & Pianta, R. C. (2007). The influence of informants on ratings of children's behavioral functioning: A latent variable approach. *Journal of Psychoeducational Assessment, 25*(3), 222-236.

Koomen, H. M. Y., Verschueren, K., Van Schooten, E., Jak, S., & Pianta, R. C. (2012). Validating the student-teacher relationship scale: Testing factor structure and measurement invariance across child gender and age in a Dutch sample. *Journal of School Psychology, 50*, 215-234.

Ladd, G. W., Birch, S. H., & Buhs, E. S. (1999). Children's social and scholastic lives in kindergarten: Related spheres of influence? *Child Development, 70*(6), 1373-1400.

Leary, T. (1957). *An interpersonal diagnosis of personality.* New York: Ronald Press Company

Pianta, R. C. (2001). *Student-Teacher Relationship Scale. Professional Manual.* Lutz, Florida: Psychological Assessment Resources.

Pianta, R. C., Hamre, B., & Stuhlman, M. (2003). Relationships between teachers and children. In *Reynolds, William M (Ed); Miller, Gloria E (Ed). (2003). Handbook of psychology: Educational psychology, Vol. 7.* (pp. 199-234). Hoboken, NJ: John Wiley & Sons.

Rimm-Kaufman, S. E., Early, D. M., Cox, M. J., Saluja, G., Pianta, R. C., Bradley, R. H., et al. (2002). Early behavioral attributes and teachers' sensitivity as predictors of competent behavior in the kindergarten classroom. *Applied Developmental Psychology, 23*, 451-470.

Sadler, P. & Woody, E. (2003). Is who you are who you're talking to? Interpersonal style and complementarity in mixed-sex interactions. *Journal of Personality and Social Psychology, 84*(1), 80-96.

Stuhlman, M. W. & Pianta, R. C. (2001). Teachers' narratives about their relationships with children: Associations with behavior in classrooms. *School Psychology Review, 31*(2), 148-163.

Thijs, J. T. & Koomen, H. M. Y. (2008). Task-related interactions between kindergarten children and their teachers: The role of emotional security. *Infant and Child Development, 17*, 181-197.

Thijs, J. & Koomen, H. M. Y. (2009). Toward a further understanding of teachers' reports of early teacher-child relationships: Examining the roles of behavior appraisals and attributions. *Early Childhood Research Quarterly, 24*(2), 186-197.

Thijs, J. T., Koomen, H. M. Y., De Jong, P. F., Van der Leij, A., & Van Leeuwen, M. G. P. (2004). Internalizing behaviors among kindergarten children: Measuring dimensions of social withdrawal with a checklist. *Journal of Clinical Child and Adolescent Psychology, 33*(4), 802-812.

Thijs, J., Koomen, H. M. Y., Roorda, D., & Ten Hagen, J. (2011). Explaining teacher-student interactions in early childhood: An interpersonal theoretical approach. *Journal of Applied Developmental Psychology, 32*(1), 34-43.

Thijs, J. T., Koomen, H. M. Y., & Van der Leij, A. (2006). Teachers' self-reported pedagogical practices toward socially inhibited, hyperactive, and average children. *Psychology in the Schools, 43*(5), 635-651.

Thijs, J. T., Koomen, H. M. Y., & Van der Leij, A. (2008). Teacher-child relationships and pedagogical practices: Considering the teacher's perspective. *School Psychology Review, 37*(2), 244-260.

Wubbels, T. & Brekelmans, M. (2005). Chapter 1: Two decades of research on teacher-student relationships in class. *International Journal of Educational Research, 43*, 6-24.

JANET M. MCGEE

5. ELEMENTARY TEACHERS NEED TO RECOGNIZE BULLYING BEFORE IT PEAKS AT THE MIDDLE SCHOOL

INTRODUCTION

Research supports that bullying often goes unnoticed in schools, especially at the elementary level. Dan Olweus, an expert and Norwegian researcher began studying bullying in the 1970s and continues his work today. The bulk of early research on bullying generally indicates younger children are bullied more than older children and declines as children get older (Hoover, Oliver, & Hazler, 1992; Rigby & Slee, 1991; Ziegler & Rosenstein-Manner, 1991; Zindi, 1994). Tom Tarshis, director of the Bay Area Children's Association, and Lynne Huffman, an associate professor of pediatrics at the Stanford School of Medicine, conducted a recent study (2007) of 270 children in grades three through six in California and Arizona, determining that "victimization and bullying are apparent at very young ages" (Huffman, Stanford University Medical Center [RxPG], 2007, paragraph 10). According to a simple questionnaire developed by Tarshis and Huffman, nine out of 10 elementary students reported their peers have bullied them. Furthermore, six in 10 children reported participating in some type of bullying in the past year. This study is consistent with earlier studies indicating that bullying begins in the early grades.

Bullying is Developmental

Often, bullying is considered a 'rite of passage' or normal life experience for students. However, researchers have found that bullying leads to many physical, emotional, and psychological problems for victims (Hay & Meldrum, 2010; Hinduja & Patchin, 2010; Kaminski & Fang, 2009). Social skills are developmental and social conflict is an inescapable component of social interactions (Bonds & Stoker, 2000). According to Olweus (1993), children in early elementary grades (K-2) tend to be self-absorbed and typically are oblivious of their influence on others. Children at this age (K-2) expect their friends to have the same desires and needs as themselves. They deal with frustration by rejecting other children that fail to live up to this expectation. By the second grade, social development progresses and children begin to grow out of the notion of friendship as a one-sided liaison. Children, in second grade, begin to engage in games with rules and spending time with others who enjoy the same activities. Since listening skills and accepting another's point of view are essential problem solving skills and

T. Wubbels et al. (eds.), Interpersonal Relationships in Education, 67–83.

not fully developed, many children have not developed the ability to compromise in opposing situations; therefore, conflicts break out as children become frustrated due to their inability to resolve opposing concerns (Olweus, 1993). Children in second and third grade can learn and develop a number of basic problem solving skills.

Normal peer conflict is a daily occurrence in the social development of children (Garrity, Jens, Porter, Sager, & Short-Camilli, 1997). Children make insensitive remarks and display hostile behaviour at all ages, however, the intermittent occurrence of tactless or argumentative conduct does not necessarily qualify as bullying. Bullying is a manifestation of one person using power in a deliberate manner to repeatedly distress another individual (Garrity et al., 1997). True bullying means that there is an imbalance of power whereas the victim of the intimidation is unable to mount a viable defence. Batsche and Knoff (1994) further discovered that the percentage of students bullied decreases significantly, as students get older and advance grades. Olweus (1991) reported that 50% of the victims of older students were in the lower grades, and the youngest students, regardless of age, were most at risk for being bullied. Boulton and Underwood (1992) discovered that, while there is a decline in direct physical bullying at the higher grade levels, there is a relatively higher level of verbal abuse that remains constant. This finding was consistent with an earlier study conducted by Perry, Kusel, and Perry (1988), where they noted nearly equal physical and verbal aggression for males at grade 3 with a reduction in the physical victimization score at grade 6 on their Peer Nomination Inventory [PNI] survey.

According to studies completed by Hoover and Oliver (1996), and Patterson, Reid and Dishion (1992), without interventions, bullies identified by the age of eight are six times more likely to be convicted of a crime by the age of twenty-four and five times more likely than non-bullies to end up with serious criminal records by the age of thirty. Olweus (1987) reported similar findings. Walker (1993) stated that aggressive behaviour is learned early and is resistant to change if it continues beyond eight years of age.

In the Maine Project Against Bullying [MPAB] (2000), a study was conducted to discover how often primary grade children reported being bullied. This intensive study, completed in 2000, supports early intervention and prevention efforts. Concentrating on third graders in Maine elementary schools during February 1999, this sample showed 22.6%-40.7% of students reported they were experiencing bullying with relative frequency. This indicated that the level of social behaviour and respect for oneself and others was lacking and caused considerable concern for the Maine Schools. Of the third graders surveyed 13%-17% reported they participated in the bullying behaviours every day, once or twice a week or once monthly.

According to Olweus (1993), children who bully early in their developmental years (K-2), tend to perpetuate these roles throughout their later school years. This was supported with a meta-analysis study examining factors that predict bullying in childhood and adolescence conducted by Cook, Williams, Gueerra, Kim, and

Sadek (2010). Cook et al. (2010) found bully-victims externalize problems and hold significantly negative attitudes and beliefs about themselves and others. Cook et al. found these children did not have adequate social problem-solving skills. He strongly urged, that it is these students that educators must help as early as possible in order to change these emerging, harmful patterns of behaviour. He also noted that harassing behaviours do not spontaneously appear in the middle schools. According to the Gale Encyclopedia of Childhood and Adolescence (1998), bullying begins at a very early age and it is not uncommon to find bullies in preschool classrooms. Up until the age of seven, bullies appear to choose their victims at random. Soon after that, they single out specific children to torment. Up until sixth grade, the bullies are usually popular with other students and most times admired for their toughness. By high school, this usually diminishes and they have only other bullies as friends (Olweus, 1993). A later study by Rodkin and Gest (2011) found that most bullies are socially integrated and networked. These bullies do not lack peer social support. They have friends that may or may not be bullies and have strong, recognizable strengths for instance; social skills, athleticism, and/or attractiveness (Rodkin & Gest, 2011).

Patterson, Reid, and Dishion (1992) further found that over the developmental age of kindergarten through sixth grade these behaviour patterns become more destructive, aversive, and have a much greater social impact. They compared this early behaviour pattern to a virus that lowers the immune system so one becomes vulnerable to a host of disease conditions over time. Following their line of thinking, elementary teachers can influence this 'bullying virus' if they are able to identify the bullying behaviours early and perceive bullying and victimization as a serious problem. Bidwell (1997) stated early intervention by teachers is important, "for every bully who is dealt with early on and learns a more empathic and respectful way of interacting with fellow students, there will likely be one or more victims who will be less afraid and unhappy in school as a result" (pp. 16-17).

Perceptions of Students

Long before anyone else knows, students know the identities of the bullies and victims within the school. Interrelational patterns are established in the first six weeks that school begins. Although the students know who these bullies are, they do not tell because they are afraid. They fear the bullying will become worse if they tell or they fear they will become the victim if they help someone else by telling. Most victims believe that no one would help them if they did tell (Olweus, 1993). A study conducted by Swearer and Cary (2003) reported that 80% of the sampled middle school students stated that the school staff did not know that the bullying occurred.

Passive victims make it easy for bullies to hide their bullying. This bullying goes on 'behind closed doors', and there exists a conspiracy of silence among children (Garrity et al., 2000); most children are afraid to tell. Research conducted in Canada, by Noelle Bidwell (1997), confirms this. Bidwell reports that when children told about bullying behaviours, most teachers immediately confronted the bully and demanded an explanation. These bullies were smart kids and they were able to figure out who told on them. They would then use intimidation to be sure the victims did not 'rat' again. The students watching and uninvolved were thankful they were not involved. They also have learned the safety of silence; do not tell, or you will be next. The Weinhold and Weinhold study (1998) discovered that 69% of all students believe that school staff responded poorly to bullying and victimization. Faulds (2001) found one quarter of 900, 10-year-old victims said they got no help despite having told adults.

Another Canadian study (Pepler & Craig, 1995) had cameras hidden on the school playground and had certain children wear microphones. Because of this study, bullying incidents were recorded every seven minutes. Since bullying occurs quickly, it is usually done before anyone, other than the victim, knows that it is happening. A shove, a quick punch, a threat, or name-calling can take place without being seen or heard by an adult. Some of the students caught on video disguised the bullying behaviour as playing, which staff members failed to catch as an unfair game.

Dan Olweus (1991), who has researched bully-victim problems for over twenty years, found "the single most effective deterrent to bullying is adult authority". So, why do children have the belief that adults in schools will not help them? What is it that teachers are or are not doing that gives the students this perception? Discovering what the teacher beliefs or perceptions are concerning bullying and the victimization problem is paramount to gaining the confidence of students in school bullying situations.

STATEMENT OF THE PROBLEM

Bullying is often associated with middle schools due to adolescent behaviours, but studies show that bullying occurs and often begins in the elementary schools. Pepler and Craig (1995) reported that every seven minutes bullying occurs on elementary school playgrounds. According to Fried (1996), student victims receive an average of 213 verbal put-downs per week, or 30 per day. More recent, Snyder (2004) found that children were targets of verbal or physical harassment about once every five minutes, based on observations of 266 kindergartners at a Wichita school playground (as cited in Baxter, 2004 blog). Snyder's study supports the notion that bullying behaviour is increasing at earlier ages. "What was most surprising was just how much of it there was", Snyder said (Baxter, 2004 blog). What complicates things is children do not believe adults will help them, so they do not tell they are being bullied. Children as young as second grade report that they are not confident that their teachers will help protect them if they reveal their fear (Lee, 1993). Secondary students examined by Athanasiades and Deliyanni-Kouimtzis (2010), indicated that bullying takes place in areas where there was no supervision by teachers. The self-reported victims admitted that they do not tell teachers about the victimization because they believe that the teachers are indifferent and ineffective (Athanasiades & Deliyanni-Kouimtzis, 2010).

More research is needed in the general area of the school environment. According to Snyder (2004) "much of the previous research relied on after-the-fact reporting" (Baxter, 2004). Research findings support the notion that messages, verbal and nonverbal, adults convey can have an important impact on students' behaviour (Batsche & Knoff, 1994; Mellor, 1993). These messages are related to teacher beliefs. If there is an inconsistent understanding by staff members of recognizing the seriousness of bullying, this situation will affect how they react to bullies and victims. This study attempts to provide insight into those beliefs. Teacher perceptions or beliefs can play a major role in decreasing bullying behaviours, especially at the elementary level. Are there dynamics that exist in elementary schools, particularly teachers' beliefs, which foster students once victimized, to become bullies, as they grow older?

Research Question

The original study was designed to explore the perceptions or beliefs of the elementary, middle, and high school teachers within one district in the north-eastern region of the United States concerning bullying and victimization. Several research questions were explored but for the purpose of this paper, only one research question will be reported on: To what extent, if any, do the teachers perceive bullying as serious and does that perception change at different school levels (elementary, middle, high)?

METHODS

Background Information

The study was conducted in one north-eastern, suburban school district with a population of about 3,200 students and 251 teachers. Many safe school programs were already in place and a full time School Resource Officer (SRO) is in the district. A Safe Schools Committee meets on a monthly basis throughout the school year. School policies have been developed for keeping students safe, and these policies seem to be followed. Each year the staff and students are provided with information on bullying and prevention strategies. As related to aggressive student behaviour, feedback is gathered from the staff to help this district coordinate future workshop and in-service topics. In the 2003-2004 school year, the district gathered information via a teacher questionnaire concerning teacher perceptions on bullying and victimization. The results of this survey formed the data set that would be analysed in this study. The data were gathered at an in-service for the elementary staff and at two separate in-services for the middle and high school staff.

Population

The district consists of three elementary schools, one middle school, and one high school. All schools are staffed with counsellors, principals and assistant principals or deans of students. The elementary schools house kindergarten through grade five students, with the middle school consisting of grades six through eight. The high school includes grades nine through twelve. Since the schools are in the same complex, the middle school and high school students ride the same buses to and from school. This situation may give middle school students opportunities to be exposed to bullying behaviours from the older students. This situation also creates an environment for older students to harass younger students.

Sample Size

This study investigated the perceptions of 251 practicing teachers in one north-eastern school district, at three elementary schools ($n = 108$), one middle school ($n = 64$), and one high school ($n = 79$), and their thoughts and ideas in the areas of victimization created primarily from bullying. Surveys were completed by all elementary teachers (108), 61 middle school teachers, and 69 high school teachers ($n = 238$). Because of the limited population sampled, the data collected in this research is specifically valid to the situation in this school district; however, the results may have validity to other school districts in the country to the extent that other districts share similar characteristics with this current school district.

Instrumentation

The district was looking to administer a survey to gauge teacher perceptions concerning bullying and victimization. Most surveys examined focused on students and their perceptions not the perceptions of teachers. One instrument, utilized by Bidwell (1997) in her study, *The Nature and Prevalence of Bullying in Elementary Schools*, was of interest. It was however in need of adaption. Bidwell's survey included a student portion as well as teachers of students in grades 5-8. The district chose to utilize this instrument for several reasons. First, the school setting was similar to that used in Bidwell's study. Second, participant size was similar however, allowing for teaching levels to include primary and high school levels. Lastly, the questions reflect perceptions of staff members concerning their beliefs and recognition of bullying and victimization, which was the ultimate goal of the district.

Description of Instrument by Sections

The survey had three sections with a total of 17 questions. Section one (questions 1-5) gathered demographic information about each teacher, this included: gender, grade levels taught, years of teaching experience, years teaching in current school, and teaching in an academic or non-academic setting. Section two (questions 6-14) directed teachers who perceived bullying as a serious problem to indicate their perceptions concerning bullying traits, and section three (questions 15-17) directed all teachers to identify preventive strategies that could be utilized by students, parents, and school personnel. For the purpose of this study, only one demographic variable, grade levels, will be reported from section one. Findings in section two and three related to grade levels will be reported.

Instrument Reliability and Validity

Bidwell (1997) had difficulty obtaining research considered as 'teachers' perspectives' concerning bullying and victimization that would allow for measuring for this purpose. Therefore, Bidwell adapted a questionnaire by Ziegler and Rosenstein-Manner (1991) from their Toronto study. In Ziegler and Rosenstein-Manner (1991) study, the researchers discovered less awareness of bullying from the teachers in comparison to the students that were included in the study. Ziegler and Rosenstein-Manner (1991) stated that both the teachers and students perceived that bullying takes place on the playground, followed by hallways, classrooms, and lunchrooms. Interestingly, the students in Ziegler and Rosenstein-Manner's study believed three times more often that the teachers did not intervene 'often/almost always', as the teachers reported. Bidwell's adapted questionnaire was piloted amongst five teachers, which then was edited to produce a final questionnaire. Bidwell's (1997) study supported Ziegler and Rosenstein-Manner's (1991) study. The majority of teachers, in Bidwell's study did not believe that bullying was a serious problem. In addition, this study had playground, hallways, classrooms, and lunchrooms identified by teachers as areas where bullying takes place. Teachers perceived they intervened much more frequently than students perceived they did. The district believed that Bidwell's questionnaire had predictive validity, as there was a relationship between the answers from both Bidwell's and Ziegler and Rosenstein-Manner's studies. Additionally, there was some measure of success in the situation of the bullying/victimization interest.

For the purpose of the current study, Bidwell's questionnaire had additional modifications to include the teachers of students in the elementary, middle, and high school levels. All questions reflect perceptions of staff members, regardless of school level, concerning their beliefs and recognition of bullying and victimization, which was the ultimate goal of this study. This district survey had a possible 251 participants with 238 completing this survey. Since bullying and victimization may look different at the different levels, it was intended that this survey, would provide important information that would lead to improved in-service training programs adapted to meet the needs at each level.

Data Collection

Permission to analyse the data was granted by the district superintendent through a written letter of request. The data for this study were gathered, though the use of an adaptive questionnaire from Bidwell's study (1997), at an October 2003 in-service for the elementary staff and at two separate in-services in September 2003 for the middle and high school staff. The participants were divided in smaller groups in order to promote active participation with the activities planned. Teachers who were absent from the in-service training were also provided a teacher survey to complete. All surveys collected were anonymous and confidential, only school levels (elementary, middle, and high) were identified.

Data Analysis

The responses from each of the levels, elementary, middle, and high school were entered into a database, and an SPSS (Statistical Program for Social Sciences) data file was created. The numeric data were formatted with variable names and response categories. The responses were analysed across the demographic variables with specific focus on perceptions indicated by responses to the survey. Where appropriate, the analysis looked at relationships that existed between or among the items. Frequencies were calculated in order to determine if teachers saw bullying as a serious problem and if this perception differed depending on the school level (elementary, middle, and high). Initial analyses utilized *chi-square*. Several categories were collapsed when utilizing the chi-square analysis to determine significant difference. The demographic variable, grades taught, K, 1, and 2, 3, 4, and 5, and K-5 categories were collapsed and represent all elementary teachers in this district to produce cell values that would provide for a more accurate computation of statistical significance. Additional correlational analyses were used to investigate potential relationships among item responses. Alpha levels were set at .05 unless otherwise stated.

Chi-square analysis was performed to investigate if there were any statistically significant differences in the responses to recognizing bullying as a serious problem compared with each of the five teacher demographic variables. The .05 level of significance was used to reject the null hypothesis that responses to the survey items were equal across the survey classifications. Although the completed study analysed all demographics, this paper will only report on findings statistically significant, related to the demographic variable, grade levels.

LIMITATIONS OF STUDY

Several intrinsic limitations should be considered when interpreting this study's findings.

Sample size. This study was limited to one school district in the north-eastern region of the United States who was participating in an ongoing professional development for their district on bullying prevention. It included all teachers teaching kindergarten through twelfth grade. The sample was unevenly distributed among the teaching levels: Elementary (n = 108), Middle School (n = 61), High School (n = 69).

Data collection. If the study took place at the end of the school year, teacher perceptions may have been different. The survey was administered in October at a workshop towards the beginning of the school year. Teachers did not know their students well enough to know if there was a 'serious' bullying problem.

Participation of aides/support staff. The majority of elementary teachers did not see playground as an area where bullying occurs and yet according to other research this was the most common place. This school district has aides and support staff that monitor the playground area. If teachers are not assigned to lunch and recess, they may be unaware that bullying is occurring. If the aides responded to the survey, the data results may have differed.

RESULTS

Two hundred and thirty-eight (238) surveys or 94.8% were completed. Almost half of the teaching staff (45.4%) is in the elementary schools. All participants answered question six on the survey, which asked, "Do you believe bullying is a serious problem in your school?" Table 1 displays the teacher responses to question six of the survey. Only those participants that reported bullying as a serious problem responded to Part II of the survey (n = 52). A sizable minority (21.8%) perceived bullying to be a serious problem (n = 52).

Table 1. Teachers who report bullying as a serious problem.

Sees bullying as a serious problem	Frequency	Percentage
Yes	52	21.8
No	186	78.2
	238	100.0

Part II asked questions related to recognition of bullying and victimization. Were the teachers able to identify bullies and victims in their school? Does their perception change at the different levels (elementary, middle, or high school) or by teaching experience? Does gender play a significant role in their perceptions of victimization?

Teacher Demographic Variables

There was no statistically significant difference with teachers recognizing bullying as a serious problem and the demographic variables: gender, years of teaching experience, years teaching in current school, and academic or non-academic setting. The majority of teachers (79%) in this district are female. Almost half of the teaching staff (45.4%) is in the elementary schools. It is a relatively 'young' district with a little over half of the teachers (51.3%) having one to ten years of teaching experience and 63.8% of the teachers have been in their current school for one to ten years. Only one demographic variable; grades taught, was found to be significantly different and is reported in Table 2.

Table 2. Frequencies, percentages, and significance test comparing teaching grade levels in relation to saying bullying is a serious problem.

Teaching grades	Sees bullying as a problem	
	Frequency	Percentage
K-5	15	13.9
6, 7, and 8	24	39.3
9, 10, 11, and 12	13	18.8
Total	52	21.8
Chi-square	DF	Significance
15.308	2	.000

There is a difference among the three levels of teaching grades. Teachers at the middle school recognize bullying as serious more often than the teachers at the elementary and high schools did ($p < .000$ level).

Where, What Grade, and How Often Teachers Intervene?

Teaching grade levels were found to be significantly different when compared with where bullying is perceived to occur, what grade/class the bullies are perceived to be in, and how often it is perceived that teachers intervene in bullying when they see it occurring. A strong majority of elementary teachers (80%) reported students are bullied on the playground, while only 17.4% of the middle school teachers reported playground. This result was very significant at the $p < .000$ level. Not surprising, teachers at the middle (87%) and high school (71.4%) reported that hallways are the most common place where students bully. The result was significant at the $p < .028$ level. Elementary teachers (86.7%) reported the bully to be in the same grade. This result was significant at the $p < .028$ level. This is again not surprising, since elementary teachers usually teach in a self-contained classroom. Although slightly over half the teachers in this district (57.7%) reported that teachers almost always intervene when they see bullying take place, slightly over half of the high school and elementary teachers reported that the teachers intervene occasionally or never. The result was significant at the $p < .020$ level.

Table 3 displays the percentages and significance test comparing teaching grade levels in relation to how often teachers intervene in bullying when they see it occurring.

Table 3. Percentages and significance test comparing teaching grade levels in relation to how often teachers intervene in bullying.

Teaching grades	Always/ Almost always	Teachers intervene in bullying		
		Occasionally	Almost never	Don't know
K-5	46.7%	40.0%	13.3%	
6, 7, and 8	79.2%	12.5%	8.3%	
9, 10, 11, and 12	30.8%	53.8%	7.7%	7.7%
Total	57.7%	30.8%	9.6%	1.9%

Chi-square	DF	Significance
15.072	6	.020

What Students, Parents and Teachers Should Do to Prevent Bullying

Part III of the survey asked questions related to prevention. The respondents were able to check all statements that applied. Therefore, the percentages reported will not equal 100% due to multiple answers from each participant. The total percentage reflects the percent of all participants ($n = 238$) that agreed with the response. Teaching grade levels was significantly different when compared with what students, parents, and teachers should do to prevent bullying. The majority of teachers regardless of teaching grade level reported that students should tell teachers when they are being bullied (97.1%). This perception slightly decreases as teaching levels increase. The result was significant at the $p < .041$ level.

Elementary teachers perceived that students should talk to the bully (46.3%) with this perception decreasing at the middle school (32.8%) and then the high school level (27.4%). The result was significant at the $p < .029$ level. Teachers at the elementary level reported that parents should tell teachers/principal that their children are being bullied (97.2%) with this belief decreasing as the grade level increases. The result was very significant at the $p < .006$ level. Lastly, the majority of teachers, regardless of teaching level reported that the teacher should talk to the bully (93.7%); the highest percentage was at the elementary level (99.1%). The result was significant at the $p < .005$ level. A higher percentage of elementary teachers reported that teachers should get the bully and victim to communicate with each other (84.3%), with this belief decreasing as grade levels increased. The result was significant at the $p < .006$ level.

DISCUSSION

The present study's purpose was to investigate and compare teachers' perceptions (kindergarten – twelfth grades) in a north-eastern school district concerning bullying and victimization with demographic variables though the use of an adapted questionnaire from Bidwell's study (1997). Because of the limited population sampled, the data collected in this research is specifically valid to the situation in this school district; however, the results may prove limited validity to other school districts in the country to the extent that other districts share similar characteristics with this current school district.

The analyses revealed several significant differences that were developed into emerging themes however; this study will report findings for one theme: *Recognition of Serious Bullying Peaks at the Middle School.* This theme has three interrelated parts.

First, *recognition of bullying looks different at different grade levels.* Teacher recognition of bullying was more prevalent at the middle school level. This result could lead one to believe that bullying increases between the elementary and middle school level in this district. There could be several reasons for an increased recognition of the problem at the middle school than at the elementary and high school. Research shows that bullying is developmental. Lober and Hay (1997) reported that the onset of aggression, in various forms, such as bullying, emerges in early adolescence. Other researchers, Boulton and Underwood (1992) discovered direct physical bullying decreases while there is a relatively higher level of verbal abuse/aggression. Second, teacher perceptions of bullying as a serious problem may be higher due to a variety of prevention programs already in place at the middle school in this district such as: Peer mediation, "Big Brothers and Sisters Program", Bullying Prevention Program in the sixth grade, "When Teasing Crosses the Line" in seventh grade, and "Sexual Harassment" in the eighth grade. Although these programs are directed towards students, teachers participate in various activities, which may create greater awareness among the middle school staff. This increased awareness and interventions in bullying and victimization situations at the middle level could explain the perception among the majority of high school teachers in this district that bullying is not a serious problem. Bullying incidents at the high school level may have decreased due to the impact of the prevention programs at the middle school on students. Further, students are maturing, learning, and using bullying avoidance strategies. Batsche and Knoff (1994) reported that the percentage of students bullied decreases significantly with age and grade.

Rigby and Slee's study (1991) indicated that younger children are bullied more often than older students are. This is confirmed in studies completed by Ziegler and Rosenstein-Manner (1991), Whitney and Smith (1993), and Zindi (1994). Research suggests aggressive behaviour is learned early in life. This evidence supports the importance of recognizing the early warning signs of aggressive behaviour. Behaviours not recognized at the elementary level may develop into behaviours that are more destructive and become more noticeable due to the socialization at the middle school.

Second, *elementary teachers are least likely to recognize bullying as a serious problem.* An important concern from this study is that only 13.9% of the elementary teachers reported that bullying is a serious problem in their classrooms. Although research indicates bullying is developmental and recognized more in early adolescence, other research suggests elementary teachers are the key to recognizing early warning signs of inappropriate developmental behaviours. Research evidence supports that students identified early can be coached during these early developmental years in behaviours that will decrease bullying in our schools. However, Olweus and Limber (2010) report that environmental factors such as; attitudes, routines, and behaviour of adults could play a role in determining the bullying problem in classrooms. If teachers do not perceive bullying to be a serious problem, they may not be able to identify the bullies or victims early enough to make a difference. The current study indicated that the elementary teachers in this study (13.9%) did not think bullying was serious. According to Olweus (1993), children who bully tend to perpetuate these roles throughout their school years. He strongly urged that educators intervene early in order to change these emerging, unacceptable behaviour patterns. Programs such as peer mentors, peer mediation, and training teachers on characteristics of bullies and victims could help elementary teachers intervene early. Olweus made an important statement in his study, "Harassing behaviors do not spontaneously appear in the middle schools" (Bonds & Stoker, 2000). In a later study, Olweus' (1994) noted that the average percentage of students bullied in elementary grades was higher than in the middle grades. It was also noted that there was a reduction of physical bullying as students develop. Perry and colleagues (1988) who reported nearly equal physical and verbal aggression for males at grade three with a significant reduction in physical victimization at grade six on their Peer Nomination Inventory survey also confirmed this. If this is true, more physical bullying is taking place in the elementary schools. Therefore, the brute nature of bullying at the elementary school level should be more observable to teachers. However, in this district, elementary teachers were less likely to recognize bullying as a problem than the middle or high school teachers were.

Sprague and Walker (2000) used a method of prospective analysis, to identify at-risk youth at an early age and follow their life course. This method yielded consistently defined pathways that progressed from early disruptive and temperamental behaviours to serious, violent, and chronic patterns of school adjustment problems, delinquency, and adult criminality. There was evidence of early warning signs that are apparent when the child enters school and escalate during the elementary years. In sharp contrast, an important finding and concern in this current study is that more than three-fourths of the teachers in this district, of which half were elementary teachers, did not perceive bullying as a serious problem. Research evidence supports that students identified early can be taught appropriate social behaviours during these early developmental years that can decrease bullying in schools. It follows that the elementary teachers in this district need to be more aware and begin to recognize bullying and victimization.

The last interrelated part, *elementary teachers recognize peers bully their peers more often than middle school teachers do.* Although the majority of teachers in this district recognize that most bullies were in the same class and/or the same grade level as the victim (67.9%), the vast majority of elementary teachers (86.7%) responded affirmatively to this survey item. This is not surprising since the elementary teachers teach in self-contained classrooms and spend the majority of the day with the same students. However, bullies in this type of setting have further opportunities to target peer victims. This is consistent with the study completed by Zindi (1994) where he noted that most bullies were in the same grade level or class as their victims. It can be concluded that bullies victimize students with whom they have increased contact and greater opportunities to detect their vulnerabilities. A study conducted by Noelle Bidwell (1997) indicated that most bullies were found to be in the same grade as their victims. At the elementary level, the students are isolated from other grade levels. Thus, bullying occurs much more frequently at the peer level and bullying techniques are more likely to involve direct physical contact. As the students reach middle school level, social groups become more prevalent and the bullying occurs more frequently by groups rather than individuals.

In conclusion bullying occurs in every school and in every grade. It begins early and continues to grow as the students go through their school years. Sometimes it turns tragic when students believe they have had enough and decide to take things into their own hands. What is more tragic is that these students believe they are alone and no one will help them.

Significance of the Study

This chapter reported on teacher perceptions concerning bullying and the importance of early recognition and awareness at the elementary school levels before bullying peaks at the middle school. Research supports the importance for recognition of early warning signs.

Although bullying issues seem to be on the rise there seems to be very little research on teacher perceptions and demographic variables that can influence teacher recognition of bullying and victimization as a serious problem. Boulton's study (1997) examined teachers' attitudes, definitions of bullying behaviour, and teachers' perceived roles in coping with bullying behaviour in the classroom. Huesmann, Eron, Guerra, and Crawshaw (1994) developed the Teacher Prediction of Peer-Nominated Aggression questionnaire in which teachers predicted peer-nominations among their students. Again, this did not make comparisons of teacher, peer, and self-perceptions of bullying. One study completed by Noelle Bidwell (1997) acquired descriptive information about bullying among students in the elementary schools through student and teacher questionnaires. Bidwell's (1997) study included grades five through eight. This study did make comparisons between student and teachers perceptions, but the focus was on students' perceptions not teachers' perceptions.

Future Studies

In the past, many programs have focused at the secondary levels, but little attention has been directed toward elementary schools. Future research should focus on the elementary level and include the lunch and playground aides and or parent volunteers. Playground duty personnel view the students in a very different capacity. Positive teacher-student interaction and strong relationships contribute to a healthy school environment. Teacher attitudes towards bullying and skills with regard to supervision and intervention will determine how teachers will react to bullying situations.

Current studies on bullying are focusing on cyberbullying, which has added considerably to the bullying issues in schools. If one is to combat bullying issues, future studies must include awareness of the influence of cyberbullying in schools. According to Hinduja and Patchin (2010) many adults do not have technological knowhow to keep track of what students are doing online and/or on cell phones. The increase in suicides for children due to bullying demonstrates a strong need for early identification. Training teachers to not only indentify bullies and victims, but encouraging proper interventions is essential to create safe havens for our children. Children should not believe that adults would not help them. Teacher, student, and parent bystanders should not be tolerated. Bullying in schools is everyone's problem.

Final Comments

In order for bullying to be prevented or decreased in our schools, school personnel need to commit to the ideal that bullying is unacceptable, is serious, and should not be tolerated. Bullying is not a rite of passage that students must work out themselves. When one incident of bullying occurs, it is serious. Silence from students does not imply acceptance. Teachers need training that will help them identify students suffering in silence. The training needs to include strategies for victims as well as bullies and school personnel need to intervene appropriately in order to gain the confidence of the students. One way to gain that confidence is that teachers need to be aware that the silent student victims will not take the initiative to tell they are being bullied and would benefit from having someone notice their circumstance and offer the needed help. There is also a large, silent majority of bystanders in our schools. Bonds and Stoker (2000) say 85% of the students in a school are neither bullies nor victims. These students are usually well-developed socially but they do not know how to reclaim the power from the bullies. Some of these students may be afraid and ignore or avoid bully situations. If we can tap into this silent majority and teach these students the skills they need we can create a positive school climate with this silent majority holding the power and helping to make the school safe and secure for all.

REFERENCES

Athanasiades, C. & Deliyanni-Kouimtzis, V. (2010). The experience of bullying among secondary school students. *Psychology in the Schools, 47*(4), 328-341.

Batsche, G. M. & Knoff, H. M. (1994). Bullies and their victims: Understanding a pervasive problem in the schools. *School Psychology Review, 23,* 165-175.

Baxter, D. J. (2004, May 12). Re: Bullying starts at young age [Blog Thread]. Retrieved from http://forum.psychlinks.ca/bullying-harassment-and-interpersonal-violence/192-bullying-starts-at-young-age.html.

Bidwell, N. M. (1997, May). *The nature and prevalence of bullying in elementary schools* (SSTA Research Center Report No. 97-06). Regina, Saskatchewan: Saskatchewan School Trustee Association.

Bonds, M. & Stoker, S. (2000). *Bullyproofing your school.* Longmont, CO: Sopris West.

Boulton, M. J. (1997). Teachers' views on bullying: definitions, attitudes and ability to cope. *British Journal of Educational Psychology, 67,* 223-233.

Boulton, J. J. & Underwood, K. (1992). Bully/victim problems among middle school children. *British Journal of Education Psychology, 62,* 73-87.

Cook, C. R., Williams, K. R., Guerra, N. G., Kim, T. E., & Sadek, S. (2010). Predictors of bullying and victimization in childhood and adolescence: A meta-analytic investigation. *School Psychology Quarterly, 25*(2), 65-83. doi:10.1037/a0020149; 10.1037/a0020149.supp (Supplemental)

Faulds, G. (2001). *Victims of school bullies say they don't receive help.* Reuters Health. Retrieved from www.rense.com.

Fried, S. (1996). *Bullies and victims: helping your child through the schoolyard battlefield.* Kansas City: MO.

Gale Encyclopedia of Childhood & Adolescence. (1998). Gale Research, in association with The Gale Group and Look Smart.

Garrity, C., Jens, K., Porter, W. W., Sager, N., & Short-Camilli, C. (1997). Bullying-proofing your school: Creating a positive climate. *Intervention in School and Clinic, 32*(4), 235-243.

Hay, C. & Meldrum, R. (2010). Bullying victimization and adolescent self-harm: Testing hypotheses from general strain theory. *Journal of Youth and Adolescence, 39*(5), 446-459. doi:10.1007/s10964-009-9502-0.

Hinduja, S. & Patchin, J. W. (2010). *Cyberbullying fact sheet: Identification, prevention, and response.* Cyberbullying Research Center. Retrieved January 30, 2011, from http://www.cyberbullying.us/Cyberbullying_Identification_Prevention_Response_Fact_Sheet.pdf.

Hoover, J. H. & Oliver, R. (1996). *The bullying prevention handbook: A guide or principals, teachers, and counsellors.* Bloomington, In: National Educational Service.

Hoover, J. H., Oliver, R., & Hazler, R. J. (1992). Bullying: Perceptions of adolescent victims in the Midwestern U.S.A. *School Psychology International, 13*(1), 5-16.

Huesmann, L. R., Eron, L. D., Guerra, N. G., & Crawshaw, V. B. (1994). Measuring children's aggression with teachers' predictions of peer nominations. *Psychological Assessment, 6,* 329-336.

Kaminski J. W. & Fang X. (2009) *Victimization by peers and adolescent suicide in three US samples.* Journal of Pediatrics, *5,* 683-8.

Lee, F. (1993). *Facing the fire: Experiencing and expressing anger appropriately.* New York: Bantam Books.

Loeber, R. & Hay, D. (1997). Key issues in the development of aggression and violence from childhood to early adulthood. *Annual Review of Psychology, 48,* 371-410.

Maine Project Against Bullying. (2000). *A survey of bullying behaviour among Maine third graders* [Electronic fact sheet]. Wiscasset, ME: Wiscasset Elementary School. Available: http://lincoln.midcoast.com/~wps/against/bullying.html [Retrieved: December 8, 2003].

Mellor, A. (1993). Finding out about bullying. *Scottish Council for Research in Education Spotlights, 43,* 1-3.

Olweus, D. (1987, Fall). Schoolyard bullying – Grounds for intervention. *School Safety, 411.*

Olweus, D. (1991). *Bully/victim problems among school children: Basic facts and effects of a school based intervention program.* In I. Rubin & E. Pepler (Eds.), *The development and treatment of childhood aggression* (pp. 411-447). Hillsdale, NJ: Erlbaum.

Olweus, D. (1993). *Bullying at school: What we know and what we can do.* Cambridge, MA: Blackwell.

Olweus, D. (1994). Bullying at school: Long-term outcomes for the victims and an effective school-based intervention program. In L. R. Huesmann (Ed.), *Aggressive behaviour: Current perspectives* (pp. 97-130). New York: Plenum.

Olweus, D. & Limber, S. P. (2010). Bullying in school: Evaluation and dissemination of the Olweus bullying prevention program. *American Journal of Orthopsychiatry, 80*(1), 124-134. doi:10.1111/j.1939-0025.2010.01015.x.

Patterson, G. R., Reid, J. B., & Dishion, T. J. (1992). *A social interactional approach: IV. Antisocial boys.* Eugene, OR: Castalia Press.

Pepler, D. J. & Craig, W. M. (1995). About bullying. Understanding this underground activity. *Orbit, 25*(3), 32-34.

Perry, D. G., Kusel, S. J., & Perry, I. C. (1988). Victims of peer aggression. *Developmental Psychology, 24*, 807-814.

Rigby, K. & Slee, P. T. (1991). Bullying among Australian school children: Reported behaviour and attitudes towards victims. *Journal of Social Psychology, 131*, 615-627.

Rodkin, P. C. & Gest, S. D. (2011). Teaching practices, classroom peer ecologies, and bullying behaviours among schoolchildren. In D. L. Espelage & S. M. Swearer (Eds.), *Bullying in North American schools* (2nd ed.) (pp. 75-90). New York, NY: Routledge.

Snyder, A. W. (2004). Autistic genius. *Nature, 429,* 470-471.

Sprague, J. & Walker, H. (2000). Early identification and intervention for youth with antisocial and violent behaviour. *Exceptional Children;* Reston, *3*, 367-379.

Stanford University Medical Center [RxPG]. (2007, April). *School bullying affects majority of elementary students.* Reviewed by Vidyarthi, Retrieved from Behavioural Science Channel website: http://www.rxpgnews.com/behaviouralscience/School_bullying_affects_majority_of_elementary_st udents_23451.shtml.

Swearer, S. M. & Cary, P. T. (2003). Perceptions and attitudes toward bullying in middle school youth: A developmental examination across the bully/victim continuum. *Journal of Applied School Psychology, 19*(2), 63-79. doi:10.1300/J008v19n02_05.

Walker, H. M. (1993). Anti-social behaviour in school. *Journal of Emotional and Behavioural Problems, 2*(1), 20-24.

Weinhold, B. K. & Weinhold, J. B. (1998). Conflict resolution: The partnership way in schools. *Counseling and Human Development, 30*(7), 1-2.

Whitney, I. & Smith, P. K. (1993). A survey of the nature and extent of bullying in junior/middle and secondary schools. *Educational Research, 35*, 3-25.

Ziegler, S. & Rosenstein-Manner, M. (1991). *Bullying at school: Toronto in an inter-national context.* Toronto: Toronto Board of Education, Research Services.

Zindi, F. (1994).Bullying at boarding school: a Zimbabwe study. *Research in Education, 51*, 23-32.

SCHOOL ORIENTED

NIENKE M. MOOLENAAR, ALAN J. DALY & PETER J.C. SLEEGERS

6. EXPLORING PATTERNS OF INTERPERSONAL RELATIONSHIPS AMONG TEACHERS

A Social Network Theory Perspective

INTRODUCTION

In the past decade, the rise of interest in interpersonal relationships in education is mirrored by an increased focus on the importance of relationships among educators. Recent studies suggest that relationships among teachers are important in building strong school communities (Penuel, Riel, Krause, & Frank, 2009), and that strong teacher networks can enhance teacher commitment and give teachers a sense of belonging and efficacy (Grodsky & Gamoran, 2003). Moreover, strong social relationships in and among schools are found to play a crucial role in policy implementation, instructional change, and teachers' professional development in support of increased student achievement (Baker-Doyle & Yoon, 2010; Daly & Finnigan, 2010; Moolenaar, 2010; Veugelers & Zijlstra, 2002).

The urge to capitalize on teacher relationships is reflected by a growing number of concepts that describe teacher interaction in support of teachers' professional development and school improvement, such as community of practice, organizational (shared, collaborative, networked) learning, professional (learning) community, and teachers' social networks (Coburn & Stein, 2006; Haythornthwaite & De Laat, 2010; Louis, Marks, & Kruse, 1996; McLaughlin & Talbert, 2001; Wenger, 1998). These concepts share an underlying assumption that interpersonal relationships among teachers are important as they provide access to information, knowledge and expertise (Frank, Zhao, & Borman, 2004), facilitate joint problem solving (Uzzi, 1997) and shape an environment of trust (Bryk & Schneider, 2002).

While the beneficial outcomes of teachers' professional communities have been well documented, what appears to be less prominent in the discourse on professional learning communities is the way in which the underlying pattern of relationships among teachers shapes these communities and their efforts at educational improvement. An emerging trend in educational research is the use of social network theory and analysis to understand how the pattern of relationships among teachers, as captured by social networks, can support or constrain teachers' learning, instructional practice, and educational change (Daly & Finnigan, 2010; McCormick, Fox, Carmichael, & Procter, 2010; Moolenaar, 2010).

Social network theory builds on the notion that social resources such as information, knowledge, and expertise are exchanged through informal networks of relationships between actors in a system; as such, these networks can facilitate or

T. Wubbels et al. (eds.), Interpersonal Relationships in Education, 87–101.

inhibit access to social capital (Lin, 2001). Network visualizations and characteristics such as density and centrality aid scholars in illuminating how social networks in schools are shaped and changed to achieve individual and organizational aims at educational improvement. As a result, applying social network theory and analysis to the study of teachers' interpersonal relationships makes the social fabric of schools and their influence more tangible than ever before.

This chapter introduces social capital theory and social network theory as a lens to understand how patterns of interpersonal relationships among educators can support or constrain efforts at school improvement. We will build on our own studies on social networks in 53 elementary school teams in the Netherlands, as well as recent studies that have been conducted in a variety of educational settings and in various countries. By changing the focus from one-to-one interpersonal relationships to the interconnected pattern of teachers' interpersonal relationships in their schools' social networks, our aim is to explore new frontiers of educational research and show the richness and potential of studying interpersonal relationships among educators for understanding educational systems.

SOCIAL CAPITAL THEORY

The fundamental notion of social capital is that social relationships provide access to resources that can be exchanged, borrowed and leveraged to facilitate achieving goals. Social capital belongs to the family of 'intangible assets' that can be accrued and leveraged by individuals, groups, or systems. Comparable to financial or human capital, in which money or knowledge and skills are the valuable assets, social capital reflects valuable sources that emerge from social relationships among linked individuals. Yet, in contrast to forms of financial capital, social capital is often argued to increase rather than diminish by using it.

In the last decade, Dika and Singh (2002) notice a sharp increase of the visibility of social capital theory in educational research. This research is mainly focused on students' social capital as a means to explain differences in educational achievement, educational attainment, high school completion, and psychosocial factors related to education like students' aspirations (Stanton-Salazar & Dornbusch, 1995), and expectations of parents (Muller & Ellison, 2001). Indicators of students' social capital range from family structure and number of close friends to extracurricular involvement. In an influential study, Coleman and Hoffer (1987) attributed significantly lower dropout rates in Catholic schools compared to public education to levels of social capital in the schools' community and the students' families. Remarkably, educational research has paid little attention to social capital from other perspectives.

Literature outside education has identified organizational social capital as a critical source of organizational advantage (e.g., Leana & Van Buren, 1999; Nahapiet & Ghoshal, 1998; Walker, Kogut, & Shah, 1997). Tsai and Ghoshal (1998) show that social capital, in the form of social interaction and trust among employees, can add significantly to a firm's value creation through innovation.

Organizations with dense informal network structures within and between organizational units generally achieve higher levels of performance than those with sparse connections (Reagans & Zuckerman, 2001). Focusing on school organizations, a social capital perspective may illuminate how schools as communities exchange resources to address common goals, and achieve the beneficial outcomes as suggested in literature on professional learning communities.

SOCIAL NETWORK THEORY

A valuable starting point for understanding how social capital is generated through the pattern of interpersonal relationships is social network theory. The most distinguishing feature of social network theory is its two-fold focus on both the individual actors and the social relationships connecting them (Wasserman & Galaskiewicz, 1994). A social network researcher is concerned with relational questions such as who knows whom, which organizations collaborate together, or which actors share common group membership. These questions can reveal the underlying social structures that are important in understanding the exchange of resources in communities and explaining a variety of social phenomena (Berkowitz, 1982; Burt, 1982).

The study of social networks is receiving increased attention in educational research. Studies have been conducted in a range of contexts, including school and teacher networks (Baker-Doyle & Yoon, 2010; Bakkenes, De Brabander & Imants, 1999; Coburn & Russell, 2008; Daly, Moolenaar, Bolivar, & Burke, 2010; Lima, 2007; Moolenaar, Daly, & Sleegers, in press; Moolenaar, Karsten, Sleegers, & Zijlstra, 2009; Penuel & Riel, 2007; Penuel, et al., 2009); leadership networks and departmental structures (Friedkin & Slater, 1994; Lima, 2003; Spillane, 2006); school-parent networks (Horvat, Weininger, & Laureau., 2003); between school networks (Lieberman, 2000; Veugelers & Zijlstra, 2002); and student networks (Lubbers, Van der Werf, Kuyper, & Offringa, 2006).

Central to the idea of social structure is the notion of social embeddedness (Granovetter, 1985; Jones, Hesterly, & Borgatti, 1997; Uzzi, 1996). Social embeddedness refers to the hierarchical, or nested, nature of a social structure. In a social network, individuals are embedded within dyadic relationships, and dyadic relationships are embedded in larger sub-groups of three, four, or more actors that eventually shape a social network. Even a social network itself is embedded in a larger social structure, for instance an organization, a community, or a country.

At least three assumptions underlie social network theory and the resulting social network research (Degenne & Forsé, 1999). First, the notion of social embeddedness implies that actors in a social network are interdependent rather than independent. Hence, changes at a single level (e.g., the interpersonal level) will have consequences for a higher-order level (e.g., the whole network) and vice versa. As such, the significance of an interpersonal relationship extends beyond the two actors (Burt, 2000; Degenne & Forsé, 1999). Second, interpersonal relationships are regarded as conduits for the exchange or flow of resources such as information, knowledge, and materials (Burt, 1982; Kilduff & Tsai, 2003). Third, patterns of interpersonal relationships may act as 'constraints' and offer opportunities for individual and collective action (Brass & Burkhardt, 1993; Burt, 1982). In the next section, we will describe four social network mechanisms to illustrate the potential of social network theory and analysis for the study of interpersonal relationships in education.

SOCIAL NETWORK MECHANISMS

Social network theory takes shape in a variety of mechanisms that may explain the flow of resources in a network. Leading examples of network mechanisms are the strength of weak ties (Granovetter, 1973, 1982), homophily (Heider, 1958), structural balance (Davis, 1963), and structural holes (Burt, 1980, 1992, 2000). While each mechanism highlights a distinctive facet of the interaction between individuals, together they offer a nuanced understanding of social structure as they explain the flow of resources among individuals and its implications for individual behaviour, opinions, and preferences.

The strength of weak ties. Relationships can vary in the strength with which individuals are connected. Ties can be classified as strong or weak depending on the frequency and duration of interactions, as well as the emotional intensity associated with the interaction (Granovetter, 1973). Strong ties, such as friendship relationships, are suggested to be important in times of uncertainty and change (Krackhardt, 1992), and the pattern of friendship ties in an organization may be critical to its ability to deal with crisis situations (Krackhardt & Stern, 1988). Being involved in many weak ties can be valuable for seeking information and innovation because of the diversity of connections (Granovetter, 1982, 1985).

Homophily. Homophily, colloquially described as 'birds of a feather flock together', is a well-established sociological principle that proposes that individuals with similar attributes will have a higher tendency to form interpersonal relationships than dissimilar individuals (Kossinets & Watts, 2006). Studies of homophily suggest that resources flowing through a network tend to be localized around a specific attribute such as age, gender, or education level (Ibarra, 1995; Marsden, 1988). Therefore, the more similar individuals are on a specific attribute, including position in a network structure, the more quickly resources will flow among these individuals. The converse is also true in that individuals who are 'distant' (different) on a specific attribute are also more 'distant' in the network. Over time, the principle of homophily shapes individuals' networks into relatively homogeneous networks in regard to many intrapersonal, interpersonal, and sociodemographic characteristics (McPherson, Smith-Lovin, & Cook, 2001). While homophily explains interpersonal relationships based on the characteristics that individuals have in common, the network mechanism of structural balance explains the pattern of interpersonal relationships based on individual efforts to maintain a balanced network.

Structural balance. In the footsteps of cognitive balance theory, structural balance theory poses that individuals will undertake action to avoid or decrease an unbalanced network (Heider, 1958). Individuals tend to balance their network by discontinuing weaker relations with 'friends of enemies' and 'enemies of friends' and creating strong relationships with 'friends of friends' (Davis, 1963; Wasserman & Faust, 1997). Moreover, individuals tend to seek mutual (reciprocal) as opposed to asymmetric relationships, and as those mutual ties provide mutual benefit to the actors, they create a reinforcing effect (Lin, 2001).

Preference for balance of strong and mutual relationships will lead to the emergence of directly connected subgroups, or 'cliques'. These cliques are suggested to stabilize the local network despite fluctuations over the larger social structure (Kossinets & Watts, 2006). Yet, while these stable networks of strong ties may provide quick and easy access to established resources, they may also reinforce existing values and routines, elicit 'group thinking', and limit individuals' access to new resources through weak and non-redundant ties (Granovetter, 1973). These weak ties are important as they are more likely to serve as bridges that can span so-called structural holes (Kilduff & Tsai, 2003).

Structural holes. Structural holes are holes in social structure that result from weaker or absent connections between individuals or groups in a social structure. Research into structural holes focuses on the importance of individuals that 'bridge' or 'broker' between individuals or groups that are themselves sparsely or weakly connected (Burt, 2000). Individuals that span structural holes in a network occupy a position that may benefit them in terms of information access, information diversity, and social control over projects that bring together people from both sides of the hole (Burt, 1992, 2000). While moving new resources, these brokers may also filter, distort, or hoard those resources which may inhibit overall organizational performance (Baker & Iyer, 1992; Burt, 1992).

Taken on balance, the above described mechanisms may explain how interpersonal relationships may be formed, maintained, or discontinued to shape social networks among educators and affect educational improvement. In the next section, we will provide an overview of recent insights in the content, formation, and effects of social networks among educators as these reflect the overall pattern of resource exchange through teachers' interpersonal relationships.

THE CONTENT OF NETWORKS IN SCHOOLS

The Content of Resources Affects the Structure of a Social Network

Social network scholars emphasize that social networks are shaped by the content or purpose of the social resources that are exchanged in the network (Coleman, 1990; Lin, 2001; Putnam, 2000; Scott, 2000; Wasserman & Faust, 1997). For instance, a social network that is maintained for the purpose of exchanging work related knowledge and expertise may look significantly different from a social network that is created for personal support.

Collegial relationships among teachers take different forms in order to optimally accommodate to the intellectual, emotional, and social demands of teaching (Little, 1990). Studies into social networks among educators have focused on various types of social networks that connect teachers within and between schools, such as discussion about curricular issues (content, teaching materials, planning), communication around reform, seeking advice, and friendship (Daly & Finnigan, 2010, Heyl, 1996; Hite, Williams, & Baugh, 2005; Pustejovsky & Spillane, 2009).

Recent findings suggest that social networks in school teams can be categorized according to their content in instrumental or expressive social networks (Coburn & Russell, 2008; Moolenaar, Sleegers, Karsten, & Daly, 2012). Instrumental networks exchange content that is purely aimed at achieving organizational goals, and are therefore referred to as work related networks. Expressive social networks are not directly aimed at fulfilling organizational needs, and are more affective by nature than instrumental relationships (Ibarra, 1995). A second categorization of teachers' social networks may be based on mutual in(ter)dependence between the individuals exchanging the content (Moolenaar, 2010). While some teacher networks are predominantly characterized by mutual interdependence between teachers (e.g., collaboration and work related advice networks), other networks appear to involve less mutual interdependence (e.g., spending breaks and personal advice networks).

Figure 1 illustrates two networks of interpersonal relationships among teachers in St. Michael Elementary School (pseudonym) (Moolenaar et al., 2012). In these social network visualizations, teachers in lower grade are represented by circles, and teachers in upper grade are represented by squares, and relationships between actors by arrowed lines representing the directional flow of work-related advice. When a teacher indicates a relationship (e.g., discuss work) with a colleague, this teacher is said to be 'seeking' a relationship, and this is represented by an arrowed line in the social network figure from the teacher who is 'seeking' the relationship to the colleague who is 'being sought'.

Apparently, the teachers of St. Michael maintain much more relationships around 'discussing work' than friendship relationships. As such, the social network around 'discussing work' is denser than the network around friendship. Moreover, in the friendship network among teachers in St. Michael, male educators (black nodes) are found to be more densely connected than female educators (white nodes). Insights in these different types of networks may facilitate the use of social networks as a meaningful tool to contextualize and target teacher interaction in support of teacher development and school improvement (e.g., collaborative practices, networked learning, and professional learning communities).

Discussing work

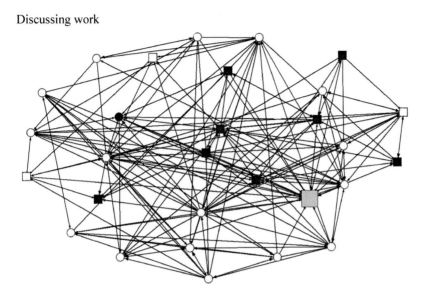

Friendship

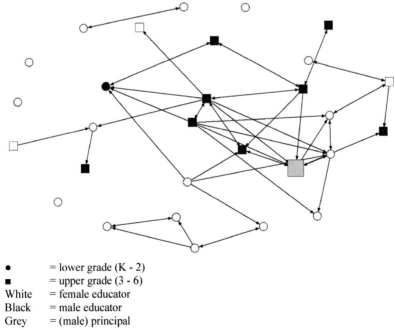

●	= lower grade (K - 2)
■	= upper grade (3 - 6)
White	= female educator
Black	= male educator
Grey	= (male) principal

Figure 1. Visualizations of two social networks of teachers in St. Michael Elementary School.

93

NETWORK FORMATION IN SCHOOLS

Characteristics of Individuals, Relationships, and Context Shape Social Networks

A developing set of studies in organizational literature is focusing on how attributes of individuals such as personality traits and individual demographics affect their social network (e.g., Burt, Jannotta, & Mahoney, 1998; Mehra, Kilduff, & Brass, 2001), and how individuals select others to engage in relationships (Kossinets & Watts, 2006; McPherson et al., 2001). Several network studies have suggested that networks are at least in part shaped by demographic characteristics of individuals, their dyadic relationships, and the larger context (Ibarra, 1995; Lazega & Van Duijn, 1997).

Recent research in education indicates that the pattern of social relationships among educators is dependent on demographic characteristics of teachers, such as gender, grade level, working hours, formal position, and experience (Daly et al., 2010; Heyl, 1996; Moolenaar, 2010). For instance, teachers who teach upper grade tend to engage more in interpersonal relationships around work discussion than lower grade teachers. Similar to research in other settings (Mehra, Kilduff, & Brass, 1998), female teachers tend to seek more relationships, and male teachers tend to be sought more for relationships. Full time employed teachers are being sought for fewer relationships than part time employees, which may be related to the amount of coordination that is needed to effectively 'share' teaching responsibility among multiple teachers. Surprisingly, older teachers and educators with more experience are being sought for fewer relationships around work related discussion than younger and less experienced teachers (Moolenaar, 2010). In addition, educators tend to seek relationships with educators with the same gender and from the same grade level, thus evidencing homophily mechanisms in school teams (Moolenaar, 2010). Moreover, it appears that the longer a school team consists of the same group of educators, the more likely they are to discuss their work in interpersonal relationships. Insights in these individual, dyadic, and network level demographics are vital to guide our expectations of networked interventions.

Individual Behaviour Shapes Social Networks

An important underlying assumption in social network literature is that individuals' behaviour may affect the shape and size of their social network. Yet, there is a dearth of research on how individual behaviour affects the emergence of interpersonal relationships among educators. A type of individual behaviour that has been suggested to shape social networks is organizational citizenship behaviour (Bolino, Turnley, & Bloodgood, 2002). Organizational citizenship behaviour (OCB) refers to behaviour that goes beyond formal role requirements and that facilitates organizational functioning (Podsakoff, MacKenzie, Paine, & Bachrach, 2000). In the context of education, OCB is believed to be important since increasing pressure to meet new standards for school performance urges educators to go well beyond their formal role to accomplish their goals (Tschannen-Moran, 2003). The interest in extra-role behaviour in education has been reflected by a growing number of studies positively linking educators' OCB to various school outcomes (Bogler & Somech, 2005; Somech & Ron, 2007). OCB may facilitate creating new interpersonal relationships and deepening existing contacts because individuals who display more extra-role behaviour will not only be in contact with others, it may also make them more likable (Denham & Holt, 1993; George, 1991). In a pioneering study in 13 Dutch school teams, teachers who reported more helping behaviour were also likely to report more work related and friendship relationships (Moolenaar, 2010). Yet, while significant, the effects were weak and leave to question whether there are other behaviours that may shape social relationships more strongly than helping behaviour. Therefore, we turn our attention to another type of behaviour that may shape social networks in schools: principals' transformational leadership behaviour.

Transformational leaders aim to motivate followers by sharing a clear vision for the school's future and attending to individual needs for professional development and intellectual growth (Bass & Avolio, 1994). Principals who are recognized as transformational leaders are found to occupy more central positions in their schools' social networks (Moolenaar, Daly, & Sleegers, 2010). Teachers with transformational principals seek out their principal more often for work related and personal advice, thus enabling principals to exert control over the resources that are disseminated within teams. Principals who occupy central positions can distribute information quicker and with more ease than less well-connected principals. Moreover, this information will have less chance of being modified as it passes from person to person. Being close to their teachers may thus be of strategic advantage for principals as these increased interpersonal relationships may enable them to maximize the skills and knowledge that reside within the network.

NETWORK EFFECTS IN SCHOOLS

Network Structure Affects Teacher and School Outcomes

An equally significant underlying assumption of social network research is that social structure may affect individuals' preferences and actions, as well as organizational outcomes. Educational researchers, practitioners, and policy-makers are increasingly recognizing the potential of networks of educators to foster systemic improvement in instructional quality and student achievement. Recent educational research using social network theory has found that the pattern and content of social relationships among teachers affects teachers' professional development, collective efficacy, shared decision-making, schools' capacity to change, innovative climate, and student achievement (Daly et al., 2010; Moolenaar, 2010; Moolenaar et al., 2010; Penuel & Riel, 2007).

Interpersonal relationships among teachers haven been closely associated with trust among teachers, both in educational literature (Bryk & Schneider, 2002; Coburn & Russell, 2008; Tschannen-Moran, 2001), and social capital theory

(Fukuyama, 1995; Nahapiet & Ghoshal, 1998; Putnam, 1993). Earlier positive experiences in interpersonal relationships may nurture trust by reducing uncertainty about the intentions and motivation of the other person involved in the relationship, thus increasing predictability, decreasing vulnerability, and infusing the relationship with routines (Uzzi, 1997). As such, interpersonal relationships among teachers may shape a context in which trust can grow by providing a blueprint for future interactions, forming mutual expectations, and outlining the norms and values of a community. Recent work in schools (Moolenaar, 2010; Moolenaar et al., 2010) demonstrates that the more interpersonal relationships educators maintain, the more they perceive their team as characterized by trust. Interestingly, the density of the schools' social networks as a whole also appeared to affect teachers' perceptions of trust, above and beyond the effect of teachers' own pattern of interpersonal relationships. This implies that the overall pattern of social relationships in the school team as a whole is *as* important to teacher trust as the individual web of interpersonal relationships.

With regard to student achievement, the influence of social networks has not yet been unambiguously reported. While some literature suggests that patterns of teachers' interpersonal relationships directly positively affect student achievement (Daly et al., 2010, Penuel et al., 2009), other research reported positive indirect effects (Moolenaar, 2010). Finally, a recent line of research has focused on the extent to which the structure of reform-related networks may affect the success of reform initiatives and suggests that the network of teachers' interpersonal relationships can support and constrain the uptake, depth, and spread of reform implementation in the schools (Daly & Finnigan, 2010, 2011; Daly & Moolenaar, 2010; Daly et al., 2010).

FUTURE DIRECTIONS

Taken together, this chapter provided deepened understanding of teachers' social networks and the conditions that shape, and result from, the interconnected pattern of interpersonal relationships that may support or constrain a variety of teacher and school outcomes. Various other questions remain to be answered. For instance, it is still unclear how teachers' interpersonal relationships permeate and change teachers' daily instructional practice and impact student achievement (McCormick et al., 2010).

Another important question remains how teachers' relationships, and the overall pattern of interpersonal relationships in school teams, relate to other stakeholders and organizations outside the boundaries of the school team, for instance preschools, university or government partnerships, similar schools, and organizations that offer teacher professional development (e.g., Lieberman, 2000; Veugelers & Zijlstra, 2002). Finally, social networks are dynamic and change over time (Kilduff & Tsai, 2003), but insights in social network change in empirical settings are limited. Therefore, longitudinal studies are indicated to enhance our knowledge of how teacher networks change to meet internal and external demands, implement change strategies, and achieve preferred and unintended outcomes over time.

IMPLICATIONS FOR EDUCATIONAL POLICY AND PRACTICE

A social network perspective on interpersonal relationships changes the focus from one-to-one relationships to a more complex web of interconnected and interdependent interpersonal relationships. Understanding these network structures may be useful for educational organizations as these networks may be leveraged to better create, use, and diffuse teacher knowledge and instructional innovation in support of increased student achievement.

One route through which educational leaders and policy-makers may increase the potential of teachers' interpersonal relationships is by stimulating the development of densely connected teacher networks, especially with regard to work related interaction. For instance, social network data may be used to identify 'blind spots' in the pattern of interpersonal relationships in a school. Moreover, this data may support efforts in connecting educators in order to stimulate and facilitate the mutual development, exchange, and use of new knowledge and practices. Better understanding of the pattern of existing relationships may assist educators in expanding interactions to include the engagement of 'weak ties' that are valuable for innovation and the creation of new ideas (Granovetter, 1973).

An additional benefit from social network data is the opportunity to yield valuable information about which individuals occupy the most strategic positions for the successful dissemination of reform information and knowledge (Daly, 2010; Daly & Finnigan, 2010). For instance, social network research demonstrates how influential individuals, so-called 'opinion leaders' who hold strategic positions in a social network, may be targeted to diffuse innovations in organizations (Valente, 1996, Valente & Pumpuang, 2007). The work around opinion leaders has examined such diverse topics as the diffusion of health promotion messages among influential young people to increase the success of tobacco prevention programs in secondary education (Starkey, Audrey, Holliday, Moore, & Campbell, 2009; Valente, Hoffman, Ritt-Olson, Lichtman, Johnson, 2003), or stimulate the spread of a rumor of a new product as a way of viral marketing (e.g., Even-Dar & Shapira, 2011). The likelihood of successful reform implementation may be increased by an intentional effort at influencing the social structure in support of the flow and uptake of reform information (Daly et al., 2010; Smylie & Evans, 2006).

While many avenues still remain open to exploration, the main road appears to be signed with the adage that 'relationships matter'. While teachers are important building blocks of a strong teacher community, teachers' interpersonal relationships are the cornerstones that connect individual knowledge, experience, and expertise in support of collective action towards powerful school outcomes.

REFERENCES

Baker, W. E. & Iyer, A. (1992). Information networks and market behavior. *Journal of Mathematical Sociology, 16*(4), 305-332.

Baker-Doyle, K. & Yoon, S. A. (2010*)*. Urban teacher support networks. In A. Daly (Ed.), *Social network theory and educational change* (pp. 115-126). Cambridge: Harvard University Press.

Bakkenes, I., De Brabander, C., & Imants, J. (1999). Teacher isolation and communication network analysis in primary schools. *Educational Administration Quarterly, 35*(2), 166-202.

Bass, B. M. & Avolio, B. J. (1994). *Improving organizational effectiveness through transformational leadership.* Thousand Oaks, CA: Sage.

Berkowitz, S. D. (1982). *An introduction to structural analysis.* Toronto, Canada: Butterworth.

Bogler, R. & Somech, A. (2005). Organizational citizenship behavior in school: How does it relate to participation in decision-making? *Journal of Educational Administration, 43*(5), 420-438.

Bolino, M. C., Turnley, W. H., & Bloodgood, J. M. (2002). Citizenship behavior and the creation of social capital in organizations. *Academy of Management Review, 27*(4), 505-522.

Brass, D. J. & Burkhardt, M. E. (1993). Potential power and power use: An investigation of structure and behavior. *Academy of Management Journal, 36*(3), 441-470.

Bryk, A. S. & Schneider, B. (2002). *Trust in schools: A core resource for school improvement.* New York, NY: Russell Sage Foundation.

Burt, R. S. (1980). Autonomy in a social topology. *American Journal of Sociology, 85*, 892-925.

Burt, R. S. (1982). *Toward a structural theory of action.* New York, NY: Academic Press.

Burt, R. S. (1992). *Structural holes: The structure of competition.* Cambridge, MA: Harvard University Press.

Burt, R. S. (2000). The network structure of social capital. *Research in Organizational Behavior, 22*, 345-423.

Burt, R. S., Jannotta, J. E. J., & Mahoney, J. T. (1998). Personality correlates of structural holes. *Social Networks, 20*, 63-87.

Coburn, C. E. & Russell, J. L. (2008). District policy and teachers' social networks. *Education Evaluation and Policy Analysis, 30*(3), 203-235.

Coburn, C. E. & Stein, M. K. (2006). Communities of practice theory and the role of teacher professional community in policy implementation. In M. I. Honig (Ed.), *Defining the field of education policy implementation* (pp. 25-46). Albany, NY: SUNY Press.

Coleman, J. S. (1990). *Foundations of social theory.* Cambridge, MA: Harvard University Press.

Coleman, J. S. & Hoffer, T. (1987). *Public and private high schools: The impact of communities.* New York, NY: Basic Books.

Daly, A. J. (2010). *Social network theory and educational change.* Cambridge MA, Harvard Education Press.

Daly, A. J. & Finnigan, K. (2010). A bridge between worlds: Understanding network structure to understand change strategy. *Journal of Educational Change, 11*, 111-138.

Daly, A. J. & Finnigan, K. (2011). The ebb and flow of social network ties between district leaders under high stakes accountability. *American Educational Research Journal, 48*(1), 39-79.

Daly, A. J. & Moolenaar, N. M. (2010). *Reform at the edge of chaos: Connecting complexity, social networks, and policy implementation.* Paper presented at the Annual Meeting of the American Educational Research Association, Denver, 2010.

Daly, A. J., Moolenaar, N. M., Bolivar, J. M., & Burke, P. (2010). Relationships in reform: The role of teachers' social networks. *Journal of Educational Administration, 48*(3), 359-391.

Davis, J. A. (1963). Structural balance, mechanical solidarity, and interpersonal relations. *American Journal of Sociology, 68*, 444-462.

Degenne, A. & Forsé, M. (1999). *Introducing social networks.* London, UK: Sage.

Denham, S. A. & Holt, R. W. (1993). Preschoolers' likability as cause or consequence of their social behavior. *Developmental Psychology, 29*(2), 271-275.

Dika, S. L. & Singh, K. (2002). Applications of social capital in educational literature: A critical synthesis. *Review of Educational Research, 72*, 31-60.

Even-Dar, A. & Shapira, A. (2011). A note on maximizing the spread of influence in social networks. *Information Processing Letters, 111*(4), 184-187.

Frank, K. A., Zhao, Y., & Borman, K. (2004). Social capital and the diffusion of innovations within organizations: Application to the implementation of computer technology in schools. *Sociology of Education, 77*(2), 148-171.

Friedkin, N. E. & Slater, M. (1994). School leadership and performance: A social network approach. *Sociology of Education, 67*, 139-157.

Fukuyama, F. (1995). *Trust.* New York, NY: Free Press.

George, J. M. (1991). State or trait: Effects of positive mood on prosocial behaviors at work. *Journal of Applied Psychology, 76*(2), 299-307.

Granovetter, M. S. (1973). The strength of weak ties. *American Journal of Sociology, 78*(1), 1360-1380.

Granovetter, M. S. (1982). The strength of weak ties: A network theory revisited. In P. V. Marsden & N. Lin (Eds.), *Social structure and network analysis* (pp. 105-130). Beverly Hills, CA: Sage.

Granovetter, M. S. (1985). Economic action and social structure: the problem of embeddedness. *American Journal of Sociology, 91*, 481-510.

Grodsky, E. & Gamoran, A. (2003). The relationship between professional development and professional community in American schools. *School Effectiveness and School Improvement, 14*(1), 1-29.

Haythornthwaite, C. & De Laat, M. F. (May 2010). Social networks and learning networks: Using social network perspectives to understand social learning. In *Proceedings of the Networked Learning Conference*, Aalborg, Denmark, May 2-3, 2010.

Heider, F. (1958). *The psychology of interpersonal relations.* New York, NY: Wiley.

Heyl, E. (1996). *Het docenten netwerk: Structuur en collegiale contacten binnen scholen* [The teacher network: Structure and collegial contacts in schools]. Unpublished doctoral dissertation. Enschede: Universiteit Twente.

Hite, J., Williams, E., & Baugh, S. (2005). Multiple networks of public school administrators: An analysis of network content and structure. *International Journal on Leadership in Education, 8*(2), 91-122.

Horvat, E., Weininger, E. & Laureau, A. (2003). From social ties to social capital: Class differences in the relations between schools and parents network. *American Educational Research Journal, 40*(2), 319-351.

Ibarra, H. (1995). Race, opportunity, and diversity of social circles in managerial networks. *Academy of Management Journal, 38*(3), 673-703.

Jones, C., Hesterly, W. S., & Borgatti, S. P. (1997). A general theory of network governance: Exchange conditions and social mechanisms. *Academy of Management Review, 22*(4), 911-945.

Kilduff, M. & Tsai, W. (2003). *Social networks and organizations.* London, UK: Sage Publications.

Kossinets, G. & Watts, D. J. (2006). Empirical analysis of an evolving social network. *Science, 311*, 88-90.

Krackhardt, D. (1992). The strength of strong ties. In N. Nohria & R.G. Eccles (Eds.), *Networks and organizations: Structure, form, and action* (pp. 216-239). Boston, MA: Harvard Business School Press.

Krackhardt, D. & Stern, R. N. (1988). Informal networks and organizational crises: An experimental simulation. *Social Psychology Quarterly, 51*, 123-140.

Lazega, E. & Van Duijn, M. (1997). Position in formal structure, personal characteristics and choices of advisors in a law firm: a logistic regression model for dyadic network data. *Social Networks, 19*, 375-397.

Leana, C. R. & Van Buren, H. J., III. (1999). Organizational social capital and employment practices. *Academy of Management Review, 24*(3), 538-555.

Lieberman, A. (2000). Networks as learning communities: Shaping the future of teacher development. *Journal of Teacher Education, 51*, 221-229.

Lima, J. A. (2003). Trained for isolation: The impact of departmental cultures on student teachers' views and practices of collaboration. *Journal of Education for Teaching, 29*(3), 197-218.

Lima, J. A. (2007). Teachers' professional development in departmentalized, loosely coupled organizations: Lessons for school improvement from a case study of two curriculum departments. *School Effectiveness and School Improvement, 18*(3), 273-301.

Lin, N. (2001). *Social capital: A theory of social structure and action.* New York, NY: Cambridge University Press.

Little, J. W. (1990). The persistence of privacy: Autonomy and initiative in teachers' professional relations. *Teachers College Record, 91*(4), 509-536.

Louis, K. S., Marks, H. M., & Kruse, S. (1996). Teacher professional community in restructuring schools. *American Educational Research Journal, 33*(4), 757-98.

Lubbers, M. J., Van der Werf, M. P. C., Kuyper, H., & Offringa, G. J. (2006). Predicting peer acceptance in Dutch youth: A multilevel analysis. *Journal of Early Adolescence, 26*(1), 4-35.

Marsden, P. V. (1988). Homogeneity in confiding relations. *Social Networks, 10*(1), 57-76.

McCormick, R., Fox, A., Carmichael, P., & Procter, R. (2010). *Researching and understanding educational networks.* New Perspectives on Learning and Instruction Series. London, UK: Routledge.

McLaughlin, M. & Talbert, J. E. (2001). *Professional communities and the work of high school teaching.* Chicago, IL: University of Chicago Press.

McPherson, J. M., Smith-Lovin, L., & Cook, J. M. (2001). Birds of a feather: Homophily in social networks. *Annual Review of Sociology, 27*, 415-444.

Mehra, A., Kilduff, M., & Brass, D. J. (1998). At the margins: A distinctiveness approach to the social identity and social networks of underrepresented groups. *Academy of Mangement Journal, 41*(4), 441-452.

Mehra, A., Kilduff, M., & Brass, D. J. (2001). The social networks of high and low self-monitors: Implications for workplace performance. *Administrative Science Quarterly, 46*, 121-146.

Moolenaar, N. M. (2010). *Ties with potential: Nature, antecedents, and consequences of social networks in school teams.* Unpublished doctoral dissertation. University of Amsterdam, The Netherlands.

Moolenaar, N. M., Daly, A. J., & Sleegers, P. J. C. (2010). Occupying the principal position: Examining relationships between transformational leadership, social network position, and schools' innovative climate. *Educational Administration Quarterly, 46*(5), 623-670.

Moolenaar, N. M, Karsten, S., Sleegers, P. J. C., & Zijlstra, B. J. H. (2009). *Professional school communities from a social capital perspective: An empirical study across multiple levels of analysis.* Paper presented at the 2009 Annual meeting of the American Educational Research Association (AERA), April 13-17, San Diego, CA USA.

Moolenaar, N. M., Daly, A. J., & Sleegers, P. J. C. (2011). Ties with potential: Social network structure and innovative climate in Dutch schools. *Teachers College Record, 113*(9), 1983-2017.

Molenaar, N. M., Sleegers, P. J. C., Karsten, S., & Daly, A. J. (2012). The social fabric of elementary schools: A network typology of social interaction among teachers. *Educational Studies.*

Muller, C. & Ellison, C. G. (2001). Religious involvement, social capital, and adolescents' academic progress: Evidence from the National Education Longitudinal Study of 1988. *Sociological Focus, 34*(2), 155-183.

Nahapiet, J. & Ghoshal, S. (1998). Social capital, intellectual capital, and the organizational advantage. *Academy of Management Review, 23*(2), 242-266.

Penuel, W. R. & Riel, M. R. (2007). The 'new' science of networks and the challenge of school change. *Phi Delta Kappan, 88*(8), 611-615.

Penuel, W. R., Riel, M. R., Krause, A., & Frank, K. A. (2009). Analyzing teachers' professional interactions in a school as social capital: A social network approach. *Teachers College Record, 111*(1), 124-163.

Podsakoff, P. M., MacKenzie, S. B., Paine, J. B., & Bachrach, D. G. (2000). Organizational citizenship behaviors: A critical review of the theoretical and empirical literature and suggestions for future research. *Journal of Management, 26*, 513–563.

Pustejovsky, J. E. & Spillane, J. P. (2009). Question-order effects in social network name generators. *Social Networks, 31*(4), 221-229.

Putnam, R. D. (1993). *Making democracy work: Civic traditions in modern Italy.* Princeton, NJ: Princeton University Press.

Putnam, R. D. (2000). *Bowling alone. The collapse and revival of American community.* New York, NY: Simon and Schuster.

Reagans, R. E. & Zuckerman, E. W. (2001). Networks, diversity and performance: The social capital of R&D teams. *Organization Science, 12*, 502-518.

Scott, J. (2000). *Social network analysis.* London, UK: Sage Publications.

Smylie, M. A. & Evans, A. E. (2006). Social capital and the problem of implementation. In: M. I. Honig (Ed.), *New directions in education policy: Confronting complexity* (pp. 187-208). Albany, NY: State University of New York Press.

Somech, A. & Ron, I. (2007). Promoting organizational citizenship behavior in schools: The impact of individual and organizational characteristics. *Educational Administration Quarterly, 43,* 38-66.

Spillane, J. P. (2006). *Distributed leadership.* San Francisco: Jossey-Bass.

Stanton-Salazar, R. D. & Dornbusch, S. M. (1995). Social capital and the reproduction of inequality: Information networks among Mexican-origin high school students. *Sociology of Education, 68,* 116-135.

Starkey, F., Audrey, S., Holliday, J., Moore, L., & Campbell, R. (2009). Identifying influential young people to undertake effective peer-led health promotion: the example of A Stop Smoking In Schools Trial (ASSIST) *Health Education Research, 24*(6), 977-988.

Tsai, W. & Ghoshal, S. (1998). Social capital and value creation: The role of intrafirm networks. *Academy of Management Journal, 41*(4), 464-476.

Tschannen-Moran, M. (2001). Collaboration and the need for trust. *Journal of Educational Administration, 39*(4), 308-31.

Tschannen-Moran, M. (2003). Fostering organizational citizenship: Transformational leadership and trust. In W. K. Hoy & C. G. Miskel, *Studies in leading and organizing schools* (pp. 157-179). Greenwich, CT: Information Age Publishing.

Uzzi, B. (1996). The sources and consequences of embeddedness for the economic performance of organizations: The network effect. *American Sociological Review, 61,* 674-698.

Uzzi, B. (1997). Social structure and competition in interfirm networks: The paradox of embeddedness. *Administrative Science Quarterly, 42*(1), 35-67.

Valente, T. W. (1996). Social network thresholds in the diffusion of innovations. *Social Networks, 18*(1), 69-89.

Valente, T. W., Hoffman, B. R., Ritt-Olson, A., Lichtman, K., & Johnson, C. A. (2003). The effects of a social network method for group assignment strategies on peer led tobacco prevention programs in schools. *American Journal of Public Health, 93,* 1837-1843.

Valente, T. W. & Pumpuang, P. (2007). Identifying opinion leaders to promote behavior change. *Health education & Behavior, 34,* 881-896.

Veugelers, W. & Zijlstra, H. (2002). What goes on in a network? Some Dutch experiences. *International Journal of Leadership in Education, 5*(2), 163-174.

Walker, G., Kogut, B., & Shah, W. (1997). Social capital, structural holes, and the formation of an industry network. *Organizational Science, 8,* 109-125.

Wasserman, S. & Faust, K. (1997). *Social network analysis: Methods and applications.* New York, NY: Cambridge University Press.

Wasserman, S. & Galaskiewicz, J. (1994). *Advances in social network analysis: Research in the social and behavioral sciences.* Thousand Oaks, CA: Sage.

Wenger, E. (1998). *Communities of practice: Learning, meaning, and identity.* New York, NY: Cambridge University Press.

HEATHER E. PRICE

7. SCHOOL PRINCIPAL-STAFF RELATIONSHIP EFFECTS ON SCHOOL CLIMATE

INTRODUCTION

The school effectiveness and school climate research solidly identifies the variables associated with successful schools; shared values and norms, openness of governance, and trusting relationships produce committed and contented school community members (Bryk, Sebring, Allensworth, Luppescu, & Easton, 2010). Principals' interactions with their staff are found to be central variables associated with these outcomes (Hoy & Henderson, 1983; Leithwood & Jantzi, 1990; Ogawa & Bossert, 1995; Rosenholtz 1985). Reviews of this research call researchers to push beyond describing these static conditions associated with positive climates and effective schools (Creemers & Kyriakides, 2008; Teddlie & Reynolds, 2000). These scholars urge researchers to consider the dynamic processes undergirding these correlates – to identify what makes them emerge, prosper, and propagate in some schools and not others. This study identifies *how* workplace relationships in schools shape the commitment and satisfaction attitudes of its members. Particular attention is paid to the dynamic, 'ripple out' effect where school members' attitudes are expected to most strongly influence those closest to them in the organizational structure. Specifically, principals' attitudes are speculated to most strongly and directly influence teachers and then indirectly influence students. Teachers' attitudes are expected to more directly influence students. This study begins exploring the dynamic process in schools with an eye toward principals in shaping staff attitudes and how this then proceeds to explain students' school attitudes.

Focusing on principal-teacher relationships within schools is one crucial portion of the dynamic process needed to understand variation in school climate and outcomes important for effective schools. Organizational, social psychological, and sociological research provide platforms from which to conceptualize a theoretical explanation for variation on school climate. The importance of affective interpersonal work ties evidenced in organizational studies and social psychology research helps understand the emergence of variation in the school organizational climate. Institutional, network, and school community theories from sociology help to explain the structural interdependence of school members and the ripple out effects of attitudes in schools.

Faculty networks are proposed as the central mechanisms that hold together schooling organizations (Bidwell & Yasumoto, 1999). This idea is extended to analyse the relationship effects from the school faculty network, defined as the summation of the interpersonal relationships between principals and teachers, on

T. Wubbels et al. (eds.), Interpersonal Relationships in Education, 103–118.

the aggregate attitudes of school members. These attitudes describe the school climate. Principal-teacher relationships are chosen as the focal interest for this analysis because principals are the persons in the structural position to initiate, develop, and maintain the network of relations in the school (Bryk et al., 2010). The effects from these principal-teacher relationships are then expected to explain the school climate.

This analysis is important because research shows that positive school climates indirectly improve student learning through improved classroom teaching and learning (Hallinger & Heck, 1998; Kyriakides, Creemers, Antoniou, & Demetriou, 2010; Lee & Bryk, 1989; Leithwood & Jantzi, 2008; Rosenholtz, 1989). But less work has been done to explain the factors that explain the emergence of positive school climate. Recent work places the onus of creating positive school climates on the principal (Bryk et al., 2010). This study specifically explores how principals' affective interpersonal work relationships with teachers create attitudinal responses that aggregate up to dynamically explained variation in school climate among all teachers and students in the school. Nationally representative US public elementary school, teacher, and principal survey data inform these analyses.

SCHOOL CLIMATE AND EFFECTIVENESS

Effective schools and schools with positive school climates share many of the same tenants and outcomes. As Teddlie and Reynolds (2000) and Creemers and Kyriakides (2008) review, most school effectiveness studies focus on achievement, but some focus on other student outcomes of attendance, identity, and academic self-confidence. School climate research focuses more on the school organization, leadership, and community influencers on the engagement indicators relevant for effective schools. This study uses both literatures to inform the outcomes of interest, namely, the teacher and student school attitudes, to explain school climates critical for effective schools.

Principals are central to the formation, development, and maintenance of the school climate (Bryk et al., 2010). Their influence goes beyond the classroom, extending into the hallways, school grounds, and surrounding community (Bryk et al., 2010). The most effective principals appear to be the ones who authentically share decision-making power with their teachers, facilitate open work environments that encourage innovation, and nurture teachers to their maximal potential through professional discourse (Bryk et al., 2010; Hoy & Henderson 1983; Leithwood & Jantzi, 1990, 2008; Rosenholtz 1989; Tschannen-Moran & Hoy, 2000). By necessity, effective principals require a certain level of autonomy from their central district office in order to most appropriately prescribe the strengths and needs of the faculty to the broader district goals (Bryk et al., 2010; Firestone & Wilson, 1985; Leithwood & Jantzi, 2008;). Schools with effective principals fuel positive work environments where teachers express higher levels of commitment and contentment/satisfaction to their schools (Bryk et al., 2010; Firestone & Pennel, 1993; Hulpia, Devos, & Rosseel, 2009; Leithwood & Jantzi,

2008; Rosenholtz, 1989). These effects spill over into the classroom and indirectly enhance student learning (Bryk et al., 2010; Creemers & Kyriakides, 2008; Hallinger & Heck, 1998; Rosenholtz, 1989).

Institutional theory from sociology frames the processes that are important to building successful school climates. Early work on institutional theory in schools proposes the network of relationships between staff as foundational blocks for the school structure (Meyer & Rowan, 1977; Ogawa & Bossert, 1995). Through relationships, principals and teachers develop and evolve a school culture out of relational trust, shared values and norms, diffuse work roles, and common experiences (Bryk & Driscoll, 1988; Bryk, Lee, & Holland, 1993; Bryk & Schneider, 2002; Bryk et al., 2010). Under these ideas, the network web of school members creates a structural interdependence that creates attitudinal ripple effects throughout the school. Therefore, as Ogawa and colleagues have proposed (Miskel & Ogawa, 1988, Ogawa & Bossert, 1995), a beneficial line of research lies in the analysis of the variation of principal practices that shape work environments for their staff.

AFFECT AND WORK RELATIONSHIPS

Affective interpersonal work ties, as evidenced in organizational studies and social psychology research, helps to understand the emergence of variation in teacher outcomes in their school workplace. In educational research there seems to be little use of these organizational and workplace theories. The hesitancy may be due to differences in assumptions between the traditionally evaluated factory line workers and professional educators. Theories regarding 'product quality' cannot be assumed to directly translate into schooling organizations since schools do not produce material products. That being said, there are good reasons to use organizational and workplace theories related to organization of professions and productive work environments to investigate positive school climates. In these theories, the dependent variables of interest are shared – schools, like other organizations, prosper with dedicated, committed, and contented school principals, teachers, and students.

The literature on affect in work relationships is quite clear: individual workers and organizations prosper when workers are content and committed to their workplace (Brief & Weiss, 2002). Strong ties benefit individuals' mental and physical health, namely, feelings of belonging and identity with co-workers subsequently increase job satisfaction (Kardos & Johnson, 2009; Miskel & Ogawa, 1988; Podolny & Baron, 1997). Strong ties benefit organizations since individual health positively correlates with work quality and a reliable, loyal, and committed work force (Brief & Weiss, 2002; Lease, 1998; Podolny & Baron, 1997). School studies find similar effects linking personal teacher satisfaction and commitment to teacher cooperation and commitment in schools (Bryk, Lee, & Holland, 1993; Bryk et al., 2010; Rosenholtz, 1989; Tschannen-Moran & Hoy, 2000).

A theme in organizational work studies is that positive attitudes are contagious – when individuals work around other workers who are satisfied with their job, others' attitudes improve and workplace production and quality increases (Brief & Weiss, 2002). When a mass of workers are satisfied and committed to their work, further increases in work quality and commitment emerge (Brief & Weiss, 2002). Similarly, effective schools are found to have higher levels of commitment and satisfaction levels among their teachers, principals, and students than other schools (Bryk, Lee, & Holland, 1993; Bryk et al., 2010; Rosenholtz, 1985). Therefore, I would expect that *the average teachers' and principal's satisfaction and commitment levels in a school explain variation in climates between schools.*

Social psychological literature helps reveal why commitment levels improve work quality. Lawler and colleagues (Lawler, Thye, & Yoon, 2000, 2006; Lawler & Yoon, 1993, 1996, 1998) discuss the affective endogenous processes that occur between interacting persons. Emotion maintains loyalty and commitment to the relationships. This process feeds back to further strengthen the relationship. Lawler and colleagues show that quality produced from affectively tied relationships becomes more reliable as commitment and loyalty continue and persist. Therefore, *the frequency of exchange between principals and teachers is expected to positively influence positive affect (satisfaction). Satisfaction should then increase relationship cohesion. Positive cohesion perceptions are then expected to increase commitment levels.* This process then feeds back to increase the frequency of interaction which further strengthens the relationship.

Most of these experimental studies by Lawler and colleagues (Lawler, Thye, & Yoon, 2000; Lawler & Yoon, 1993, 1996, 1998) are based on equally distributed power. It is only recently that these effects have been tested under imbalanced power situations (Lawler, Thye, & Yoon, 2006). Similar to the worker, co-worker, and supervisor workplace findings (Lease, 1998; Riggio & Cole, 1992), the magnitudes of worker affect effects differs by the amount of power balance between the two interacting persons. Balanced power relationships experience larger effect sizes from the frequency of exchanges and emotion than experienced in imbalanced relationships. *Thus, principals who share school decision-making powers with the teachers are expected to magnify the impact on the school attitudes of their teachers and students.*

A caveat in social psychological and organizational studies is that 'match' matters. Match matters for the individual and for the relationship. Holland's Theory of Vocational Choice (TVC) (1959) outlines that individuals whose personal traits align with the organizations' traits should experience more positive outcomes than workers whose personalities do not fit as well. Yet, empirical findings on TVC effects are mixed (Spokane, Meir, & Catalano, 2000). To test TVC effects, *principal preparations*, as measured by prior assistant principal experience and/or pre-principal training programs, *are expected to increase the likelihood of aligning job requirements to personality traits of principals. These preparatory experiences should moderate the individual levels of principal satisfaction and commitment.*

Definition of the situation theory explains the importance of matched expectations between two people. Within a relationship, if one's own expectations of the other person match the actual behaviours of other, then the exchange is more successful than if there is mismatch (Thomas & Thomas in Hewitt, 2007). Matched definition of situation depends on both actors' interpretation and adherence to role expectations upon entering the exchange (Fazio, 1986). Moreover, the frequency and likelihood of future exchanges increases when definitions match (Fazio, 1986). Thus, *if principals and teachers match on their perception of the school environment, the frequency of their interactions should increase and subsequently improve their satisfaction and commitment levels.*

In summary, this study focuses on how the qualities of principals and the relationships they form with their teachers affect the attitudes of teachers. This interaction-relationship mechanism provides explanation as to the effect of workplace affect on job satisfaction and organizational commitment, which then translates into higher quality work outcomes. In the case of schools, this explanation helps unpack the 'black box' of school climate effects on school effectiveness. The effects from principal-teacher relationships are expected to then ripple out to affect the students.

In the section to follow, a description of the data and methods outlines the analytic plan. Following that, the relationship processes between the principals and their teachers are discussed. This sets the stage to explain how school attitudes among teachers and students that define the school climate. Unlike other research, this study focuses on how the effects of relationships ripple out to affect the aggregate, school levels of commitment and satisfaction. This focus helps elucidate the central importance of interpersonal relationships in schools.

DATA AND METHOD

Data

The Schools and Staffing Survey (SASS) is a nationally representative survey of districts, schools, teachers, principals, and librarians in the US conducted every four years. For this study, principal and teacher surveys are matched by school for the 2003-2004 school year. Research discusses the organizational leadership complexities of secondary education institutions (Bidwell & Yasumoto, 1999; Kyriakides et al., 2010). To gain the least confounded and most clear understanding of the relationship processes outlined in this study, only US public elementary schools are analysed.

To assess the relationship process between principals and their teachers, several latent variables are constructed from Likert-rated question responses. The degree of principals' *power sharing* with teachers is captured by principals rating the extent to which their teachers have equal voice in six decisions on the curriculum, discipline, programming, teacher evaluations, hiring, and budget ($\alpha = 0.55$). Frequency of *joint professional exchange* reflects the number of joint principal and teacher professional development activities during the year (0, 1-2, 3-5, more than 5). *Matched definition of the Situation* is a dichotomous variable regarding whether the teachers and the principal 'match' on their staff climate perceptions. *Principal satisfaction* uses the general question: "I like the way things are run in this district". *Principal cohesion* assesses the principal's perception of teacher unity in the school. *Principal commitment* is latently constructed from three questions regarding whether the job is worth the stress, low pay, and/or the transferring hassle ($\alpha = 0.62$). Appendix A describes the covariance matrix for these variables.

Exogenous to this relationship process are the moderating effects of principal autonomy and aligned expectations. *Principal autonomy* assesses the principal's assessment of their level of direct control in their schools over personnel policies, termination decisions, bureaucratic processes, and tenure assignment. *Principal preparation*, whether or not the principal was formerly an assistant principal and/or whether she participated in a principal training program, reflects vocational choice theory ideas about alignment benefits.

Four measures indicate positive school climate and assess the effects of the principal-teacher relationships on school climate (see Table 1). Averaged teacher ratings of teacher satisfaction, teacher commitment, respectful student attitudes, and positive student behaviours reflect the school climate.[i] *Teacher satisfaction* factors answers regarding teachers' satisfaction with the amount of principal communication, recognition, and support as well as satisfaction with their class size, salary, and teaching ($\alpha = 0.74$). *Teacher commitment* factors questions related to intentions to switch careers (reverse coded), transfer schools (reverse coded), and remain in teaching ($\alpha = 0.61$). *Respectful student attitudes* reverse codes teacher assessments of classroom disorder, verbal abuse, acts of disrespect toward teachers, student vandalism, and student conflicts ($\alpha = 0.85$); higher scores on these indicators represent fewer incidences. *Positive student behaviours* reverse codes student levels of problematic tardiness, class cutting, absenteeism, and unpreparedness ($\alpha = 0.84$); higher scores represent fewer incidences of misbehaviour.

Method

Structural equation modelling (SEM) techniques model the proposed endogenous processes involved in the principal-teacher relationship processes. SEM allows for the series of embedded, simultaneous processes between independent and dependent variables to be modelled (Bollen, 1989). SEM determines the overall standardized effect of the variable on the entire relationship process and the separate effect of the variables on each portion of the process (Bollen, 1989). This modelling deconstructs the relationships to better understand the attitude levels of job satisfaction, cohesion perceptions, and commitment among principals.

Table 1. Descriptive characteristics of principals, schools, relationships, and school climate.

	Mean/ Proportion	Std. Dev.	Min	Max
School climate, aggregate level				
Teacher satisfaction	2.996	0.257	1	4
Teacher commitment	3.115	0.268	1	4
Student respectful attitudes	3.445	0.508	1	5
Student positive behaviour	2.553	0.457	1	4
Principal attitudes				
Principal satisfaction	3.058	0.837	1	4
Principal cohesion perception	3.447	0.780	1	4
Principal commitment	3.346	0.639	1	4
Relationship characteristics				
Matched definition of the situation	0.370		0	1
Power sharing	2.083	0.495	0	3
Joint professional interactions	3.417	0.506	1	4
Exogenous influences				
Principal autonomy from district	2.375	0.926	1	4
Assistant Principal	0.498		0	1
Principal Training	0.498		0	1
Assistant Principal & Training	0.388		0	1
Dyadic characteristics, controlled				
All female dyads	0.416		0	1
All male dyads	0.405		0	1
All white, non-Hispanic administration	0.826		0	1
Principal characteristics				
Female	0.464		0	1
White, non-Hispanic	0.792		0	1
Age	50.474	7.942	26	70
Years as principal at this school	4.802	4.931	0	36
School characteristics				
Urban	0.294		0	1
Suburban	0.428		0	1
Rural	0.279		0	1
Student enrolment	469.844	224.215	6	3023
Free and reduced lunch %	45.6%	28.5	0	100
Minority student %	37.1%	32.6	0	100
Limited English proficiency %	7.5%	14.9	0	100
Special education %	12.0%	8.5	0	100

n = 11,620 relationships.
All n's rounded to the nearest 10, in accordance with NCES restricted data reporting standards.

Elements that are theoretically exogenous to this affective relationship process, namely, the amount of autonomy of principals over school decisions and principal preparatory training, are also accounted. Controls for principal gender, racial-ethnic background, age, and years of principal experience are also accounted in the models, but not reported out due to space constraints. Proper principal weights are applied (afnlwgt).

To test the main portion of the analysis regarding the effects of the principal-teacher relationships on overall school climate, this study uses ordinary least squares (OLS) linear regression modelling. With this technique, the qualities of principal relationships with their teachers and the principal attitudes are used to explain variation at the school level of attitudes of teachers and students indicative of positive school climates. The standard deviations on these outcomes are low because individual scores are aggregated up to the school level.[ii] The standard errors of the models are adjusted accordingly since the models show the effects of principal-teacher relationships at the school level, $n = 1800$, not the teacher level, $n = 11,620$. To model the ripple out scenario, teacher attitudes are additionally nested into these models mediate principal effects on student attitudes. School urbanicity, size, proportion of student body of colour, poverty, limited English, and special needs are controlled in the models to properly account for the between school demographic variation which may otherwise influence the conclusions. Due to space constraints, the control variable effects are not reported here. School weights are applied to reflect national representation (sfnlwgt). This modelling heeds a call from researchers to begin analysing school effects at the school level (Creemers & Kyriakides, 2008; Teddlie & Reynolds 2000).

FINDINGS

Figure 1 shows that most of the principal-teacher relationship processes act as hypothesized on principal attitudes.[iii] Power sharing and matched definitions of the situation directly and positively influence the frequency of joint professional interactions between principals and teachers. Sharing school decision-making power indirectly influences principals' levels of satisfaction and perceptions of staff cohesion, but not commitment. Matched definition of the situation does not directly influence satisfaction levels as hypothesized, but it does indirectly and positively influence commitment. The frequency of joint professional interactions mediates matched definition of situation effects on commitment and directly increases job satisfaction. Satisfaction levels strongly improve perceptions of faculty cohesion and principal commitment. Cohesion perceptions also influence principals' commitment levels. Exogenous influences of principal autonomy from the district and principal preparation moderates these relationship effects.

This study specifically extends the results of the SEM model presented in Figure 1 in order to investigate how these relationship characteristics and principal attitudes ripple out to affect the overall teacher and student attitudes in schools. Table 2 shows the importance of the principal-teacher relationship processes on the indicators of positive school climate. For the teacher attitudes, including the principal-teacher relationship mechanisms dramatically improves the explained variance (R^2) in the models. There is a five-fold increase of R^2 on teacher satisfaction and a three-fold increase of R^2 on teacher commitment levels, where the prior model included principal pre-training and all controls. For the student outcomes, including the principal-teacher relationships improves the model fit 25% for student attitudes and 10% for student behaviour. This improvement is quite laudable considering the school controls account for 17.2% and 26.0% of the between school variation for student attitudes and behaviours, respectively.

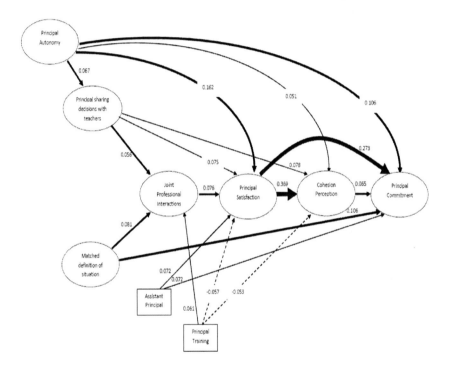

Figure 1. Reduced form model of principal-teacher relationship effects.

Matched definition of the situation between teachers and principals explains a substantial portion of the model variances. Teacher satisfaction and commitment increase 0.83 and 1.01 standard deviations, respectively, when teachers' and principal's definition of the situation match. In addition, the frequency of joint professional principal-teacher interactions significantly improves school climate. Every 2-3 additional professional interaction activities for principals and teachers in a school year increase the teacher workplace satisfaction levels by 2/3 of a

Table 2. School level regression models of principal relationship effects on school climate indicators.

	Principal-Teacher Relationship Effects on Teacher and Student Attitudes			
	(1) Teacher Satisfaction	(2) Teacher Commitment	(3) Student Respectful Attitudes	(4) Student Positive Behaviour
Relationship characteristics				
Matched definition situation	0.303***	0.364***	0.305***	0.191***
	(0.030)	(0.037)	(0.058)	(0.045)
Power sharing	0.006	-0.007	-0.018	-0.023
	(0.020)	(0.023)	(0.037)	(0.029)
Joint professional interactions	0.241***	0.088**	0.090*	0.078*
	(0.022)	(0.027)	(0.042)	(0.033)
Principal attitudes				
Principal satisfaction	0.012	-0.018	0.023	0.001
	(0.014)	(0.017)	(0.028)	(0.024)
Principal cohesion perception	0.041*	0.046	0.092**	0.090***
	(0.017)	(0.024)	(0.033)	(0.027)
Principal commitment	0.005	0.019	-0.020	-0.004
	(0.017)	(0.018)	(0.032)	(0.026)
Exogenous Influences				
Principal autonomy	0.027*	0.009	0.045*	0.031
	(0.011)	(0.012)	(0.022)	(0.017)
Asst. principal experience	-0.010	-0.006	-0.047	-0.126**
	(0.028)	(0.030)	(0.051)	(0.039)
Principal training program	-0.016	-0.011	-0.044	-0.060
	(0.034)	(0.036)	(0.058)	(0.046)
AP and training program	0.025	-0.021	0.082	0.101
	(0.042)	(0.047)	(0.076)	(0.059)
Teachers attitude and behaviour				
Teacher satisfaction, school average				
Teacher commitment, school average				
Constant	1.770***	2.456***	3.037***	2.579***
	(0.125)	(0.149)	(0.234)	(0.190)
Observations	1800	1800	1800	1800
Model F-statistic	17.50***	11.70***	19.66***	27.61***
R-squared	0.240	0.178	0.251	0.331

Models control for principal age and experience, demographic characteristics of the dyads, and school demographics. All n's rounded to the nearest 10, in accordance with NCES restricted data reporting standards.
Standard errors in parentheses *** $p < 0.001$, ** $p < 0.01$, * $p < 0.05$.

Table 2 continued. School level regression models of principal relationship effects on school climate indicators.

	Mediating Role of Teachers on Student Attitudes	
	(5) Student Respectful Attitudes	(6) Student Positive Behaviour
Relationship characteristics		
Matched definition of the situation	0.073	0.035
	(0.057)	(0.043)
Power sharing	-0.021	-0.025
	(0.035)	(0.027)
Joint professional interactions	-0.072	-0.034
	(0.042)	(0.034)
Principal attitudes		
Principal satisfaction	0.018	-0.004
	(0.025)	(0.022)
Principal cohesion perception	0.060*	0.069**
	(0.028)	(0.024)
Principal commitment	-0.025	-0.007
	(0.029)	(0.025)
Exogenous Influences		
Principal autonomy	0.027	0.018
	(0.020)	(0.016)
Assistant principal experience	-0.040	-0.121**
	(0.048)	(0.037)
Principal training program	-0.033	-0.052
	(0.056)	(0.046)
Both AP and training program	0.068	0.091
	(0.071)	(0.057)
Teachers attitude and behaviour		
Teacher satisfaction, school average	0.628***	0.444***
	(0.071)	(0.057)
Teacher commitment, school average	0.115	0.060
	(0.062)	(0.054)
Constant	1.645***	1.645***
	(0.266)	(0.220)
Observations	1800	1800
Model F-statistic	29.79***	32.61***
R-squared	0.361	0.402

Models control for principal age and experience, demographic characteristics of the dyads, and school demographics. All n's rounded to the nearest 10, in accordance with NCES restricted data reporting standards.
Standard errors in parentheses *** $p < 0.001$, ** $p < 0.01$, * $p < 0.05$.

standard deviation. Personal principal satisfaction or commitment levels do not directly affect teachers and students. However, principals' perception of staff cohesion positively influences school climate.

Exogenously, the amount of principal autonomy from the district moderates teacher satisfaction and student respectful attitudes, but does not translate into differences in teacher commitment or student behaviour. Principal preparations explain little variation on school climate with the exception that assistant principal experience significantly worsens student behaviour.

When the teacher levels of satisfaction and commitment are added to the student models in models 5 and 6 (Table 2), only the principal perception of cohesion continues to directly affect student attitudes and behaviours. With the exception the principals' cohesion perception, the affective relationship processes between principals and teachers no longer affects the students. More simply, the principal-teacher relationship mechanisms indirectly affect student attitudes through their teachers' attitudes. For example, schools with one standard deviation higher average teacher satisfaction and commitment correlate with a student body whose attitudes and behaviours are one-third of a standard deviation higher than otherwise similar schools.

DICUSSION

The relationship process hypotheses blended from the social psychology, organizational, and sociology literatures explain a substantial portion of the variance in attitudes important to school climate and effective schools. As the experimental findings in social psychology would predict, the elements of the relationship, from sharing power to perceptions of staff cohesion, influence principals' attitudes. In this non-experimental school setting, positive affect (satisfaction) and sense of cohesion strongly predict principals' commitment behaviours. Similarly, power dynamics moderate the effect sizes; the effects from the interpersonal exchange magnify as the power between principals and teachers balance. The principals' autonomy from the district also enhances the overall positive relationship effects on their attitudes. As the organizational literature proposed, personal satisfaction and cohesion levels strongly predict individuals' commitment to their organization. In this case, principals' satisfaction is the strongest predictor of their commitment. These relationship processes then ripple out to influence school climate.

Faculty networks appear to act as the glue that holds together schools (Bidwell & Yasumoto, 1999).The principal-teacher relationship processes significantly affect aggregate teacher and student attitudes critical for effective schools. Principals' interactions with their staff and perceptions of staff cohesion strongly associate with teachers' satisfaction and commitment and students' attitudes and behaviour levels. The relationship processes, not the individual principals' attitudes, matters most to teachers and students. In Price and Collett (forthcoming), the co-worker influence of the individual teachers' satisfaction and commitment levels significantly and positively influence aggregate teacher matched definition of the situation. Dramatic increases occur in teacher satisfaction and commitment levels when principals and staff agree on the definition of the school situation. Student attitudes and behaviours also respond positively to this. Theory of vocational choice effects, as defined by prior principal trainings, show mixed results on principal and student attitudes and does not affect teachers.

Teachers' attitudes moderate the majority of the principal effects on the students. Schools' average teacher satisfaction and commitment levels strongly influence the student body's attitudes and behaviours. Students' attitudes and behaviours respond to their teachers' satisfaction and commitment levels and the teachers' attitudes and behaviours respond to their relationships with their principals. This ripple out structure shows the centrality of principal relationships in the formation, development, and maintenance of positive school climates.

Limitations

First, the processes described here have an obvious non recursive nature where staff relationships affect the school climate and the school climate then cycles back to influence the relationships. This likely feedback loop enhances the importance of the findings regarding principal-staff relationships on the school climate. Second, due to data limitations, school climate is narrowly defined as principal, teacher, and student attitudes. Other stakeholders' attitudes that makeup the school climate, such as parents, are not analysed in this study. Also, this study does not focus on the intrinsic psychological factors which may exogenously influence commitment levels. Previous studies cite the influence of teacher self-efficacy on their commitment to teaching and their school (Tschannen-Moran & Hoy, 2000). Finally, there are more dimensions to positive affect discussed in the social psychology literature than empirically tested in this study. Interest, for example, is an affective dimension relevant to these theories. Interest levels are captured adequately on the SASS teacher survey, but it is not captured adequately on the principal survey. In a companion study where teacher-teacher relationships are tested, teacher interest is included as a second positive affect dimension and it is found to improve commitment levels (Price & Collett, forthcoming). Future research will incorporate other interpersonal relationships in the school to better map the interdependence of the school network structure.

Policy Implications

In this study, principal-teacher relationships explain a significant portion of between-school variance on attitudes associated with positive school climate and effective schools. These relationships help identify one relevant and dynamic dimension of school climate (Bryk et al., 2010; Ogawa & Bossert, 1995). Principal, teacher, and student attitudes improve with positive principal-teacher relationships.

Building positive staff relationships could be a tangible policy initiative to improve teacher and student pro-school attitudes and the school learning climate. Given the definition of the situation effect sizes, explicit communication between teachers and principals could be one effective strategy to improve attitudes and behaviours among school staff. Joint principal-teacher professional interactions and activities also improve relationships. Attention to these relationships could reduce serious costs incurred by schools, school districts, and their students which occur from exorbitant rates of teacher attrition (Barnes, Crowe, & Schaefer 2007).

APPENDIX A. COVARIANCE MATRIX FOR THE SEM PRINCIPAL MODEL

	Principal autonomy	Power sharing	Matched definition of the situation	Assistant principal experience	Pre-principal training	Joint Professional interactions	Principal satisfaction	Principal cohesion perception
Power sharing	0.0836							
Matched definition of the situation	-0.0126	0.0094						
Assistant principal experience	-0.1149	-0.0807	-0.0488					
Pre-principal Training	-0.0465	0.0240	-0.0113	0.1348				
Joint professional interactions	0.0101	0.0681	0.0752	0.0112	0.0861			
Principal satisfaction	0.1820	0.0901	0.0112	0.0054	-0.0843	0.0655		
Principal cohesion perception	-0.1494	-0.1312	0.0104	0.0159	0.1113	-0.0510	-0.4167	
Principal commitment	0.1492	0.0388	-0.0688	0.0864	0.0474	0.1168	0.2911	-0.1714

NOTES

[i] Teacher reports of these types of school climate indicators are found to be "highly reliable and precise" indicators of actual school occurrences (Wolfe, Ray, & Harris, 2004).

[ii] The standard deviations for the individual level measures are not low. For $n = 11,620$, teacher satisfaction $\mu = 3.00$ $\sigma = 0.524$; teacher commitment $\mu = 3.115$ $\sigma = 0.608$; student attitudes $\mu = 3.156$ $\sigma = 0.553$; student behaviour $\mu = 2.178$ $\sigma = 0.618$.

[iii] The fit statistics for the most efficient model, as shown in Figure 1, are: Chi-square = 1043.885; $p = .000$; AIC = 1205.885; CFI = 0.910; RMSEA = 0.048. For a more detailed account of the SEM model building, fits, and analyses, see Price (2012).

REFERENCES

Barnes, G., Crowe, E., & Schaefer, B. (2007). *The cost of teacher turnover in five school districts: A pilot study.* National Commission on Teaching and America's Future, Washington.

Bidwell, C. E. & Yasumoto, J. Y. (1999). The collegial focus: Teaching fields, collegial relationships, and instructional practice in American high schools. *Sociology of Education, 72*, 234-256.

Bollen, K. A. (1989). *Structural Equations with Latent Variables.* New York: Wiley-Interscience.

Brief, A. P. & Weiss, H. M. (2002). Organizational behavior: Affect in the workplace. *Annual Review of Psychology, 53*, 279-307.

Bryk, A. S. & Driscoll M. (1988). *The high school as community: Contextual influences and consequences for students and teachers.* National Center on Effective Secondary Schools, Madison: University of Wisconsin.

Bryk, A. S., Lee, V. E., & Holland, P. B. (1993). *Catholic schools and the common good.* Cambridge: Harvard University Press.

Bryk, A. S. & Schneider, B. L. (2002). *Trust in schools: A core resource for improvement.* New York: Russell Sage Foundation.

Bryk, A. S., Sebring, P. B., Allensworth, E., Luppescu, S., & Easton, J. Q. (2010). *Organizing schools for improvement: Lessons from Chicago.* Chicago The University of Chicago Press.

Creemers, B. P. M. & Kyriakides, L. (2008). *The dynamics of educational effectiveness: A contribution to policy, practice and theory in contemporary schools.* London/New York: Routledge.

Fazio, R. H. (1986). How do attitudes guide behavior?. In R. M. Sorrentino & E. T. Higgins (Eds.), *Motivation & cognition: Foundations of social behavior.* New York: The Guilford Press.

Firestone, W. A. &. Pennell, J. R. (1993). Teacher commitment, working-conditions, and differential incentive policies. *Review of Educational Research, 63*, 489-525.

Firestone, W. A. & Wilson, B. L. (1985). Using bureaucratic and cultural linkages to improve instruction – The principals contribution. *Educational Administration Quarterly, 21*, 7-30.

Hallinger, P. & Heck, R. H. (1998). Exploring the principal's contribution to school effectiveness: 1980-1995. *School Effectiveness and School Improvement, 9*(2), 157-150.

Hewitt, J. P. (2007). *Self and society: A symbolic interactionalist social psychology,* 10th ed. Boston, MA: Allyn & Bacon.

Holland, J. L. (1959). A theory of vocational choice. *Journal of Counseling Psychology, 6*, 35-45.

Hoy, W. K. & Henderson, J. E. (1983). Principal authenticity, school climate, and pupil-control orientation. *Alberta Journal of Educational Research, 29*, 123-130.

Hulpia, H., Devos, G., & Rosseel, Y. (2009). The relationship between the perception of distributed leadership in secondary schools and teachers' and teacher leaders' job satisfaction and organizational commitment. *School Effectiveness and School Improvement, 20*, 291-317.

Kardos, S. M. & Johnson, S. M. (2009). On their own and presumed expert: New teachers' experiences with their colleagues. *Teachers College Record, 109*(102).

Kyriakides, L. B., Creemers, P. M., Antoniou, P., & Demetriou, D. (2010). A synthesis of studies searching for the school factors: Implications for theory and research. *British Educational Research Journal, 36*(5), 807-830.

Lawler, E. J., Thye, S. R., & Yoon, J. (2000). Emotion and group cohesion in productive exchange. *American Journal Of Sociology, 106*, 616-657.

Lawler, E. J., Thye, S. R., & Yoon, J. (2006). Commitment in structurally enabled and induced exchange relations. *Social Psychology Quarterly, 69*, 183-200.

Lawler, E. J. & Yoon, J. (1993). Power and the emergence of commitment behavior in negotiated exchange. *American Sociological Review, 58*, 465-481.

Lawler, E. J. & Yoon, J. (1996). Commitment in exchange relations: Test of a theory of relational cohesion. *American Sociological Review, 61*, 89-108.

Lawler, E. J. & Yoon, J. (1998). Network structure and emotion in exchange relations. *American Sociological Review, 63*, 871-894.

Lease, S. H. (1998). Annual review, 1993-1997: Work attitudes and outcomes. *Journal of Vocational Behavior, 53*, 154-183.

Lee, V. E. & Bryk, A. S. (1989). A multilevel model of the social distribution of high-school achievement. *Sociology Of Education, 62*, 172-192.

Leithwood, K. & Jantzi, D. (1990). *Transformational leadership: How principals can help reform school cultures.* Paper presented at the Annual Meeting of the Canadian Association for Curriculum Studies, Victoria. June, 1990.

Leithwood, K. & Jantzi, D. (2008). Linking leadership to student learning: The contributions of leader efficacy. *Educational Administration Quarterly, 44,* 496-528.

Meyer, J. W. & Rowan, B. (1977). Institutionalized organizations – Formal-structure as myth and ceremony. *American Journal of Sociology, 83,* 340-363.

Miskel, C. & Ogawa, R. (1988). Work motivation, job satisfaction, and climate. In N. Boyan (Ed.) *Handbook of educational administration* (pp. 279-303). New York: Longman.

Ogawa, R. T. & Bossert, S. T. (1995). Leadership as an organizational quality. *Educational Administration Quarterly, 31,* 224-43.

Price, H. E. (2012). Principal-teacher interactions: How affective relationships shape principal and teacher attitudes. *Educational Administration Quarterly, 48,* 39-85.

Price, H. E. & Collett, J. (Forthcoming). The role of exchange and emotion on commitment: A study of teachers. *Social Science Researcher.*

Podolny, J. M. & Baron, J. N. (1997). Resources and relationships: Social networks and mobility in the workplace. *American Sociological Review, 62,* 673-693.

Riggio, R. E. & Cole, E. J. (1992). Agreement between subordinate and superior ratings of supervisory performance and effects on self and subordinate job-satisfaction. *Journal of Occupational and Organizational Psychology, 65,* 151-158.

Rosenholtz, S. J. (1985). Effective schools: Interpreting the evidence. *American Journal of Education, 93,* 352-388.

Rosenholtz, S. J. (1989). Workplace conditions that affect teacher quality and commitment: implications for teacher induction programs. *The Elementary School Journal, 89,* 421-439.

Singh, K. & Billingsley, B. S. (1998). Professional support and its effects on teachers' commitment. *Journal of Educational Research, 91,* 229-239.

Spokane, A. R., Meir, E. I., & Catalano, M. (2000). Person-environment congruence and Holland's theory: A review and reconsideration. *Journal of Vocational Behavior, 57,* 137-187.

Teddlie, C. & Reynolds, D. (2000). *The international handbook of school effectiveness research.* London/New York: Falmer Press.

Tschannen-Moran, M. & Hoy, W. K. (2000). A multidisciplinary analysis of the nature, meaning, and measurement of trust. *Review of Educational Research, 70,* 547-593.

Wolfe, E. W., Ray, L. M., & Harris, D. C. (2004). A Rausch analysis of three measures of teacher perception generated from the school and staffing survey. *Educational and Psychological Measurement, 64,* 842-860.

MARIA GEORGIOU AND LEONIDAS KYRIAKIDES

8. THE IMPACT OF TEACHER AND PRINCIPAL INTERPERSONAL BEHAVIOUR ON STUDENT LEARNING OUTCOMES

A Large Scale Study in Secondary Schools of Cyprus

INTRODUCTION

Educational Effectiveness Research (EER) addresses the questions on what works in education and why. Over the last two decades, the quality of EER has increased considerably by the use of improved research designs, sampling strategies, and statistical techniques. Methodological advances, particularly the availability of particular software for the analysis of multilevel data, have enabled more efficient estimates of teacher and school differences in student achievement to be obtained (Goldstein, 2003). There is also substantial agreement on appropriate methods of estimating school differences/effects and on the types of data that are required to make valid comparisons. As far as the theoretical component of the field is concerned, progress was made by a more precise definition of the concepts used and the relations between the concepts (Scheerens & Bosker, 1997). Moreover, models which refer to factors operating at different levels – such as the student, teacher, school, and system levels – have been developed (e.g., Creemers, 1994; Scheerens, 1992; Stringfield & Slavin, 1992). The multilevel nature of these models is supported by various effectiveness studies, which revealed that factors operating at different levels are associated with learning outcomes (Teddlie & Reynolds, 2000). However, an important constraint of the existing approaches of EER is the fact that the whole process does not contribute significantly to the improvement of school effectiveness. In this context, a dynamic model of educational effectiveness (Creemers & Kyriakides, 2008) has been developed. This model attempts to define the dynamic relations between the multiple factors that were found to be associated with effectiveness.

However, the dynamic model is based on a rather strict approach when defining classroom and school factors. Specifically, based on the main findings of teacher effectiveness research (e.g., Brophy & Good, 1986; Darling-Hammond, 2000; Doyle, 1990; Muijs & Reynolds, 2000; Rosenshine & Stevens, 1986; Scheerens & Bosker, 1997), the dynamic model refers to eight factors which describe the teachers' instructional role and are associated with student outcomes: *orientation, structuring, questioning, teaching-modelling, applications, management of time, teacher role in making classroom a learning environment, and classroom assessment*. These eight factors do not refer to only one approach of teaching, such

T. Wubbels et al. (eds.), Interpersonal Relationships in Education, 119–135.

as the direct and active teaching approach (Joyce, Weil, & Calhoun, 2000) or the constructivist approach (Schoenfeld, 1998), but cover, at least partly, the main approaches to learning and teaching. For example, the collaboration technique is included under the overarching factor 'contribution of teacher to the establishment of the classroom learning environment'. Moreover, most of the constructivist approaches to teaching are subsumed in the factors 'teaching modelling' and 'orientation'. These two factors are also in line with the principles of teaching for understanding, and they promote the achievement of new goals of education such as the development of meta-cognitive skills. But although the dynamic model refers to the teacher contribution in creating the classroom learning environment, only the observable interactions between the teacher and his/hers students are taken into account in measuring the classroom learning environment (see Creemers & Kyriakides, 2008).

The definition of the school level is based on the assumption that factors at the school level are expected to not only have direct effects on student achievement, but also indirect effects that are even more important. School factors are expected to influence classroom-level factors, especially the teaching practice. This assumption is based on the fact that EER has shown that the classroom level is more significant than the school level (e.g., Kyriakides, Campbell, & Gagatsis, 2000; Teddlie & Reynolds, 2000). Moreover, defining factors at the classroom level is seen as a prerequisite for defining factors at the school level (Creemers, 1994). As a consequence, the dynamic model refers to factors at the school level which are related to the same key concepts of quantity of teaching, provision of learning opportunities, and quality of teaching which are used to define the classroom-level of the model. More specifically, emphasis is given to the following two main aspects of the school policy which affect learning at both the teacher and student level: a) school policy for teaching, and b) school policy for creating a specific learning environment (see Creemers & Kyriakides, 2008). But although one of the overarching school level factors of the dynamic model is concerned with the school learning environment, the interpersonal relations between teachers and the principal are not taken into account. The dynamic model is only concerned with those interactions among teachers that have a significant impact on their professional development.

Three longitudinal studies (Creemers & Kyriakides, 2010; Kyriakides & Creemers, 2008, 2009) and a meta-analysis (Kyriakides, Creemers, Antoniou, & Demetriou, 2010) provided empirical support for this model, but a significant percentage of the variance remained unexplained. In this context, the study reported here attempts to expand the dynamic model by searching for the impact of teacher and principal interpersonal behaviour on student outcomes.

RESEARCH ON TEACHER AND PRINCIPAL INTERPERSONAL BEHAVIOUR

The effect of teacher behaviour on student outcomes has also been studied within the domain of classroom environment research, which found its origin in early teacher effectiveness studies and studies on the interaction between persons and environment (Moos, 1979; Walberg, 1979). Over the past thirty years, classroom environment research has shown the quality of the classroom environment in schools to be a significant determinant of student learning (Dorman, 2003; Fraser, 1994). For example, Goh and Fraser (1998) managed to establish associations between student outcomes and perceived patterns of teacher-student interaction in primary school mathematics classes in Singapore. Thus, a particular line of research has evolved that focuses on classroom communication processes, studying teaching from the perspective of the interpersonal relationship between teacher and students (Wubbels & Brekelmans, 1998). In line with a systems approach to communication that was originally developed by Watzlawick and his colleagues (Watzlawick, Beavin, & Jackson, 1967), group students and their teacher are studied as ongoing systems. In the systems approach to communication the focus is on the effect of communication on the persons involved.

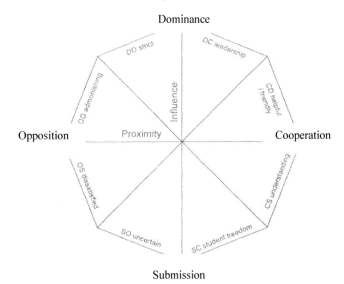

Figure 1. Model for interpersonal teacher behaviour.

Wubbels, Créton, and Hooymayers (1987) adapted a general model of interpersonal communication, for which the work of Leary (1957) was a starting point, to describe the perceptions students have of the behaviour of their teacher. Underlying the original Leary model are dimensions that Leary labelled Dominance-Submission and the Hostility-Affection. While the two dimensions have occasionally been given other names, they have generally been accepted as universal descriptors of human interaction. Adapting the Leary model to the context of education, Wubbels et al. (1987) named the dimensions *Influence* (describing who is in control in the teacher-student relationship) and *Proximity* (describing the degree of cooperation between teacher and students) in their model. The influence dimension is characterized by teacher dominance (D) on one end of the dimension, and teacher submission (S) on the other end. The proximity dimension is characterized by teacher cooperation (C) on one end, and by teacher opposition (O) on the other. The two dimensions are independent and can be depicted in a two-dimensional plane that can be further subdivided into eight categories or sectors of behaviour: leadership (DC), helpful/friendly behaviour (CD), understanding behaviour (CS), giving responsibility/freedom (SC), uncertain behaviour (SO), dissatisfied behaviour (OS), admonishing behaviour (OD) and strictness (DO). In the Model for Interpersonal Teacher Behavior (MITB) these eight categories of behaviour are also expected to be ordered with equal distances to each other on a circular structure and maintain equal distances to the middle of the circle (see Figure 1).

The Questionnaire on Teacher Interaction (QTI) was designed in order to map students' perceptions of teacher interpersonal behaviour according to the MITB. The items of the QTI refer to the eight sectors of behaviour, mentioned above, that jointly make up the MITB. Since its development, the QTI has been the focus of more than 120 learning environment studies in many countries (Den Brok, Brekelmans, Levy, & Wubbels, 2002) and has been translated into more than 15 languages (Wubbels, Brekelmans, Van Tartwijk, & Admiraal, 1997). Classroom environment and educational effectiveness studies that have included interpersonal teacher behaviour measured using the QTI, identified positive relationships between student perceptions of Influence and Proximity or their related (sub)sectors and cognitive student outcomes (Den Brok, Brekelmans, & Wubbels, 2004; Kyriakides, 2006).

Following the same rationale and the structure of QTI, the Principal Interaction Questionnaire (PQI) attempts to measure the perceptions of teachers for the interpersonal behaviour of their principal. In both primary and secondary schools, teachers are in constant communication with other people in the normal course of their duties. In the classroom, the communication of a teacher with his/her students is an essential part of the learning process. But teachers are also in communication with other teachers, parents, and the principal. An important aspect of most teachers' work is the communication and relationship that they have with the principal (Cresswell & Fisher, 1995). For example, some teachers may feel threatened by a dominant principal and will respond with a set of behaviours that is defensive and cautious. Other teachers might respond aggressively to this situation. It is therefore important to explore the type of interaction that principals have with their teachers as perceived by them. The importance of looking at the principal interpersonal behaviour can also be attributed to the fact that the link between school environment and student outcomes has been found to be less direct and not as strong as the link between classroom environment and student outcomes (Dorman, Fraser, & McRobbie, 1995). Although some studies provided support to the argument that there is a measurable link between school environment and student outcomes, there is a need for research investigating the joint associations between the principals' interpersonal behaviour, classroom environment and student outcomes (Fisher & Cresswell, 1998).

In this context, the study reported here attempts to identify whether: a) principal interpersonal behaviour has any effect on the interpersonal behaviour of his/her teachers by examining whether the primary communication dimensions of the principal behaviour (*Influence – Proximity*) have any effect on the relevant primary communication dimensions of their teachers when communicating with their students, and b) the primary communication dimensions of teacher and principal have any effect on student achievement. This study also attempts to test the construct validity of the Greek version of QTI and PQI in the context of secondary education in Cyprus. The methods and the main results of this study are therefore presented in the next two sections of this chapter.

METHODS

Participants

Stratified sampling was used to select 22 out of 30 upper secondary schools (lyceums) in Cyprus. Nineteen schools participated in this study. Data were gathered among all the students (n = 2603) who attended grade 11 of these schools. The total sample consisted of 1489 (57.2%) girls and 1114 (42.7%) boys. A chi-square test did not reveal any statistically significant difference between the research sample and the population in terms of students' sex (X^2 = 0.86, d.f. = 1, p = 0.39). Although this study refers to other variables, such as the socio-economic status of students, there are no data available about these characteristics of all Greek Cypriot grade 11 students. Therefore, it was not possible to examine whether the sample was nationally representative in terms of any other characteristic than students' sex.

Dependent Variable: Student Achievement in Greek Language at the End of Grade 11

Data on student achievement in Greek language were collected by using external forms of assessment, designed to assess knowledge and skills in Greek language, which are used in the Cyprus Curriculum for grade 11 students (Ministry of Education, 1994). Criterion-reference tests are more appropriate than norm-referenced tests for relating achievement to what a student should know, and for testing competence rather than general ability. Thus, a criterion-reference test was constructed and students were asked to answer at least two different tasks related to each objective in the teaching program of Greek language for grade 11 students. Scoring rubrics, used to differentiate among four levels of task proficiency (0-3) on each task, were also constructed. Thus, ordinal data about the extent to which each student had acquired each skill included in the grade 11 curriculum of Greek language were collected.

The construction of the test was subject to control for reliability and validity. Specifically, the Extended Logistic Model of Rasch (Andrich, 1988) was used to analyze the emerging data. A scale that refers to student knowledge and skills in Greek language was created and analyzed for reliability, fit to the model, meaning and validity. Analysis of the data revealed that this scale had satisfactory psychometric properties. Specifically, the indices of cases (i.e., students) and item separation were found to be higher than 0.84 indicating that the separability of each scale was satisfactory (Wright, 1985). Moreover, the infit mean squares and the outfit mean squares were near one and the values of the infit t-scores and the outfit t-scores were approximately zero. Furthermore, all items had item infit with the range 0.83 to 1.20. It can therefore be claimed that there was a good fit to the Rasch model (Keeves & Alagumalai, 1999). Thus, for each student a score for his/her achievement at the end of grade 11 was generated, by calculating the Rasch person estimate.

Explanatory Variables at Student Level

Aptitude: prior knowledge Aptitude refers to the degree in which a student is able to perform the next learning task. For the purpose of this study, it consists of prior knowledge in Greek language, emerged from student responses to a written test administered to students at the beginning of the school year (i.e., baseline assessment). The baseline test was in line with the national curriculum for grade 10 students (Ministry of Education, 1994). The Extended Logistic Model of Rasch was used to analyze the emerging data and a scale which refers to student knowledge in Greek language at the beginning of year 11 was created. The psychometric properties of this scale were also satisfactory and a score for each student was generated, by calculating the relevant Rasch person estimate in this scale.

Student background factors Information was collected on two student background factors: sex (0 = boys, 1 = girls) and socioeconomic status (SES). Five SES variables were available: father's and mother's education level (i.e., graduate of a primary school, graduate of secondary school, or graduate of a college/university), the social status of father's job, the social status of mother's job, and the economical situation of the family. Following the classification of occupations used by the Ministry of Finance, it was possible to classify parents' occupation into three groups which have relatively similar sizes: occupations held by working class (35%), occupations held by middle class (37%), and occupations held by upper-middle class (28%). Relevant information for each child was taken from the school records. Then standardized values of the above five variables were calculated, resulting in the SES indicator.

Explanatory Variable at Classroom Level: Teacher Interpersonal Behaviour

The Greek version of QTI was administered to the student sample in order to measure the interpersonal relations of their teachers. Results concerning the internal reliability and the construct validity of the QTI are presented below.

Reliability, consistency and variance at class level A learning environment instrument is expected to differentiate between perceptions of students in different classes. Students within a class usually view the learning environment similarly but differently from students in other classes. Thus, reliability was computed for each of the scales of the QTI by calculating multilevel λ (Snijders & Bosker, 1999) and Cronbach alpha for data aggregated at the class level. The value of Cronbach alpha represents consistency across items whereas multilevel λ represents consistency across groups of students. Reliability coefficients were found to be very high (around 0.90). Using the Mplus (Muthén & Muthén, 1999), the intra-class correlations of the scales were computed. The intra-class correlations indicate the amount of variance of the QTI which is located at the between level. It was found out that the percentages of variance at the between level (class level) were between 26 and 37 and can be considered as satisfactory (see Snijders & Bosker, 1999).

Construct validity Construct validity of the QTI was investigated by subjecting the scale scores to a multilevel factor analysis using Mplus. Two models were tested, an *ideal interpersonal circumplex model* (see Fabrigar, Visser, & Browne, 1997) representing Figure 1, and an *irregular circumplex model* (a model with two independent dimensions and free factor loadings). The ideal circumplex model, specifying scale positions exactly as shown in Figure 1, displayed reasonable fit ($X^2 = 88.7$, d.f. = 26 $p = .001$; CFI = .97; TLI = .93; RMSEA = .06 and SRMR = .17 for the between level). While some of these model fit indicators imply that there is an acceptable model fit (e.g., CFI was above .95 and RMSEA close to .05), others indicated that the model fit could be improved (TLI was below .95; SRMR above .05). Moreover, in the ideal circumplex model, most of the structural relations between variables indicated high amounts of unexplained variance, another sign that the model tested could be improved. On the other hand, the model fit for the irregular circumplex model was sufficient ($X^2 = 18.12$, d.f. = 13, $p = 0.21$, CFI = .99; TLI = .96; RMSEA = .04; SRMR = .06 for the between level). Thus, a model with two, uncorrelated factors (i.e., the interpersonal dimensions) and free factor loadings (i.e., the interpersonal sectors were allowed to deviate from their positions as hypothesized in Figure 1) seemed to fit to the data. The factor loadings resulting from this model are presented in Table 1. We can observe that the factor loadings more or less follow a circular ordering, but they are clearly not equally spaced in the circle. To investigate the consequences of these dislocations for the two interpersonal dimensions (Influence and Proximity), we computed correlations between the two dimension scores based on the *theoretical* structure and the relevant scores based on the *empirical* structure (estimated by using the factor loadings of Table 1). The correlations were very high: .991 (Influence) and .988 (Proximity). These findings provide partial support for the Model of Interpersonal Teacher Behavior since the eight scale scores were not only generated but they were also found to be ordered in a circle and represented by two independent dimensions. However, it was not found that the eight sectors of teacher interpersonal behaviour are equally distributed over the circle or equally distanced to the circle centre. This implies that student responses to the Greek version of QTI helped us generate empirical evidence supporting the three main assumptions upon which the design of QTI was based. In addition, the findings of this study reveal that we can use the two dimension scores, rather than the eight sector scores, in order to investigate the relationship between interpersonal teacher behaviour and student outcomes. Finally, it is important to note that this study generated very similar evidence about the construct validity of the Greek version of QTI with those emerged from the study conducted in Cypriot primary schools (see Kyriakides, 2006). Therefore, the two dimension scores (estimated by using the factor loadings presented in Table 1) were used in order to evaluate teacher interpersonal behaviour.

Table 1. Factor loadings for the unequally spaced circumplex model.

Scales of QTI	Factor 1	Factor 2
DC	0.98	0.33
CD	0.30	0.92
CS	0.09	1.02
SC	-0.38	0.62
SO	-0.93	0.12
OS	-0.20	-0.82
OD	-0.04	-0.88
DO	0.36	-0.72

The scales of the QTI are as follows: leadership (DC), helpful/friendly behaviour (CD), understanding behaviour (CS), giving responsibility/freedom (SC), uncertain behaviour (SO), dissatisfied behaviour (OS), admonishing behaviour (OD) and strictness (DO).

Explanatory Variable at School Level: Principal Interpersonal Behaviour

The Greek version of PQI was administered to all teachers ($n = 112$) who taught Greek language to the student sample. A very satisfactory response rate was obtained (i.e., 87.5%). A chi-square test did not reveal any statistically significant differences between the distribution within this sample of teachers and the distribution within the whole population of language teachers working at the 19 participating schools. Therefore, the sample was representative to the whole population in terms of how the teachers are distributed in each of these 19 schools.

Results concerning the internal reliability and the construct validity of the PQI are presented below.

Reliability, consistency and variance at school level   Since it is expected that teachers within a school view the interpersonal behaviour of their principal similarly, but differently from teachers in other schools, a Generalizability study was initially conducted. For almost all questionnaire items of the PQI (i.e., 44 out of 48), the object of measurement was the school. Thus, reliability was computed for each scale of PQI by calculating multilevel λ (Snijders & Bosker, 1999) and the Cronbach alpha for data aggregated at the school level emerged from the 44 items found to be generalizable at the level of school. The reliability coefficients which emerged were very high (i.e., higher than 0.92). The intra-class correlations of the scales were also computed and were found to be satisfactory (i.e., between 0.28 and 0.33).

Table 2. Factor loadings for the unequally spaced circumplex model.

Scales of PQI	Factor 1	Factor 2
DC	0.99	0.35
CD	0.27	1.02
CS	0.02	1.12
SC	-0.37	0.52
SO	-0.97	0.20
OS	-0.27	-0.78
OD	0.03	-0.82
DO	0.57	-0.62

The scales of the PQI are as follows: directive behaviour (DC), encouraging behaviour (CD), understanding behaviour (CS), giving independence behaviour (SC), uncertain behaviour (OS), aggressive behaviour (OD), and strict/inflexible behaviour (DO).

Construct validity   Construct validity of the PQI was investigated by using the same approach as in the case of QTI. Specifically, the scale scores were subjected to a multilevel factor analysis. From this analysis, it was found that an unequally-spaced circumplex model fitted the data well ($X^2 = 13.73$, d.f. = 13, $p = 0.33$, CFI = 0.98, TLI = 0.96; RMSEA = 0.03; SRMR = 0.05 for the between level). The factor loadings resulting from this model are presented in Table 2. This model provides empirical support for the assumption that the eight scale scores are ordered in a circle and represented by two independent dimensions. However, the eight sectors of principal interpersonal behaviour were not found to be equally distributed over the circle. This implies that teachers' responses to the Greek version of PQI helped us generate empirical evidence supporting the main assumptions upon which the design of PQI was based. Nevertheless, neither the SEM analysis of QTI nor the relevant analysis of PQI provided support to the assumption that the eight scales measuring interpersonal behaviour are equally distributed over the circle or equally distanced to the circle centre. This implies that there is a need to reconsider this theoretical assumption especially since we are not aware of any study which provided empirical support to this assumption. For the purposes of this study, we decided to use the two dimension scores in order to evaluate both teacher and principal interpersonal behaviour (which were estimated by using the factor loadings presented in Tables 1 and 2 respectively) and to search for effects of interpersonal behaviour on student achievement in Greek language.

RESULTS

Having established the construct validity of QTI and PQI and generating measures of the two overarching factors (i.e., influence and proximity) at the teacher and school level, a two-level SEM analysis was used to identify any relations among principal's interpersonal behaviour and their teachers' interpersonal behaviour. A number of researchers have developed methods to apply SEM on multilevel data (e.g., Goldstein & McDonald, 1988; Muthén & Satorra, 1989). Hox (2002) gives an overview of the different approaches to multilevel SEM. In this paper, we use the approach of Muthén (1997) through the use of the software package MPlus (Muthén & Muthén, 2001). The basic idea for this technique is the decomposition of the individual scores in an individual component (the deviation of the individual score from the groups' mean score) and a group component (the disaggregated group mean score) (Heck, 2001). This decomposition is used to calculate two independent covariance matrices: a between and a within matrix. To test a multilevel SEM model, both matrices are used. Different authors describe this technique more extensively (e.g., Heck, 2001; Heck & Thomas, 2000; Hox, 2002; Muthén, 1994; Stapleton, 2006). For the purposes of this analysis, MPlus was used to investigate whether the measures of influence and proximity at the school level have any effect on relevant measures of these two factors at the teacher level. The model illustrated in Appendix A was found to fit well with the data ($X^2 = 15.12$, d.f. $= 18$, $p = 0.41$, RMSEA $= 0.04$, CFI $= 0.961$) and revealed statistically significant effects of influence and proximity at the school level upon the relevant teacher level factors concerned with teacher interpersonal behaviour. The parameter estimates shown in Appendix A are the result of the Muthén's limited information maximum likelihood (MUML) estimation and revealed that the sizes of these relations are very small.

Multilevel regression analysis was also conducted in order to identify the effects of principals' and teachers' interpersonal behaviour upon student achievement in Greek language. The first step in the analysis was to determine the variance at school, teacher, class, and student level without any explanatory variables (i.e., empty model). In subsequent steps, explanatory variables at different levels were added. Explanatory variables, except grouping variables, were centred as Z scores with a mean of 0 and a standard deviation of 1.

Table 3. Parameter estimates and standard errors for the multilevel analysis of student achievement in language.

Factors	Model 0	Model 1	Model 2	Model 3
Intercept	-0.87 (.15)	-0.67 (.15)	-0.56 (.15)	-0.56 (.15)
Student level				
Sex (0 = boys, 1 = girls)		0.19 (0.05)*	0.18 (0.05)*	0.18 (0.05)*
Prior achievement		0.41 (0.12)*	0.42 (0.12)*	0.42 (0.12)*
SES		0.28 (0.09)*	0.29 (0.09)*	0.28 (0.08)*
Classroom level				
Context				
Percentage of girls		0.06 (0.05)	0.06 (0.05)	0.06 (0.05)
Average prior achievement		0.26 (0.09)*	0.26 (0.09)*	0.26 (0.09)*
Average SES		0.08 (0.07)	0.08 (0.07)	0.08 (0.07)
Teacher level				
Interpersonal behaviour				
Proximity			0.07 (0.02)*	0.07 (0.02)*
Influence			0.09 (0.03)*	0.09 (0.03)*
School level				
Context				
Percentage of girls		0.04 (0.05)	0.04 (0.04)	0.04 (0.04)
Average prior achievement		0.12 (0.05)*	0.12 (0.05)*	0.12 (0.05)*
Average SES		0.06 (0.05)	0.06 (0.05)	0.06 (0.05)
Interpersonal behaviour				
Proximity				0.02 (0.04)
Influence				0.04 (0.02)*
Variance Components				
School	5.1%	4.1%	4.0%	3.2%
Teacher	15.8%	14.0%	11.0%	10.8%
Class	6.1%	5.1%	5.1%	5.1%
Student	73.0%	41.0%	40.0%	39.9%
Explained		35.8%	39.9%	41.0%
Significance test				
X^2	1132.6	1027.7	944.4	933.1
Reduction		104.9	43.3	11.3
Degrees of freedom**		5	2	1
P – value		.001	.001	.001

* Statistically significant effect at .05 level.
** Each model was estimated without the variables that did not have a statistically significant effect at 0.05 level.

This is a way of centring around the grand mean (Bryk & Raudenbush, 1992) and yields effects that are comparable. Thus, each effect expresses how much the dependent variable increases (or decreases, in case of a negative sign) by each additional deviation on the independent variable (Snijders & Bosker, 1999). Grouping variables were entered as dummies with one of the groups as baseline (e.g., boys = 0). The models presented in Table 3 were estimated without the variables that did not have a statistically significant effect at 0.05 level.

The empty model indicates that of the total variance 73% was accounted for by the student, 6% by the class, 16% by the teacher and 5% by the school level. The variance at each level reached statistical significance ($p < 0.05$). The following observations arise from the empty model. Most of the explained variance was at the student level. This finding is in line with findings of previous studies conducted in secondary education both in Cyprus (Kyriakides & Luyten, 2009) and in other countries (Teddlie & Reynolds, 2000). Moreover, the explained variance situated at the teacher level was found to be much stronger than both the classroom and school variance.

In Model 1, the context variables at the student, classroom, and school levels were added to the empty model. The following observations arise from the figures of the third column illustrating the results of Model 1. First, Model 1 explains approximately 36% of the total variance of student achievement, and most of the explained variance is at the student level. However, more than 40% of the total variance remained unexplained at the student level. Second, the likelihood statistic (X^2) shows a significant change between the empty model and Model 1 ($p < 0.001$), which justifies the selection of Model 1. Third, the effects of all contextual factors at the student level (i.e., SES, prior knowledge, sex) are significant. Finally, prior knowledge (i.e., aptitude) has the strongest effect in predicting student achievement at the end of the school year. It was also found that aptitude is the only contextual variable that had a consistent effect on student achievement when aggregated either at the classroom or school level.

In Model 2, the variables measuring teacher influence and proximity, which emerged from student responses to the Greek version of QTI, were entered. Both teacher influence and proximity were found to be associated with student achievement in Greek language. We can also observe that the explanatory variables emerged from student responses to the QTI helped us explain 4% of the total variance in achievement of Greek language and most of it (i.e., 3 out of 4%) was situated at the level of teacher. It is finally important to note that the likelihood statistic reveals a statistically significant reduction ($p < 0.001$) from Model 1 to Model 2, which justifies the selection of Model 2.

Finally, we entered the variables that concerned principal interpersonal behaviour at Model 2. Principal influence was found to be associated with student achievement in Greek language but the effect size was very small. We can also observe that although this factor helped us explain approximately 1.0% of the total variance, the likelihood statistic reveals a statistically significant reduction ($p <$ 0.001) from Model 2 to Model 3.

DISCUSSION

The study reported here revealed that reliable and valid data on the interpersonal teacher behaviour can be gathered among Cypriot students of grade 11. Moreover, reliable and valid data on principal interpersonal behaviour can be provided by the teachers. This study has also shown that data on teacher interpersonal behaviour derived from student responses to the Greek version of QTI helped us explain variance on achievement of Cypriot secondary students. Given that similar results emerged from a study investigating the impact of teacher interpersonal behaviour on achievement of Cypriot primary students (Kyriakides, 2006), it can be claimed that teacher interpersonal behaviour is an important variable for EER. These findings also imply that teacher interpersonal behaviour could be considered as an important teacher factor and its relation with other teacher factors concerned with their teaching skills could be investigated. Further national and comparative studies should be conducted in order to identify the importance of treating variables associated with teacher interpersonal behaviour as educational effectiveness factors. Research from cross-national studies and cross-cultural studies using the QTI indicate that the instrument and the model are cross-culturally valid (Den Brok, Levy, Wubbels, & Rodriguez, 2003; Wubbels & Levy, 1991). This implies that researchers can use the QTI in large-scale international effectiveness studies. Such studies may help us find out the extent to which teacher interpersonal behaviour explain effectiveness across countries and at different phases of schooling and whether teacher interpersonal behaviour should be treated as a generic teacher factor explaining student achievement gains in different outcomes of schooling and at different phases of education (Kyriakides & Creemers, 2009).

With regard to the impact of principal interpersonal behaviour, influence was found to be associated with student achievement but its effect size was very small. Although further research is needed to test the generalizability of the findings of this study, the results of this study seem to be in line with the results of three meta-analyses of school effectiveness studies which reveal that principal leadership style has a very weak effect on student achievement (see Kyriakides et al., 2010; Scheerens, Seidel, Witziers, Hendriks, & Doornekamp, 2005; Witziers, Bosker, & Kruger, 2003). Moreover, this study revealed that principal interpersonal behaviour has a very small effect upon the interpersonal behaviour of their staff. Since data on both teacher and principal interpersonal behaviour were collected, it was possible to search for indirect effects of principal interpersonal behaviour, by investigating the impact that principals could have on the quality of teaching practice. However, it was not possible to identify any indirect effect of principal interpersonal behaviour on student achievement. Further research is needed to study the impact that principal interpersonal behaviour may have on other school factors rather than on teacher interpersonal behaviour more systematically. For example, principal interpersonal behaviour may have an effect on the school learning environment factor included in the dynamic model which was found to be associated with student achievement (Creemers & Kyriakides, 2010). Such studies may also help us to further expand the dynamic model and better understand the complex nature of effectiveness in education, and may provide further support to the validity of the model implying that factors not included in the model at the school level have very small effect on student achievement and should not be treated as important factors for effectiveness.

REFERENCES

Andrich, D. (1988). A general form of Rasch's Extended Logistic Model for partial credit scoring. *Applied Measurement in Education, 1*(4), 363-378.

Brophy, J. & Good, T. L. (1986). Teacher Behavior and Student Achievement. In M. C. Wittrock (Ed.), *Handbook of research on teaching* (pp. 328-375). New York: MacMillan.

Bryk, A. S. & Raudenbush, S. W. (1992). *Hierarchical linear models.* Newbury Park: CL: Sage.

Creemers, B. P. M. (1994). *The effective classroom.* London: Cassell.

Creemers, B. P. M. & Kyriakides, L. (2008). *The dynamics of educational effectiveness.* London: Routledge.

Creemers, B. P. M. & Kyriakides, L. (2010). School factors explaining achievement on cognitive and affective outcomes: establishing a dynamic model of educational effectiveness. *Scandinavian Journal of Educational Research, 54*(3), 263-294.

Cresswell, J. & Fisher, D. (1995). *Assessing principal's interpersonal behaviour.* Paper presented at Annual Conference of AARE. Hobart.

Darling-Hammond, L. (2000). Teacher quality and student achievement: A review of state policy evidence. *Education Policy Analysis Archives, 8*(1), http://epaa.asu.edu/epaa/v8n1/.

Den Brok, P., Brekelmans, M., Levy, J., & Wubbels, T. (2002). Diagnosing and improving the quality of teachers' interpersonal behavior. *International Journal of Educational Management, 4*, 176-184.

Den Brok, P., Brekelmans, M., & Wubbels, T. (2004). Interpersonal teacher behaviour and student outcomes. *School Effectiveness and School Improvement, 15*(3-4), 407-442.

Den Brok, P., Levy, J., Wubbels, T., & Rodriguez, M. (2003). Cultural influences on students' perceptions of videotaped lessons. *International Journal of Intercultural Relations, 27*, 268-288.

Dorman, J. P. (2003). Cross national validation of the What Is Happening in This Class questionnaire using confirmatory factor analysis. *Learning Environments Research, 6*, 231-245.

Dorman, J. P., Fraser, B. J., & McRobbie, C. J. (1995). Associations between school-level environment and science classroom environment in secondary schools. *Research in Science Education, 25*, 333-351.

Doyle, W. (1990). Classroom knowledge as a foundation for teaching. *Teachers College Record, 91*(3), 347-360.

Fabrigar, L. R., Visser, P. S., & Browne, M. W. (1997). Conceptual and methodological issues in testing the circumplex structure of data in personality and social psychology. *Personality and Social Psychology Review, 1*, 184-203

Fisher, D. & Cresswell. J. (1998). Actual and ideal principal interpersonal behaviour. *Learning Environments Research, 1*, 231-247.

Fraser, B. J. (1994). Research on classroom and school climate. In D. Gabel (Ed.), *Handbook of research on science teaching and learning* (pp. 493-541). New York: Macmillan.

Goh, S. C. & Fraser, B. J. (1998). Teacher interpersonal behaviour, classroom environment and student outcomes in primary mathematics in Singapore. *Learning Environments Research, 1*, 199-229.

Goldstein, H. (2003). *Multilevel statistical models* (3rd Edition). London: Edward Arnold.

Goldstein, H. & McDonald, R. (1988). A general model for the analysis of multilevel data. *Psychometrika, 53*, 455-467.

Heck, R. H. (2001). Multilevel modeling with SEM. In G. A. Marcoulides & R. E. Schumacker (Eds.), *New developments and techniques in structural equation modelling* (pp. 89-127). Mahwah, NJ: Lawrence Erlbaum Associates Publishers.

Heck, R. H. & Thomas, S. L. (2000). *An introduction to multilevel modelling techniques.* Mahwah, NJ: Lawrence Erlbaum Associates Publishers.

Hox, J. (2002). *Multilevel analysis. Techniques and applications.* Mahwah, NJ: Lawrence Earlbaum Associates Publishers.

Joyce, B., Weil, M., & Calhoun, E. (2000). *Models of teaching.* Boston: Allyn & Bacon.

Keeves, J. P. & Alagumalai, S. (1999). New approaches to measurement. In G. N. Masters & J. P. Keeves (Eds.), *Advances in measurement in educational research and assessment* (pp. 23-42). Oxford: Pergamon.

Kyriakides, L. (2006). Measuring the learning environment of the classroom and its effect on cognitive and affective outcomes of schooling. In D. Fisher & M. S. Khine (Eds.), *Contemporary approaches to research on learning environments* (pp. 369-408). Singapore: World Scientific.

Kyriakides, L., Campbell, R. J., & Gagatsis, A. (2000). The significance of the classroom effect in primary schools: An application of Creemers' comprehensive model of educational effectiveness, *School Effectiveness and School Improvement, 11*(4), 501-529.

Kyriakides, L. & Creemers, B. P. M. (2008). Using a multidimensional approach to measure the impact of classroom level factors upon student achievement: A study testing the validity of the dynamic model. *School Effectiveness and School Improvement, 19*(2), 183-205.

Kyriakides, L. & Creemers, B. P. M. (2009). The effects of teacher factors on different outcomes: Two studies testing the validity of the dynamic model. *Effective Education, 1*, 61-86.

Kyriakides, L., Creemers, B. P. M., Antoniou, P., & Demetriou, D. (2010). A synthesis of studies searching for school factors: Implications for theory and research. *British Educational Research Journal, 36*(5), 807-830.

Kyriakides, L. & Luyten, H. (2009). The contribution of schooling to the cognitive development of secondary education students in Cyprus: An application of regression discontinuity with multiple cut-off points. *School Effectiveness and School Improvement, 20*(2), 167-186.

Leary, T. (1957). *Interpersonal diagnosis of personality.* New York: Ronald Press Company.

Ministry of Education. (1994). *The new curriculum.* Nicosia, Cyprus: Ministry of Education.

Moos, R. H. (1979). *Evaluating educational environments: Procedures, measures, findings and policy implications.* San Francisco: Jossey-Bass.

Muijs, D. & Reynolds, D. (2000). School effectiveness and teacher effectiveness in mathematics: Some preliminary findings from the evaluation of the mathematics enhancement programme (primary). *School Effectiveness and School Improvement, 11*(3), 273-303.

Muthén, B. O. (1994). Multilevel covariance structure analysis. *Sociological Methods and Research, 22*(3), 376-398.

Muthén, B. O. (1997). Latent growth modelling with longitudinal and multilevel data. In A. E. Raftery (Ed.), *Sociological methodology* (pp. 453-480). Boston: Blackwell.

Muthén, L. K. & Muthén, B. O. (1999). *Mplus user's guide.* Los Angeles, CA: Muthén & Muthén.

Muthén, L. K. & Muthén, B. O. (2001). *MPlus user's guide.* Los Angeles, CA: Muthén & Muthén.

Muthén, B. O. & Satorra, A. (1989). Multilevel aspects of varying parameters in structural models. In R.D. Bock (Ed.), *Multilevel analysis of educational data* (pp. 87-99). San Diego, CA: Academic Press.

Rosenshine, B. & Stevens, R. (1986). Teaching functions. In M. C. Wittrock (Ed.), *Handbook of research on teaching* (pp. 376-391). New York: MacMillan.

Scheerens, J. (1992). Effective schooling: *Research, theory and practice.* London: Cassell.

Scheerens, J. & Bosker, R. J. (1997). *The foundations of educational effectiveness.* Oxford: Pergamon.

Scheerens, J., Seidel, T., Witziers, B., Hendriks, M., & Doornekamp, G. (2005). *Positioning and validating the supervision framework.* Enschede/Kiel: University of Twente, Department of Educational Organisational and Management.

Schoenfeld, A. H. (1998). Toward a theory of teaching in context. *Issues in Education, 4*(1), 1-94.

Snijders, T. & Bosker, R. (1999). *Multilevel analysis: An introduction to basic and advanced multilevel modeling.* London: Sage.

Stapleton, L. M. (2006). Using multilevel structural equation modeling techniques with complex sample data. In G. R. Hancock & R. O. Mueller (Eds.), *Structural equation modeling: a second course* (pp. 345-384). Greenwich, CT: Information Age Publishing.

Stringfield, S. C. & Slavin, R. E. (1992). A hierarchical longitudinal model for elementary school effects. In B. P. M. Creemers & G. J. Reezigt (Eds.), *Evaluation of educational effectiveness* (pp. 35-69). Groningen: ICO.

Teddlie, C. & Reynolds, D. (2000). *The international handbook of school effectiveness research.* London: Falmer Press.

Walberg, H. J. (1979). *Educational environments and effects: Evaluation, policy, and productivity.* Berkely: McCutchan.

Watzlawick, P., Beavin, J. H., & Jackson, D. (1967). *The pragmatics of human communication.* New York: Norton.

Witziers, B., Bosker, J. R., & Kruger, L. M. (2003). Educational leadership and student achievement: The elusive search for an association. *Educational Administration Quarterly, 39*(3), 398-425.

Wright, B. D. (1985). Additivity in psychological measurement. In E. E. Roskam (Ed), *Measurement and personality assessment* (pp. 101-112). Amsterdam: Elsevier Science Publishers.

Wubbels, T. & Brekelmans, M. (1998). The teacher factor in the social climate of the classroom. In B. J. Fraser & K. G. Tobin (Eds.), *International handbook of science education* (pp. 565-80). London: Kluwer Academic Publishers.

Wubbels, T., Brekelmans, M., Van Tartwijk, J., & Admiraal, W. (1997). Interpersonal relationships between teachers and students in the classroom. In H. C. Waxman & H. J. Walberg (Eds.), *New directions for teaching practice and research* (pp. 151-170). Berkeley, CA: McCutchan Publishing Company.

Wubbels, T., Créton, H. A., & Hooymayers, H. P. (1987). A school based induction programme. *European Journal of Teacher Education, 10*, 81-94.

Wubbels, T., & Levy, J. (1991). A comparison of interpersonal behavior of Dutch and American teachers. *International Journal of Intercultural Relations, 15*, 1-18.

APPENDIX A

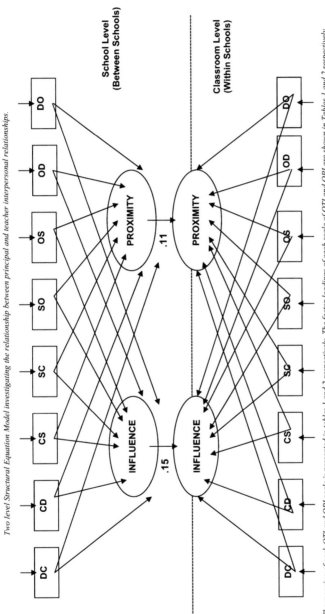

Two level Structural Equation Model investigating the relationship between principal and teacher interpersonal relationships.

The meaning of each QTI and QPI scale is presented in tables 1 and 2 respectively. The factor loadings of each scale of QTI and QPI are shown in Tables 1 and 2 respectively.

WALTER DOYLE AND DENNIS ROSEMARTIN[i]

9. THE ECOLOGY OF CURRICULUM ENACTMENT

Frame and Task Narratives

INTRODUCTION

The fundamental issue we address in this chapter is the relationship between the curriculum and the teacher. Despite decades of efforts to reform education through curriculum development, it is common to find that teachers do not enact curricula according to design (Hume & Coll, 2010; Olsen, 1981). Shavelson and his colleagues (Shavelson et al., 2008), for example, carefully and collaboratively designed a curriculum to include embedded formative assessments and provided six middle school teachers from across the United States intensive professional development in the use of a guide for enacting the curriculum. Yet they found that the teachers enacted only parts of the intended practices. They note: "Teachers have a huge impact on the efficacy of any education reform, and we can add formative assessment to the list. The gap between what [...] we envisioned and the reality is quite significant" (p. 310).

Remillard (2008) has pointed out that research and practice in the area of curriculum-teacher relationships "lacks a theoretical and conceptual base" (p. 85), in part, we suspect, because the fields of curriculum and teaching represent quite distinct academic communities and citation networks (see Doyle, 1992). Our goal in this chapter is to construct a way of thinking about the curriculum-teacher relationship that offers the possibility of greater continuity between these two domains. It is our contention that an explication of the curriculum enactment process itself is essential to understanding how curriculum and teaching are related. In the context of this collection of papers, our analysis includes the interpersonal relationships that operate in classroom settings (see Wubbels, Brekelmans, Den Brok, & Van Tartwijk, 2006).

FRAMING THE ARGUMENT

Depending upon one's viewpoint, the gap between design and enactment is either (1) a design/management failure – the curriculum or the curriculum surveillance system fails to persuade or compel teachers to align their decisions with it – or (2) a cause for celebration – teachers are exercising their professional judgment and autonomy.

On the side of curriculum, curriculum developers who design innovative or reform curriculum materials are often primarily interested in matching the teacher to the curriculum. From this perspective, a curriculum is a systematic

T. Wubbels et al. (eds.), Interpersonal Relationships in Education, 137–147.

program, often benefiting from substantial expertise and resources, to achieve valuable educational purposes. It is reasonable, then, that such materials should be used (see Davis & Krajcik, 2005; Remillard, Herbel-Eisenmann, & Lloyd, 2008). The emphasis, in other words, is on utilization of the materials, and a variety of strategies are proposed to insure implementation, including the strategic design of the materials themselves and the extensive professional development of teachers to use the materials (see Hord & Huling-Austin, 1986; Remillard, 2000). In some schools and districts, of course, surveillance is used to ensure teachers' compliance with the curriculum. The overall emphasis here tends to be on the fidelity or at least the integrity of the teachers' use of the curriculum materials and on the capacities teachers need to use curriculum appropriately and effectively. In this context, teachers are often seen as obstacles to be overcome in the successful implementation of a curriculum.

Those who focus on the teacher, on the other hand, tend to emphasize professional expertise, autonomy, and creativity in the adaptation of curriculum and curriculum materials to specific learners and situations. Achinstein and Ogawa (2006) have underscored "principled resistance" in which teachers use their professional discretion to protect students from what they perceive as potentially misguided ideas in mandated curricula. At the extreme end of this ideological continuum there is an anti-materials bias in which the highest form of professional practice is to create one's own curriculum, and one should never be caught using a textbook. For example, Shkedi (2009) quotes a teacher of eight grade Bible Studies, a subject (with textbook) mandated by the Israeli compulsory curriculum: "I teach what seems relevant to me without any connection to the curriculum and without any sense of obligation to it" (p. 833).

The overall picture that emerges is one of discontinuity. Developers propose and teachers dispose. In Olsen's (1981) terms, teachers domesticate the project doctrine (e.g., inquiry) into familiar practices (e.g., direct instruction). As a result, it is often difficult to find curricula being enacted in the form intended by developers, and the further one gets away from the site of the original development the less likely one is to find the curriculum in action. As Berliner (1985) once said of individualized instruction, it's like water in Arizona: Hard to find and it evaporates quickly.

This picture obviously generates frustration, especially for curriculum developers. As a result, considerable attention has been given to the issue of curriculum implementation (see Snyder, Bolin, & Zumwalt, 1992). This concern has given rise to an emerging field of inquiry around issues of curriculum implementation and enactment (see Remillard, Herbel-Eisenmann, & Lloyd, 2008). The direction of much of this work is from the curriculum to the teacher. It is our contention that the issue is more complex than finding better ways to get teachers to cooperate with developers' intentions. Rather, the issue rests on a more complete understanding of enactment as a core processes in the curriculum-teacher relationship.

METAPHORS FOR BRIDGING THE GAP

Several attempts have been made recently to conceptualize more fully the nature of the curriculum-teacher relationship. Brown (2008), for example, uses two metaphors to elucidate the relationship: (1) musical score and musical performance and (2) tool-designer interaction. In the first instance, he uses jazz as the model, noting that any two jazz musicians are likely to render a song in very different ways. We think the score-performance image is powerful, in part because it implies that the score must be studied in order to perform. However, the choice of jazz tends to emphasize improvisation. Perhaps classical music is a better example: you don't have to write the Mozart sonata to perform it, and, while there is room for interpretation, it must sound like Mozart or the audience may well walk out. The second metaphor – curriculum as tool or artifact to be used in solving problems and in the design of teaching – emphasizes materials (texts, lesson plans, worksheets) and the teacher's knowledge, orientation, and capacity in the use of these materials. The teacher, in other words, is artisan or craftsperson in the construction of learning tasks and activities that implement the curriculum.

Although these images are quite promising, they seem narrow in at least two ways. First, metaphors of curriculum as musical score or tool fail to capture what curriculum is and give a somewhat static or inert sense of curriculum products. Curriculum is more than just the content, and these metaphors do not provide a base for exploring what that something more is. Second, in both images, context is nearly invisible. In a musical performance, the audience is spectator, but in a classroom the students are participants. Similarly, a teacher uses tools to design not only for content and learners but also for a complex classroom environment that is more than just background. As will be seen, classroom setting is a central part of a more complete conception of enactment.

ELEMENTS OF CURRICULUM ENACTMENT

What does it mean to 'enact' a curriculum? What does one look for to ascertain whether a teacher is actually using a curriculum? Any attempt to answer these questions soon reveals that the concept of curriculum enactment is itself surprisingly ambiguous. Does it mean following a script? If so, then one would look for replications of the curriculum's scripts in the classroom. Or is the curriculum an idea that can take different forms depending upon local circumstances. But then how 'different' can a classroom look and still represent an instance of a curriculum in use?

Addressing these core issues in curriculum enactment requires an explication of what a curriculum, the object of enactment, is. Numerous attempts have been made over the years to define the term 'curriculum' (for a classic treatment, see Zais, 1976). Most definitions revolve around two common elements: experience and outcomes. To write curriculum, then, is to posit an association between an experience with a particular content and an educative outcome – between, say, practicing a particular song on the piano and the acquisition of a particular performance skill along a continuum toward becoming a fluent pianist, between reading a particular story and movement toward developing literary sensibility, between doing a particular laboratory experiment and developing an understanding of some aspect of science or the scientific process.

One way to illustrate this process is with an example derived loosely from Sontag's (1966) book, *Against Interpretation* (see Doyle & Carter, 2003). A painting on the wall of a museum is minimally interpreted in the sense that a decision was made to purchase the work, implying some importance in the art world, and to display it as an instance of a particular genre, style, era, or the like, implying membership in a category. But unless one listens to the visitor's recorded guide, one is free to assign whatever meaning one wants to the painting, if any. However, if the painting is brought into a classroom, it is curricularized, that is, interpreted as content that gives rise to a particular disposition, skill, or item of knowledge. Personal meanings can and do operate in classrooms, but the curricularization of the painting gives it a formal meaning with respect to the educative process and judgments can then be made with respect to an individual's accomplishment of the purpose that is now educationally associated with this art work.

From this perspective, to posit an association between an experience with a particular content and an educative outcome means one must interpret or theorize the content, i.e., decide what the content represents or what it is a case of. Is a story an example of a genre or style (pulp fiction, realism, etc.) or an opportunity to explore personal meanings and insights or a chance to practice recognizing certain semantic or syntactic constructions? Embedded in this interpretation of the content is also a degree of pedagogical framing, i.e., a specification of what the educative potential of the content is, what the trajectory is for learning the content, and what counts as appropriate activity with respect to the content.[ii] Pedagogical framing begins, in other words, as curriculum is being written because a theory of the content as educative material includes an analysis of how the content is to be experienced by novices.

At a very basic level, then, curriculum is the product of an interpretation or theory of content with respect to a purpose, a result of a process of transforming content in the world into content for schooling, i.e., into a school subject, and ultimately into a classroom event. Although curriculum is fundamentally about content, it is more than a statement of what to teach. A curriculum is an argument about the educative potential of content, the path (sequence) of learning that content, and educative activity with respect to the content. It is in this sense that a curriculum can be said to be a theory of a content.

FRAME AND TASK NARRATIVES

We would like to adapt two constructs from Shkedi's (2009) recent analysis – frame narrative and task narrative – to explicate further the essential dimensions of curriculum. As we are using the terms, a *frame narrative* is a theory of the content as educative potential and as pedagogical representation – this is an interpretation of what counts, educationally, as mathematics, history, literature, etc., and this is how it should be represented. A frame narrative is in essence the interpretive foundation of a curriculum. An important function of a frame narrative is to activate beliefs or commitments that elicit and sustain pedagogical investment.

One example of a frame narrative is the following description of the elements of what might be called 'ambitious instruction', an approach to inquiry or problem-based teaching (adapted from the work of Cobb, Smith, Jackson, & Wenzel, 2010, and Coffey & Hammer, 2010). These elements are:

Ambitious, model-based inquiry
Goal: Develop students' ability to produce evidence-based causal explanations
Process:
    Task Design:
Puzzling and complex cases reflecting big ideas
    Task Launch:
Focus on unobservable (model) processes, events, entities, & relationships linked to observable natural phenomena
    Task Maintenance:
Building on students' ideas from everyday experience
Model-based reasoning and testing
Rich discourse/dialogic episodes
    Task Assessment:
Press for evidence-based causal (scientific) explanations

This frame narrative is perhaps best seen as an "envelope" that contains a "set of allowed solutions" (Ben-Peretz, 1990, p. 31). Teachers' classroom actions can then be seen as instantiations of this "theoretical ideal" (Furtak et al., 2008).

A *task narrative* is a description of classroom forms, discourse practices, activities, and exercises or assignments that seem most consistent with the frame narrative. A task narrative, in other words, is an interpretation in a concrete form of the actions that fit a particular frame narrative, that is, a pedagogical instantiation of a frame narrative.

Every curriculum or set of curriculum materials has a frame and a task narrative, although curricula vary widely on the extent to which these narratives are explicit, transparent, or complete. In the case of scripted curricula, the task narrative is quite explicit and 'visible' to the extent that it might embody or even overshadow the frame narrative. In more holistic approaches, the emphasis is often on the frame narrative with the task narrative 'invisible' or illustrative rather than mandatory (on visible and invisible pedagogies, see Bernstein, 1990). Regardless, interpreting a curriculum document essentially means identifying and understanding the embedded frame and task narratives.

What is often overlooked, however, is that every teacher has, at least implicitly, a frame narrative and a task narrative for her or his curriculum practice. Curriculum work, i.e., the interpretation of content, does not stop at the classroom door. Teachers continue to do curriculum work as they interpret content to design and maintain tasks within the complex setting of classrooms. In cases in which a teacher agrees with the frame and task narratives of a particular design, fidelity of implementation would be expected to be quite high. In cases of a discrepancy between design and classroom practice, it could be that a teacher does not agree with or understand the frame or task narratives of the curriculum. Disagreement with or failure to understand the frame narrative, for example, means that a teacher will not or cannot align with the theory of educative potential and possibility upon which the design is based. In such instances, one would expect that the teacher would make no effort to implement the design.

We suspect, however, that issues of implementation have a great deal more to do with task narratives and especially with the "practical constraints of the learning context" (Edelson, Gordin, & Pea, 1999). Given the demands of their work, teachers are embedded daily in task narratives that are quite local and situated. Curricular task narratives are necessarily decontextualized and idealized, intended for a wide array of classroom situations. Even the most scripted task narrative cannot account for all the local contingencies of a particular enactment. As a result, implementation is always a design process for teachers, a fitting or scaling of a curriculum to a particular situation. In cases of many reform or innovative curricula, the task narratives are quite complex and are often substantially different from the typical activity narratives of conventional classrooms (for a perspective on this complexity see Schoenfeld, 2002, and Nystrand, Wu, Gamoran, Zeiser, & Long, 2003). Furtak and her colleagues (2008), for example, note that the teachers in their study typically thought of assessment as summative and therefore had to switch frames to use embedded formative assessments. In these circumstances, a teacher's design and implementation tasks can be formidable (see Harris & Rooks, 2010). Furthermore, we suspect these complex task narratives take a long time to learn. Finally, curriculum authors sometimes have limited understanding of or experience with some or all of the contexts in which classroom activity takes place so that their task narratives (and perhaps even their frame narratives) may lack ecological validity, which further contributes to the complexity of a teacher's design task in scaling a curriculum to a locale.

To explicate more fully the complexity of a teacher's design or scaling task in curriculum implementation, we summarize briefly a conception of classroom ecology that highlights some of the features of classroom life a teacher must take into account.

CLASSROOM ECOLOGY

Doyle (2006) has argued, largely from the insights of Paul Gump (1969) and Jack Kounin (1970), that classrooms are multidimensional activity settings or ecologies in which teachers must establish, orchestrate, and sustain events that elicit student cooperation over long periods of time and across challenging daily, weekly, monthly, and seasonal variations. These events are jointly constituted by a teacher and her or his students and contain, at their core, action vectors that pull participants along and hold order in place. Seatwork, for example, is a familiar event in which students typically work individually on well-structured assignments or worksheets that sustain their involvement. A class discussion, on the other hand, is a more complex action system involving bidding for turns, multiple speakers whose contributions may or may not address the central topic, and unpredictable sequences and directions. From this perspective, enacting a curriculum means translating a document into sustainable events. As will be seen, curriculum materials, as tools or artifacts, represent only a part of this process.

Embedded in classroom events are tasks that specify the products students are to generate and the nature of their accountability for these products. Are students to remember the examples the teacher is providing or learn the principles to later apply to new examples? At one level this means that the curriculum on the floor – what students actually do with the content – is embodied in the tasks they accomplish. In other words, the content delivered is the content the students must use to accomplish the classroom tasks posed by the teacher. Thus, how teachers interpret the content of a curriculum in constructing work for students will shape what curriculum the students' experience.

We also know that the ability and willingness of students to engage in classroom tasks affects the flow of activity that holds order in place in classrooms. Familiar and routine tasks involving memory or predictable formulas (e.g., addition or subtraction) that all students can easily accomplish often create strong engagement for sustained periods of time. "When familiar work is being done, the flow of classroom activity is typically quite smooth and well ordered. Tasks are initiated easily and quickly, work involvement and productivity are typically high, and most students are able to complete tasks successfully" (Doyle, 1988, p. 174).

Novel tasks that require comprehension and inventiveness by students – write a compelling description of a scene or decide which of several formulas can be used to solve a complex word problem in mathematics – do not always have the same holding power. Studies have shown that (1) students prefer predictable tasks and have developed reliable strategies for accomplishing these tasks (see Schoenfeld, 1988), and (2) when a novel task is on the floor, launching the task takes more time, errors and non-completion rates are higher, and student engagement is delayed, in part because students often negotiate to simplify work demands or otherwise resist engagement (see Doyle, 1988; Doyle & Carter, 1984; Herbst, 2006). "In sum, novel work stretches the limits of classroom management and intensifies the complexity of the teacher's task of orchestrating classroom events" (Doyle, 1988, p. 174). As a result, novel task systems are often fragile.

INTERPERSONAL RELATIONSHIPS

Another important aspect of sustainable events in classroom is the interpersonal relationships that evolve within a classroom community. Wubbels and his colleagues (e.g., Wubbels et al., 2006) have, for example, established, with an impressive series of studies, the central importance of the dimensions of (a) influence or control and (b) proximity or affiliation in teacher-student relationship in classrooms. Teachers who are perceived by their students to have moderately high influence in directing classroom events and moderately high levels of interpersonal connection or affiliation have high student involvement and achievement.

It is our contention that these dimensions of influence and proximity are linked closely to the features of familiarity and novelty in classroom work systems and that radical changes in a classroom task narrative can disrupt these perceptions in fundamental ways. In familiar task systems, work requirements are explicit, workflow is smooth, engagement and productivity are high, and the teacher is a reliable source of information and affirmation. Such conditions would seem to afford excellent circumstances for establishing moderate levels of influence and proximity in a classroom.

In novel work situations, however, products and procedures are necessarily less explicit so that the students will assume responsibility for their own analysis and understanding. The teacher, in turn, must shift from director and arbitrator to coach and inquisitive expert, i.e., become a less reliable source of information to accomplish or judge work. These conditions increase the likelihood of student discomfort and error as they grapple with the demands of achieving understanding, and the teacher's role in alleviating this discomfort is restricted. "In tasks structured for student decisions, predictability is low and cognitive and emotional demands are high because there is considerable ambiguity about products and a measure of risk that answers will be incorrect" (Doyle, 1988, p. 174; see also Davis & McKnight, 1976; Herbst, 2006). As a teacher shifts toward novel work, then, it is reasonable to expect that students' perceptions of a teacher's influence and proximity would be disrupted and such a disruption would have consequences for students' involvement in classroom events. It is also likely that teachers would experience these shifts in student affiliation directly and act to compensate for the changes in classroom organization and management.

More work is certainly needed to understand what happens to teacher-student relationships during curricular transformations. But it is clear that interpersonal dimensions are often overlooked in curricular task narratives despite their centrality in classroom life and, it would seem, a teacher's perceptions of the consequences of adopting a curriculum.

This analysis of familiar and novel tasks and their consequences for interpersonal relationships in classrooms is especially relevant to the present discussion because most contemporary reform curricula are designed precisely to focus on meaning and understanding. The curricular emphasis, in other words, is on novel tasks for students, on problems and student ideas, conjectures, and explanations with the teacher serving as an indirect resource. This analysis suggests that one reason reform curricular may not be implemented is that their frame and task narratives come into direct conflict with powerful situational patterns – i.e., teacher and students 'technologies' – that have grown up around current practices. As Edelson, Gordin, and Pea (1999, p. 400) note: "A failure to work within the available technology [...] in a school will doom a design to failure".

IMPLICATIONS

From this analysis, we argue that the common thread connecting curriculum and teaching is interpretation. A curriculum is a product of a theory or interpretation of content, a definition of the educative potential of some portion of a subject. The curriculum on the floor in a classroom is contained in the tasks a teacher is able to establish and maintain in that environment, and these tasks are products of the teacher's interpretation or theory of the content, an interpretation that is grounded not only in subject matter but also in a teacher's knowledge of and experience with classroom contexts. A teacher knows, for example, what subtraction events look like and how they unfold over time with particular groups of students.

Each enactment, then, is an instantiation of an interpretation of curriculum, the product of a design process by the teacher to scale a program to a locale. There would seem to be three important implications of this perspective. First, there would seem to be a need for much greater explicitness by both curriculum authors and teachers about the frame and task narratives embedded in any curriculum. Our sense is that most frame and task narratives are implicit and underspecified and that most curriculum narratives lack situated understanding. Second, enactment needs to be seen less as a unidirectional process of moving from curriculum to the teacher and more of a mutual, collaborative processes that is grounded deeply in an understanding of classroom contexts. Closing the gap between curriculum and teaching requires changes on both sides. Finally, it is important that tools be developed to help teachers capture their curricula in motion at a local level so that these systems can become objects of analysis and understanding.

What are less clear are the mechanisms that need to be invented to make this collaborative and mutually adaptive process between curriculum and teaching possible. Perhaps if teaching were seen as not only a matter of student motivation, classroom management, or instructional method but also as a curriculum process it would be possible to highlight the coming together of document and action in teacher education and professional development. Similarly if the challenges of practical constraints and practical action were made more an essential part of the curriculum design process there would be greater emphasis on constructing tools that bridge curricular frames and classroom practice (see Janssen, Van Driel, & Verloop, 2010). It is our hope that this analysis will at least point in the direction of more ecologically valid designs for connecting curriculum and teaching.

NOTES

[i] The authors are grateful to Nico Verloop, Fred Janssen, Dineke Tigelaar, Klass van Veen, and Jan van Driel of ICLON, Leiden University Graduate School of Teaching, The Netherlands, for their very thoughtful discussion of a draft of this chapter.

[ii] This formulation was informed substantial by the project by Westbury, Hopmann, and Riquarts (2000) on German didactic theory.

REFERENCES

Achinstein, B. & Ogawa, R. T. (2006). (In)fidelity: What the resistance of new teachers reveals about professional principles and prescriptive educational policies. *Harvard Educational Review, 76*, 30-63.

Ben-Peretz, M. (1990). *The teacher-curriculum encounter: Freeing teachers from the tyranny of texts.* Albany, NY: State University of New York Press.

Berliner, D. (1985). Why is individualized instruction like water in Arizona? In M. C. Wang & H. Walberg (Eds.), *Adapting instruction to individual differences* (pp. 298-312). Berkeley: McCutchan.

Bernstein, B. (1990). *The structuring of pedagogic discourse: Volume IV of class, codes and control.* London/New York: Routledge.

Brown, M. W. (2008). The teacher-tool relationship: Theorizing the design and use of curriculum materials. In J. T. Remillard, B. A. Herbel-Eisenmann, & G. M. Lloyd (Eds.), *Mathematics teachers at work: Connecting curriculum materials and classroom instruction* (pp. 17-36). New York: Routledge.

Cobb, P., Smith, T., Jackson, K., & Wenzel, S., (2010). *Supporting mathematics teachers' development of ambitious and equitable instructional practices on a large scale.* Presentation at the DR K12 PI Meeting, Washington, DC, December 1-3.

Coffey, J. & Hammer, D., (2010). *A model for interactive, web-based curricula to support responsive teaching and student inquiry in elementary science classrooms.* Presentation at the DR K-12 PI Meeting, Washington, DC, December 1-3.

Davis, E. A. & Krajcik, J. S. (2005). Designing educative curriculum materials to promote teacher learning. *Educational Researcher, 34*(3), 3-14.

Davis, R. B. & McKnight, C. (1976). Conceptual, heuristic, and S-algorithmic approaches in mathematics teaching. *Journal of Children's Mathematical Behavior, 1* (Suppl. I), 271-286.

Doyle, W. (1988). Work in mathematics classes: The context of students' thinking during instruction. *Educational Psychologist, 23,* 167-180.

Doyle, W. (1992). Curriculum and pedagogy. In P. W. Jackson (Ed.), *Handbook of research on curriculum* (pp. 486-516). New York: Macmillan.

Doyle, W. (2006). Ecological approaches to classroom management. In C. Evertson & C. Weinstein (Eds.), *Handbook of classroom management: Research, practice, and contemporary issues* (pp. 97-125). New York: Erlbaum.

Doyle, W. & Carter, K. (1984). Academic tasks in classrooms. *Curriculum Inquiry, 14,* 129-149.

Doyle, W. & Carter, K. (2003). Narrative and learning to teach: Implications for teacher-education curriculum. *Journal of Curriculum Studies, 35,* 129-137.

Edelson, D. C., Gordon, D. N., & Pea, R. D. (1999). Addressing the challenges of inquiry-based learning through technology and curriculum design. *The Journal of the Learning Sciences, 8,* 391-450

Furtak, E. M., Ruiz-Primo, M. A., Shemwell, J. T., Ayala, C. C., Brandon, P. R., Shavelson, R. J., & Yin, Y. (2008). On the fidelity of implementing embedded formative assessments and its relation to student learning. *Applied Measurement in Education, 21,* 360-389.

Gump, P. V. (1969). Intra-setting analysis: The third grade classroom as a special but instructive case. In E. Williams & H. Rausch (Eds.), *Naturalistic viewpoints in psychological research* (pp. 200-220). New York: Holt, Rinehart & Winston.

Harris, C. J. & Rooks, D. L., (2010). Managing inquiry-based science: Challenges in enacting complex science instruction in elementary and middle school classrooms. *Journal of Science Teacher Education, 21,* 227-240.

Herbst, P. G. (2006). Teaching geometry with problems: Negotiating instructional situations and mathematical tasks. *Journal of Research in Mathematics Education, 37,* 313-347.

Hord, S. M. & Huling-Austin, L. (1986). Effective curriculum implementation: Some promising new insights. *Elementary School Journal, 87,* 96-115.

Hume, A. & Coll, R. (2010). Authentic student inquiry: The mismatch between the intended curriculum and the student-experienced curriculum. *Research in Science and Technological Education, 28,* 43-62.

Janssen, F. J. J. M., Van Driel, J. H., & Verloop, N. (2010). Naar praktische ontwerpondersteuning voor docenten [Towards practical design support for teachers]. *Pedagogische Studiën, 87,* 412-431.

Kounin, J. S. (1970). *Discipline and group management in classrooms.* New York: Holt, Rinehart & Winston.

Nystrand, M., Wu, L. L., Gamoran, A., Zeiser, S., & Long, D. A.(2003). Questions in time: Investigating the structure and dynamics of unfolding classroom discourse. *Discourse Processes, 35,* 135-198.

Olson, J. (1981). Teacher influence in the classroom: A context for understanding curriculum translation. *Instructional Science, 10,* 259-275.

Remillard, J. T. (2000). Can curriculum materials support teachers' learning? Two fourth-grade teachers' use of a new mathematics text. *Elementary School Journal, 100,* 331-350.

Remillard, J. T. (2008). Considering what we know about the relationship between teachers and curriculum materials. In J. T. Remillard, B. A. Herbel-Eisenmann, & G. M. Lloyd (Eds.), *Mathematics teachers at work: Connecting curriculum materials and classroom instruction* (pp. 85-92). New York: Routledge.

Remillard, J. T., Herbel-Eisenmann, B. A., & Lloyd, G. M. (Eds.). (2008). *Mathematics teachers at work: Connecting curriculum materials and classroom instruction.* New York: Routledge.

Schoenfeld, A. H. (1988). When good teaching leads to bad results: The disasters of "well-taught" mathematics courses. *Educational Psychologist, 23,* 145-166.

Schoenfeld, A. H. (2002). A highly interactive discourse structure. *Social Constructivist Teaching, 9,* 131-169.

Shavelson, R. J., Young, D. B., Ayala, C. C., Brandon, P. R., Furtak, E. M., Ruiz-Primo, M. A., Tomita, M. K., & Yin, Y. (2008). On the impact of curriculum-embedded formative assessment on learning: A collaboration between curriculum and assessment developers. *Applied Measurement in Education, 21,* 295-314.

Shkedi, A. (2009). From curriculum guide to classroom practice: Teachers' narratives of curriculum application. *Journal of Curriculum Studies, 41,* 833-854.

Snyder, J., Bolin, F., & Zumwalt, K. (1992). Curriculum implementation. In P. W. Jackson (Ed.), *Handbook of research on curriculum.* New York: Macmillan.

Sontag, S. (1966). *Against interpretation and other essays.* New York: Farrar, Straus, & Giroux.

Westbury, I., Hopmann, S., & Riquarts, K. (2000). *Teaching as reflective practice: The German didactik tradition.* Mahwah, NJ: Erlbaum.

Wubbels, T., Brekelmans, M., Den Brok, P., & Van Tartwijk, J. (2006). An interpersonal perspective on classroom management in secondary classrooms in the Netherlands. In C. Evertson & C. Weinstein (Eds.), *Handbook of classroom management: Research, practice, and contemporary issues* (pp. 1161-1191). Mahwah, NJ: Lawrence Erlbaum Associates.

Zais, R. S. (1976). *Curriculum: Principles and foundations.* New York: Crowell.

TEACHER ORIENTED

PHILIP RILEY, HELEN M.G. WATT, PAUL. W. RICHARDSON AND
NILUSHA DE ALWIS[i]

10. RELATIONS AMONG BEGINNING TEACHERS' SELF-REPORTED AGGRESSION, UNCONSCIOUS MOTIVES, PERSONALITY, ROLE STRESS, SELF-EFFICACY AND BURNOUT[ii]

INTRODUCTION

Disturbing evidence documenting some teachers' aggressive classroom management (mis)behaviour is growing. Relative to the importance of this issue, the level of research activity into the area is small (Sava, 2002). Writing about teacher aggression is widespread in the non-English literature: in France, Romania, Russia, and Spain (Sava, 2002). Reports have also appeared in Australia (Lewis & Riley, 2009), China and Israel (Lewis, Romi, Katz, & Qui, 2008), Poland (Piekarska, 2000), Scotland (Munn, Johstone, & Sharp, 2004), and Japan (Treml, 2001). In Europe, the term *didactogeny* has been coined for the experience of "a faulty education that harms children" medically, psychologically, or educationally (Sava, 2002, p. 1008). While children may appear to cope with the experience of teacher aggression in classrooms and schools, negative consequences accrue over time for some children more than others (Brendgen, Wanner, Vitaro, Bukowski, & Tremblay, 2007).

Background

Schools are complex environments where a range of emotional experiences is generated between students and teachers through their interpersonal relationships (Frenzel, Goetz, Lüdtke, Pekrun, & Sutton, 2009; Riley, 2011; Sutton, Mudrey-Camino, & Knight, 2009). Until relatively recently (Blackmore, 1996), little attention has been directed toward researching teachers' emotions and their associated 'emotional geographies' (Hargreaves, 2001). Teachers' work is inherently interpersonal; therefore it is both subjective and inter-subjective. A teacher's interpretation of his or her relationships with students and the resulting effects on teaching and learning are dynamically influenced, as are the students' interpretations of the teacher-student relationship (Riley, 2011). These relationships are grounded in their daily interactions and influenced by the interpretations or attributions each makes of the other's behaviour. These interactions produce a wide range of positive and negative teacher emotions in response to student behaviour.

T. Wubbels et al. (eds.), Interpersonal Relationships in Education, 151–166.

When students misbehave, teachers have a responsibility to manage the situations as they arise, and employ strategies to reduce the incidence of misbehaviour over time. In doing so, they must manage their own emotional reactions to students and this in turn affects their own classroom behaviour. Keeping emotions under control is not always easy to achieve, particularly when student emotional volatility is high (Finn et al., 2009). Teachers' strategies for managing student misbehaviour and their own emotional reaction to it will depend on a range of factors. Sometimes, student misbehaviour will provoke an aggressive teacher response (Sava, 2002) which can take many forms; from overt acts of commission such as yelling angrily at students, through to more subtle, even covert acts, such as not rewarding or acknowledging the prosocial behaviours of students considered to be 'bad'. This is labelled 'teacher misbehaviour' in the literature (for a full review of the taxonomy of teacher misbehaviour see Lewis & Riley, 2009). Aggressive teacher misbehaviour has a powerful negative influence on the interpersonal relationships formed between teachers and students. It tends to increase the types of student misbehaviour it seeks to diminish as students react to feelings of rejection by the teacher (Lewis, et al, 2008). Aggression by teachers also leads to diminution of student self-esteem (Poenaru & Sava, 1998); student negativity toward teachers (Romi, Lewis, Roache, & Riley, 2011); and, negatively affects the quality of relationships between teachers and students over time (O'Connor, 2010). Poor quality teacher-student relationships have been shown to contribute to student disengagement (Romi et al., 2011) and job dissatisfaction among teachers (Johnson, et al., 2005; Liu, Wei, & Jiang, 2009).

In this chapter we focus on three aspects of aggressive teacher responding to student misbehaviour. Each behaviour type is a display by the teacher directed toward students in response to student misbehaviour. The three types of aggressive behaviour are: deliberately embarrassing students, usually in front of their peers; using sarcasm to discredit a student, also usually in front of peers; and, yelling angrily to intimidate. Each behaviour, whilst often directed at an individual or small group, can also affect other students in the class in multiple ways; these range from distraction from the work tasks to more serious health effects (Hyman & Snook, 1999). The three aggressive behaviours were chosen because they have been reported as typical negative teachers' classroom reactions to student misbehaviour in Australia and elsewhere (Lewis et al., 2008).

The emergent field of research concerning teachers' aggressive behaviour has predominantly focussed on situational correlates. From this literature, teacher aggression appears to be both common, and under-reported. More than 60% of Australian teachers have been identified as sometimes employing at least one of these aggressive techniques in their classroom interactions with students (Lewis, 2008); it has also been estimated in the US that between one and two percent of all students may be suffering from education-induced post-traumatic stress disorder (PTSD; Hyman & Snook, 1999). In this chapter we widen consideration of the range of factors that may be involved, by the inclusion of dispositional bases. We investigate three commonly reported modes of aggressive responding to student misbehaviour and seek to relate these to a range of relatively unexplored background dimensions. The impetus for our study was to investigate the prevalence, salience, sources, and correlates of aggressive classroom responding displayed by beginning teachers. We were especially interested to examine possible relationships with a range of relatively unexplored dimensions including personality factors; unconscious motives; self-efficacy for managing difficult student behaviour; role stress from teaching situations and environments; and, teachers' burnout.

Sources of Aggression for Beginning Teachers

Potential sources of aggression displayed by beginning teachers toward students are likely to be complex aggregations of individual causes, in different school contexts. Despite changes to the nature of their work, for many teachers, the classroom remains the arena in which emotions are activated throughout the day. Hope, fear, joy, anxiety, anger, and a host of other affective dimensions propel teachers and students in classrooms for different reasons. This affects teachers' perceptions and appraisal of students (Frenzel et al., 2009), and, consequently, relationships within the classroom (Riley, 2011). Increasingly, teachers' interpersonal work is framed by an apparatus of management structures that monitor and assess how teaching and learning is organised and conducted. These factors all contribute to teaching as a highly stressful occupation (Montgomery & Rupp, 2005). This places beginning teachers in a very vulnerable position where fears, concerns, and problems associated with learning how to teach are exacerbated by multiple demands, lack of time to prepare, lack of rest, and lack of professional preparation for the socio-emotional and relational demands of teaching.

How these stressors are handled initially by a beginning teacher, is likely to set in train the course of a teacher's long-term classroom behaviours. In some social contexts, displays of aggression are condoned or even promoted, and become embedded in everyday assumptions, interactions, practices, and values. Left unexamined, these can become accepted modes of classroom behaviour and management for teachers and students. If a school culture overtly or covertly condones aggressive behaviours such as yelling at students, or anger to maintain classroom control, novice teachers may be encouraged to adopt them. Hence school cultures are replicated and sustained over time, and aggression becomes acceptable and invisible to review. This is in contrast to positive school cultures which are also self-replicating, with benefits flowing to both teachers and students, and, their interpersonal relationships.

Beginning teachers' reactions to students' poor behaviour may have utilitarian goals, by seeking to alter the future behaviour; be retributive, oriented toward 'retaliation for a past wrong', to avenge, rather than to prevent future misbehaviour (Reyna & Weiner, 2001, p. 309); reflect a disposition or personality type; or, be a reactive response provoked by a sudden stressful situation. Aggression theories range from genetic inheritance, cognitive neo-association, script, excitation transfer, through to social learning and social interaction (Anderson & Bushman, 2002). The latter perspective informs our study; as well, we include dispositional bases discussed below.

Personality. The Five-Factor model of personality (Judge & Ilies, 2002) proposes that five basic dimensions underlie human personality: Openness, Conscientiousness, Extraversion, Agreeableness and Neuroticism. Personality dimensions may appear an intuitively obvious source for teacher aggression, but have not previously been systematically examined as such, or in combination with the other sources investigated in our study. We anticipated that Neurotic teachers may be more likely to perceive personal threat in student misbehaviour and respond aggressively. Conversely, we expected that Open, Conscientious, and Agreeable teachers would be less aggressive. We had no clear expectations regarding Extraversion; more enthusiastic teachers may either be less likely to behave negatively to students, or, on the other hand, may be more likely to 'let off steam' when provoked and aggravated.

Self-efficacy. Teachers' self-efficacy for the management of difficult students is likely to impact teacher aggression (Sava, 2002). Beginning teachers who report poor disciplinary and management skills may be more likely to employ aggressive responding during episodes of elevated stress when dealing with a difficult classroom situation. Teacher behaviours that 'work' to keep the teacher feeling in control during such a stressful experience are likely to be repeated. These behaviours may be learned through trial and error, observation of, and listening to other teacher colleagues, outside the classroom.

Role stress. Stress and lack of effective support have been identified as causal factors for aggressive behaviour in many life circumstances (Bowlby, 1975). Documenting the difficulties that many teachers deal with on a daily basis indicates the high level of background stress involved in school teaching (Friedman, 2006). Beginning teachers who appraise their setting as stressful may engage in aggressive behaviours, especially when they lack the confidence to appropriately respond to challenging students.

Unconscious motives. Unconscious motives refer to those motives or drives of which the individual is not fully aware; these could be more relevant than *conscious* motivations as a source of teacher aggression, as teachers may be powerfully influenced by their need for attachment to their students (Riley, 2009). Attachment theory (Bowlby, 1969/82) provides plausible explanations for at least some types of teacher aggression, as it closely describes the underlying feelings that can develop as part of emotional transfer or reciprocity between teachers and students and the subsequent vulnerabilities that can result for both (see Cassidy & Shaver, 2008; Mikulincer & Shaver, 2007).

Teaching is an intensely interpersonal arena; therefore teachers' and students' perceptions of the relationship are central to teaching effectiveness (Riley, 2011). According to attachment theory the teacher's *internal working model* of self and other, or mental representation of the relationship with the student(s), is likely to be a determining factor affecting the teacher's level of aggressive behaviour, provoked in the teacher by a combination of student behaviour and the symbolic meaning it unconsciously primes in the teacher. A perceived threat to the current relationship with students is likely to cause emotional dissonance for the teacher (Lewis & Riley, 2009). This could result from the students becoming too close or too distant for the beginning teacher to feel comfortable in the relationship. This is further complicated by the interplay with the students' attachment needs, but has not yet been widely researched (Riley, 2009).

Attachment avoidance. This refers to the desire to remain emotionally distant and independent from others. For the avoidant teacher, aggressive responding should increase the emotional distance between him/herself and students, reducing tension and providing emotional stability. Students in turn may learn that increased emotional distance reduces aggressive interactions with the teacher. It is possible that as Attachment avoidance increases, so too does aggressive behaviour.

Attachment anxiety. Attachment anxiety is founded on a fear of being unloved or abandoned. When confronted with student misbehaviour, this perceived lack of care and concern for the teacher by the students is likely to confirm the teacher's internal working model of how the world works – of being let down or abandoned – prompting what in attachment theory is termed 'separation protest' behaviours, which are invariably aggressive (Bowlby, 1975). This state of tension and distress is likely to arouse aggressive responding in the teacher who has high levels of Attachment anxiety.

Burnout. Burnout is widely researched along dimensions of reduced Personal accomplishment, Depersonalisation, and Emotional exhaustion (Maslach, Jackson, & Leiter, 1996). Perhaps teachers who are more 'burned out' may care less about students, and therefore treat them with less concern and respect; alternatively, the same symptoms may manifest as more apathetic and less aggressive responses to challenging student behaviour. Aggressive responding by teachers may serve to 'let off steam', thereby reducing the pathway to burnout. On the other hand, if beginning teachers behave in aggressive ways, thereby lowering self-efficacy and reducing work satisfaction, aggressive responding may increase burnout.

Some antecedents of aggression may be more readily addressed than others: for example, teacher personality characteristics are likely to be less malleable, but may be modified using interventions such as counselling, motivational retraining, and anger management. In contrast, aggression brought about by stressful school settings may be amenable to intervention through methods such as classroom management skills and coping strategies. Where we might be able to identify different kinds of beginning teachers for whom aggression is a problem as a result of personality, or where it arises in response to a particular environment, there is a better chance to design appropriate interventions to prevent or reduce aggression. This underpins our concern to understand the range of individual and situational factors associated with teacher aggression.

The Present Study

Using surveys with 412 Australian beginning primary and secondary school teachers, we examined the extent of teacher-reported aggressive behaviours in response to student misbehaviour (Yell angrily, Deliberately embarrass, Sarcastic comments); and correlations with dimensions of teacher personality, unconscious motives, self-efficacy for student behaviour management, role stress, and burnout symptoms. We were also interested to explore whether there were subgroup differences according to gender, primary or secondary strand, and undergraduate Bachelor or graduate-entry teaching qualification. Our major aims were to establish the extent and level of these teachers' self-reported aggressive behaviours; relate aggression to personality characteristics, unconscious motives, self-efficacy for student behaviour management, role stress, and burnout symptoms; and, recommend practical and policy implications.

METHOD

Participants

The 412 participants were primary (162 females, 21 males) and secondary (165 females, 64 males) beginning teachers from the 'FIT-Choice' ongoing research program of Watt and Richardson (www.fitchoice.org). At the time of the survey, participants had up to five years of teaching experience. Those who had undertaken teacher education through an undergraduate Bachelor degree typically had one year's teaching experience ($n = 192$); graduate-entry teachers typically had four years' teaching experience ($n = 220$).

Instrumentation

Data came from the FIT-Choice surveys, and included measures of:
- personality (TIPI; Gosling, Rentfrow, & Swann, 2003);
- unconscious motives: Anxiety about close relationships, and Avoidance of intimacy (2 items per subscale selected from Brennan, Clark, & Shaver, 1998);
- self-efficacy for managing difficult student behaviour (items from: the Sentiments, Attitudes and Concerns about Inclusive Education [SACIE] scale: Loreman, Earle, Sharma, & Forlin, 2007; and from Watt & Richardson, 2008)

- experience of role stress (single item);
- teacher aggression (3 items based on Lewis, et al., 2008); and
- teacher burnout symptoms (Maslach Burnout Inventory – Educators Survey [MBI-ES]; Maslach & Jackson, 1986), containing subscales Emotional exhaustion, Personal accomplishment, and Depersonalisation;

Table 1 reports details of the measures. Cronbach alpha measures of internal consistency were adequate for all measures except the TIPI Agreeableness (α = .38) and Openness (α = .35) subscales (as has also been found in previous studies, see Gosling et al., 2003). For the dimension of Attachment anxiety intimacy, Cronbach's alpha for the two selected items was .86; consistent with the alphas reported for the whole scale (.91; Brennan et al., 1998). However, reliability for the two items from the Avoidance scale, .55, was substantially different from the full subscale .92, reported by Brennan and colleagues (1998). We had no alternative measure of avoidance, and strong theoretical reasons for its inclusion.

Although Cronbach's alpha among the 3 self-reported aggression items was adequate overall (alpha = .67), Yell angrily had similarly low correlations with each of Deliberately embarrass (rho = .33) and Sarcastic comments (rho = .33, p <.001, n = 360). However, the correlation between Deliberately embarrass and Sarcastic comments was substantially higher (rho = .57, p < .001). For exploratory purposes we analysed both the composite aggression factor, as well as disaggregating the 3 aggression items, to allow for indications of possibly different patterns of relationships for different kinds of teacher aggression.

Procedure and Analyses

Participants completed an online survey interrogating the factors described above. Spearman correlations determined the relative strength of association between each of personality, unconscious motives, self-efficacy for the management of difficult students, role stress, burnout symptoms, and the central teacher aggression outcomes. The single timepoint correlational data in our present study do not allow us to tease out directionality, but they do allow us to probe for associations between dimensions of burnout and teacher-reported aggression. MANOVA also tested for differences between men and women; primary and secondary strand; and undergraduate versus graduate-entry on the teacher aggression items, and potential correlates of teacher aggression. In view of the exploratory nature of the study, and number of tests being conducted, statistical significance was set at $p < .01$.

RESULTS

Prevalence of Self-Reported Teacher Aggression

Fifty-four percent of beginning teachers reported Deliberately embarrassing their students at least sometimes, while 45.9% reported they never engaged in this

Table 1. Details of measures.

Higher-order factor (where applicable)	Subscale	N Items	Sample item	Cronbach's alpha
	Aggression	3	To what extent do students in <u>your</u> classes feel ... you deliberately embarrass students who misbehave? *(1 = not at all, 7 = a lot)*	.67
	Self-efficacy for managing difficult student behaviour	3	How confident are you that you have the ability to ... manage badly behaved students? *(1 = not confident at all, 7 = extremely confident)*	.89
	Role stress	1	In general, how stressful do you find being a teacher? *(1 = not at all, 5 = extremely stressful)*	n/a
Personality			I see myself as ... *(1 = disagree strongly, 7 = agree strongly)*	
	Extraversion	2	Extraverted, enthusiastic	.70
	Agreeableness	2	Critical, quarrelsome (reversed)	.38
	Conscientiousness	2	Dependable, self-disciplined	.60
	Neuroticism	2	Anxious, easily upset	.62
	Openness	2	Open to new experiences, complex	.35
Unconscious motives	Attachment anxiety	2	I am afraid that I will lose other people's love *(1 = disagree strongly, 7 = agree strongly)*	.86
	Attachment avoidance	2	I prefer not to show how I feel deep down *(1 = disagree strongly, 7 = agree strongly)*	.55
Burnout symptoms	Emotional Exhaustion	9	I feel emotionally drained from my work *(1 = never, 7 = everyday)*	.90
	Personal Accomplishment	8	I have accomplished many worthwhile things in this job *(1 = never, 7 = everyday)*	.82
	Depersonalisation	5	I've become more callous toward people since I took this job *(1 = never, 7 = everyday)*	.74

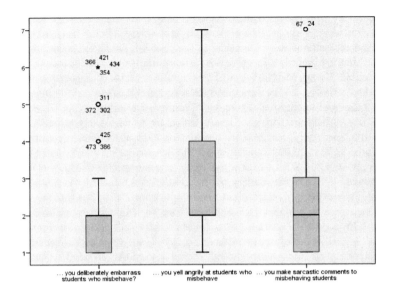

1 = *not at all* to 7 = *a lot.*
The box length is the interquartile range and the solid bar represents the median value.
'o/*' denotes outliers with values between 1.5 and 3 box lengths from the upper edge
of the box.

Figure 1. Distributions for teacher-reported aggressive behaviours.

behaviour. On the other hand, 78.5% of teachers reported Yelling angrily, and 63.8% reported becoming Sarcastic with students at least some of the time. Figure 1 shows the spread of teachers who reported using aggressive behaviours in response to student misbehaviour.

Different Aggression Levels for Different Teachers

A 3-way ANOVA explored differences in Aggression between graduate and undergraduate trained, primary and secondary, and male and female teachers. A univariate effect of gender was found, F (1, 352) = 11.58, p = .001, partial η^2 = .032, with male teachers reporting higher Aggression levels (M = 2.83, SD 1.18) than females (M = 2.24, SD 1.02). Additionally, a univariate effect of teaching strand was present, F (1, 352) = 11.05, p = .001, partial η^2 = .030, with secondary teachers reporting higher Aggression (M = 2.54, SD 1.14) than primary teachers (M = 2.16, SD 0.96). A significant interaction between strand and degree type, F (1, 352) = 8.81, p = .004, partial η^2 = .023 (secondary graduates: M = 2.36, SD = 1.10; secondary undergraduates: M = 2.85, SD = 1.16; primary graduates: M = 2.22, SD = 0.92, primary undergraduates: M = 2.12, SD = 0.98), suggested higher

159

Aggression by undergraduate- relative to graduate-trained secondary teachers, in comparison to no degree differences among primary school teachers; no such significant interactions were identified in the following analyses according to type of aggression, and so this effect was not further interpreted.

A similar 3-way MANOVA was repeated with the 3 aggression items as dependent variables, to explore potentially different subgroup findings for the different kinds of aggression. There was a multivariate effect of strand, F (3, 350) = 6.33, $p < .001$, partial $\eta^2 = .051$, accounted for by univariate effects of higher scores from secondary than primary teachers on each of Deliberately embarrass, F (1, 352) = 7.00, $p = .009$; partial $\eta^2 = .019$ (Secondary: $M = 2.10$, $SD = 1.37$; Primary: $M = 1.83$, SD 1.01); and Sarcastic comments, F (1, 352) = 18.92, $p < .001$; partial $\eta^2 = .051$ (Secondary: $M = 2.64$, $SD = 1.50$; Primary: $M = 1.96$, SD 1.26). A multivariate effect of gender was significant F (3, 350) = 6.24, $p < .001$; due to men reporting higher scores than women for Deliberately embarrass, F (1, 352) = 7.26, $p = .007$; partial $\eta^2 = .020$ (Male: $M = 2.60$, SD 1.43; Female: $M = 1.81$, $SD = 1.10$). Therefore, there were no significant subgroup differences at all for Yelling angrily, implying similar scores regardless of gender, strand, and degree type. There were no significant effects of degree type on any of the 3 aggression items.

Factors Which Relate to Teacher Aggression

The following factors correlated significantly with the Aggression factor: Agreeableness, Personal accomplishment, Depersonalisation, Self-efficacy for managing student behaviour, Conscientiousness, Emotional exhaustion, Neuroticism and Openness (arranged from highest in strength to lowest). There were some differences in the patterns of relationships with the 3 different kinds of aggression: Yell angrily was the only kind which did not significantly relate to self-efficacy; Sarcastic comments was the only kind which did not relate to Attachment anxiety and Conscientiousness, and, the only kind which did relate to Emotional exhaustion; Deliberately embarrass was the only kind which did not relate to Neuroticism, and, the only kind which did relate to Openness ($p < .01$).

Teacher Differences on Correlates of Aggression

A MANOVA investigated differences in correlates of the Aggression factor and the individual aggression items, by gender, type of teaching qualification, and strand of teaching. A multivariate effect of gender was found, F (12, 277) = 3.41, $p < .001$, partial $\eta^2 = .129$, with univariate effects for Agreeableness, F (1, 288) = 17.18, $p < .001$, partial $\eta^2 = .056$, and Conscientiousness, F (1, 288) = 17.18, $p < .001$, partial $\eta^2 = .056$. Females reported higher levels of Agreeableness ($M = 5.63$, $SD = 1.00$) and Conscientiousness ($M = 6.02$, $SD = 1.01$) than male teachers (A: $M = 5.10$, $SD = 1.18$; C: $M = 5.38$, $SD = 1.189$). A multivariate effect of strand, F (12, 277) = 3.41, $p < .001$, partial $\eta^2 = .129$, was accounted for by a univariate effect on

Depersonalisation F (1, 288) = 6.33, p = .01, partial η^2 = .022. Secondary teachers reported higher levels of depersonalisation (M = 2.29, SD = 1.16) than primary teachers (M = 1.97, SD = 0.92).

Table 2. Spearman correlates of teacher aggression (component items and factor scores).

Higher-order factor (where applicable)	Subscale	N	Delibe-rately embarrass	Sarcastic com-ments	Yell angrily	Aggression (composite factor)
	Self-efficacy	347	-.173*	-.206*	-.122	-.213*
	Role stress	336	-.105	.071	-.072	-.031
Personality	Conscientiousness	330	-.212*	-.091	-.206*	-.197*
	Neuroticism	331	.120	.171*	.147*	.184
	Extraversion	328	.000	-.057	.072	.010
	Agreeableness	326	-.258*	-.249*	-.308*	-.342*
	Openness	325	-.153*	-.125	-.083	-.156*
Unconscious motives	Attachment anxiety	329	.156*	.052	.180*	.135
	Attachment avoidance	327	.058	-.046	.008	-.006
Burnout symptoms	Personal accomplishment	326	-.212*	-.334*	-.226*	-.342*
	Emotional exhaustion	324	.130	.187*	.128	.193*
	Depersonalisation	326	.246*	.253*	.271*	321*

* p < .01.

DISCUSSION

The implications of aggressive teacher strategies include a dislike by students of those teachers (Friedel, Marachi, & Midgley, 2002). The different techniques appear to result in different student perceptions of the interpersonal relationships they form with teachers. For example, deliberate embarrassment attacks a student's self-esteem (Parrott, Sabini, & Silver, 1988) in that it is a personal attack, rather than a management strategy based on demonstrating care toward students, even when admonishing them, such as the way in which yelling might be interpreted. On the other hand, sarcasm is not necessarily personal in nature, and if identified by students as irony, could even be interpreted as witty. Students may think that the teacher has understood the situation and reacted intelligently, if not ideally, to it. Previous studies (Romi et al., 2011) suggest that students are not as put off by teachers who yell at them, perhaps seeing this behaviour as driven by identifiable classroom events. At times they may be yelled at by people who care about them, such as parents, as a result of frustration or stress, understanding that the underlying interpersonal relationship remains one of care, even in difficult situations.

The prevalence of beginning teachers' self-reported aggressive responding to student misbehaviour was similar to the 60% reported in previous studies (Lewis et al., 2008). However, the frequency with which these beginning teachers reported engaging in aggressive responding was generally quite low. Yelling angrily was the most common form of aggression displayed by these teachers, and also the most ubiquitous, unaffected by gender or strand. Men were more likely to deliberately embarrass students, a type of aggression which is likely to cause harm to the student-teacher relationship (Romi et al., 2011). Secondary teachers also deliberately embarrassed and were more sarcastic to students than their primary colleagues. Perhaps this stems from the lesser time available to secondary teachers with the same group of students, to be able to build strong interpersonal relationships. Such an interpretation is supported by secondary teachers' higher reported levels of depersonalisation.

The fact that a range of dispositional dimensions did relate to aggressive teacher responding to student misbehaviour, suggests that teachers may not be choosing to behave this way deliberately. In a separate study with 233 experienced teachers who reported responding aggressively, the authors suggested many teachers may simply react to student misbehaviour (Riley, Lewis & Brew, 2010). Men's higher use of deliberately embarrassing students was partly accounted for by their lower scores on Agreeableness and Conscientiousness. The relationship between teachers' aggressive responding and their self-efficacy for managing difficult student behaviour further points to the importance of developing a suite of effective class management skills for beginning teachers. If aggressive responding is chosen deliberately, it may be that the technique has been evaluated as efficacious in the short term, while conforming to the accepted school culture.

There were no significant differences between those with typically four years of teaching experience (graduate-entry) versus those who had typically only one year's experience (undergraduates) on levels of aggressive responding to student misbehaviour. Also, no significant relationship existed between how stressful teachers found their role and their reported levels of aggression. Our speculation about time spent teaching in a stressful setting predicting aggressive responding was therefore not supported. The findings support an interpretation of teacher aggression arising from dispositional and personality based dimensions, and self-efficacy for class management skills. Therefore aggressive teachers are likely to need more profound interventions than are typically available as professional development. This has implications for the higher education sector and suggests a holistic approach where initial teacher education and ongoing professional development are integrated, not distinct from each other. For example, if school culture is the underlying cause, only interventions aimed at cultural change in a particular school would be likely to succeed in lessening teacher aggression. There is a substantial literature that suggests this is very much long-term work (Neville & Dalmau, 2008), even longer than the length of a teacher's initial training.

Our speculation that 'burned out' teachers would engage in more aggressive behaviours was supported. Teachers experiencing higher levels of Personal accomplishment were less likely to engage in aggressive behaviours. It seems that teachers who lack skills to sensitively respond to student misbehaviour are those more likely to resort to aggressive forms of response. On the other hand, the Emotional exhaustion and Depersonalisation dimensions of burnout showed a positive relationship; teachers higher on those dimensions reported more frequent aggressive student management. Because Emotional exhaustion has been well documented in samples of beginning teachers (Goddard, O'Brien, & Goddard, 2006), the relationships we report, while weak, are important. Depersonalisation showed a stronger relationship with aggression. Depersonalisation has been hypothesised to occur as a result of Emotional exhaustion (Maslach, 2003) whereby individuals attempt to disengage in order to cope with emotional strain (Schwarzer & Hallum, 2008), representing a more chronic aspect of the burnout syndrome. The higher incidence of aggression among secondary teachers may be partly explained by their higher Depersonalisation scores. For example, the number of students a secondary teacher deals with each day and the frequency of transitions from class to class may exacerbate the risk of Depersonalization. The impacts of different kinds of job demands, classroom structures and accountability systems for primary and secondary teachers require further investigation.

As hypothesised, teachers who reported elevated scores on Agreeableness, Conscientiousness or Openness reported lower aggression; whereas, teachers higher on Neuroticism had higher aggression scores, and Extraversion showed no significant relationship. It may be that greater Openness and Conscientiousness predict seeking alternative, constructive strategies and solutions to resolving student misbehaviour; while Agreeable teachers should be less likely to behave in an aggressive way even if provoked. In our continuing work, we will examine which constellations and combinations of factors interact together to produce aggressive teacher behaviours using longitudinal data.

Attachment anxiety correlated with two aggression items (Deliberately embarrass and Yell angrily). This finding suggests that aggression in the classroom may be founded on an unconscious need to be 'loved' by the students. Student misbehaviour could prompt teacher separation protest behaviours, which are largely beyond conscious control (Bowlby, 1975). The lack of a reliable short measure of Attachment avoidance made interpretation of the lack of association with teacher-reported aggression more difficult. Because avoidant people are not likely to seek help, and, are less likely to accept it if offered, this relationship requires further exploration using more sensitive measures. Teachers, who perceived themselves to have lower self-efficacy for managing student misbehaviour, were also more likely to use aggressive behaviours, particularly making sarcastic comments, supporting an interpretation that this was because they lacked a suite of alternative effective strategies and skills.

Limitations and Future Directions

This study relied on self-report measures to tap levels of beginning teachers' aggression in response to student misbehaviour in their classroom. It is possible this approach may underestimate aggressive teacher behaviours, given a possible social desirability bias. Future research could fruitfully incorporate observational and student-report data to overcome this limitation. Effect sizes, where significant effects were identified, were typically small, suggesting that other factors are at play and should be examined in relation to teacher aggression. A greater range of situational factors may be worthwhile to study in this regard, alongside more dispositional dimensions such as we have included. The poor alphas for certain subscales, and the single-item indicator for measured perceived role stress, provide insufficiently sensitive measures which also reduce power to identify and precision to estimate significant effects, likely contributing to the small effect sizes identified. The fact that significant effects were still able to be identified, points to the need to develop improved measures in order to productively pursue this line of research inquiry. What is clear is that this is a rich area for researchers to explore, and develop interventions to improve, teachers' professional development.

NOTES

[i] The authors contributed equally to the chapter.

[ii] The research was supported by a Monash University Small Grant and supplemented by ARC Discovery grant DP0987614 awarded to Watt and Richardson. The authors would like to thank Dr Umesh Sharma for early discussions about the ideas in this paper.

REFERENCES

Anderson, C. A. & Bushman, B. J. (2002). Human aggression. *Annual Review of Psychology, 53*(1), 27-51.

Blackmore, J. (1996). Doing emotional labour in the educational market place: Stories from the field of women in management. *Discourse, 17*(33), 337-350.

Bowlby, J. (1969/82). *Attachment* (2nd ed. Vol. 1). London: Harper Collins.

Bowlby, J. (1975). *Separation: Anxiety and anger* (Vol. 2). Harmondsworth: Penguin.

Brendgen, M., Wanner, B., Vitaro, F., Bukowski, W. M., & Tremblay, R. E. (2007). Verbal abuse by the teacher during childhood and academic, behavioral, and emotional adjustment in young adulthood. *Journal of Educational Psychology, 99*(1), 26-38.

Brennan, K. A., Clark, C. L., & Shaver, P. R. (1998). Self-report measures of adult attachment: An integrative overview. In J. A. Simpson & W. S. Rholes (Eds.), *Attachment theory and close relationships* (pp. 46-76). New York: Guilford Press.

Cassidy, J. & Shaver, P. R. (2008). *Handbook of attachment: Theory, research, and clinical applications* (2nd ed. ed.). New York Guilford.

Finn, A. N., Schrodt, P., Witt, P. L., Elledge, N., Jernberg, K. A., & Larson, L. M. (2009). A meta-analytical review of teacher credibility and its associations with teacher behaviors and student outcomes. *Communication education, 58*(4), 516-537.

Frenzel, A. C., Goetz, T., Lüdtke, O., Pekrun, R., & Sutton, R. E. (2009). Emotional transmission in the classroom: Exploring the relationship between teacher and student enjoyment. *Journal of Educational Psychology, 101*(3), 705-716.

Friedel, J., Marachi, R., & Midgley, C. (2002). *"Stop embarrassing me!" Relations among student perceptions of teachers, classroom goals, and maladaptive behaviors.* Paper presented at the annual meeting of the American Educational Research Association, New Orleans, LA.

Friedman, I. A. (2006). Classroom management and teacher stress and burnout. In C. M. Evertson & C. S. Weinstein (Eds.), *Handbook of classroom management: Research, practice, and contemporary issues* (pp. 925-944). New Jersey: Laurence Erlbaum and Associates Inc.

Goddard, R., O'Brien, P., & Goddard, M. (2006). Work environment predictors of beginning teacher burnout. *British Educational Research Journal, 32*(6), 857-874.

Gosling, S. D., Rentfrow, P. J., & Swann, W. B. (2003). A very brief measure of the Big-Five personality domains. *Journal of Research in Personality, 37*(6), 504-528.

Hargreaves, A. (2001). The emotional geographies of teachers' relations with colleagues. *International Journal of Educational Research, 35*(5), 503.

Hyman, I. A. & Snook, P. A. (1999). *Dangerous schools: What we can do about the physical and emotional abuse of our children.* San Francisco: Jossey Bass.

Johnson, S., Cooper, C., Cartwright, S., Donald, I., Taylor, P., & Millet, C. (2005). The experience of work-related stress across occupations. *Journal of Managerial Psychology, 20*(2), 178-187.

Judge, T. A. & Ilies, R. (2002). Relationship of personality to performance motivation: A meta-analytic review. *Journal of Applied Psychology, 87*(4), 797-807.

Lewis, R. (2008). *The developmental management approach to classroom behaviour: Responding to individual needs.* Camberwell, Vic: ACER Press.

Lewis, R. & Riley, P. (2009). Teacher misbehaviour. In L. J. Saha & A. G. Dworkin (Eds.), *The international handbook of research on teachers and teaching* (pp. 417-431). Norwell, MA, USA: Springer.

Lewis, R., Romi, S., Katz, Y. J., & Qui, X. (2008). Students' reaction to classroom discipline in Australia, Israel, and China. *Teaching and Teacher Education, 24*(3), 715-724.

Liu, J., Wei, X., & Jiang, G. (2009). Relationship between teacher's adult attachment and teacher interaction style. *Chinese Journal of Clinical Psychology, 17*(1), 104-106.

Loreman, T., Earle, C., Sharma, U., & Forlin, C. (2007). The development of an instrument for measuring pre-service teachers' sentiments, attitudes, and concerns about inclusive education. *International Journal of Special Education, 22*(2), 150-159.

Maslach, C. (2003). Job burnout: New directions in research and intervention. *Current Directions in Psychological Science, 12*(5), 189-192. doi: http://dx.doi.org/10.1111/1467-8721.01258.

Maslach, C. & Jackson, S. E. (1986). *The Maslach Burnout Inventory manual* (2nd ed.). Palo Alto, CA: Consulting Psychologists Press.

Maslach, C., Jackson, S. E., & Leiter, M. P. (1996). *Maslach burnout inventory manual* (3rd ed.). Palo Alto, California: Consulting Psychologists Press.

Mikulincer, M. & Shaver, P. R. (2007). *Attachment in adulthood: Structure, dynamics, and change.* New York: Guilford Press.

Montgomery, C. & Rupp, A. A. (2005). A meta-analysis for exploring the diverse causes and effects of stress in teachers. *Canadian Journal of Education, 28*(3), 458.

Munn, P., Johnstone, M., & Sharp, S. (2004). *Discipline in Scottish schools: A comparative survey over time of teachers' and headteachers' perceptions.* Edinburgh: Scottish Executive Education Department.

Neville, B. & Dalmau, T. (2008). *Olympus Inc. Intervening for cultural change in organisations.* Greensborough: Flat Chat Press.

O'Connor, E. (2010). Teacher-child relationships as dynamic systems. *Journal of School Psychology, 48*(3), 187-218.

Parrott, W. G., Sabini, J., & Silver, M. (1988). The roles of self-esteem and social interaction in embarrassment. *Personality & Social Psychology Bulletin, 14*(1), 191-202.

Piekarska, A. (2000). School stress, teachers' abusive behaviors, and children's coping strategies. *Child Abuse & Neglect, 24*(11), 1443-1449.

Poenaru, R. & Sava, F. A. (1998). *Teacher abuse in schools: Ethical, psychological and educational aspects.* Bucharest: Editura Danubius.

Reyna, C. & Weiner, B. (2001). Justice and utility in the classroom: An attributional analysis of the goals of teachers' punishment and intervention strategies. *Journal of Educational Psychology, 93*(2), 309-319.

Riley, P. (2009). An adult attachment perspective on the student-teacher relationship & classroom management difficulties. *Teaching and Teacher Education, 25*(5), 626-635.

Riley, P. (2011). *Attachment theory and the student-teacher relationship.* London: Routledge.

Riley, P., Lewis, R., & Brew, C. (2010). Why did you do that? Teachers explain the use of legal aggression in the classroom. *Teaching and Teacher Education, 26*(4), 957-964.

Romi, S., Lewis, R., Roache, J., & Riley, P. (2011). The impact of teachers' aggressive management techniques on students' attitudes to schoolwork and teachers in Australia, China, and Israel. *Journal of Eduational Research, 104*(4), 231-240.

Sava, F. A. (2002). Causes and effects of teacher conflict-inducing attitudes towards pupils: A path analysis model. *Teaching and Teacher Education, 18*(2002), 1007-1021.

Schwarzer, R. & Hallum, S. (2008). Perceived teacher self-efficacy as a predictor of job stress and burnout: Mediation analyses. *Applied Psychology: An International Review, 57*, 152-171.

Sutton, R. E., Mudrey-Camino, R., & Knight, C. C. (2009). Teachers' emotion regulation and classroom management. *Theory into Practice, 48*(2), 130-137.

Treml, J. N. (2001). Bullying as a social malady in contemporary Japan. *International Social Work, 44*, 107-117.

Watt, H. M. G. & Richardson, P. W. (2008, 30 Nov-4 Dec). *A new multidimensional measure of teaching self-efficacy: The SET Scale.* Paper presented at the AARE Annual Conference, Brisbane.

KATHARINA FRICKE, ISABELL VAN ACKEREN,
ALEXANDER KAUERTZ AND HANS E. FISCHER

11. STUDENTS' PERCEPTIONS OF THEIR TEACHERS' CLASSROOM MANAGEMENT IN ELEMENTARY AND SECONDARY SCIENCE LESSONS AND THE IMPACT ON STUDENT ACHIEVEMENT

INTRODUCTION

Research investigating teacher effects on student outcomes indicates that "effective teaching demands the orchestration of a wide array of skills that must be adapted to specific contexts" (Brophy, 1986, p. 1069). One of these skills is teachers' classroom management (CM) ability, which not only influences teacher-student interactions (Brophy, 2006), but also the amount of academic learning time. This is particularly so in well-organized classrooms, "where activities run smoothly, transitions are brief and orderly, and little time is spent getting organized or dealing with misconduct" (Brophy, 1986, p. 1070). In 1996, Jones identified five main features of classroom management: an understanding of students' needs, the use of instructional methods, the maximization of time-on-task behaviour, the assistance of students with behaviour problems and the creation of positive teacher-student relationships (Jones, 1996, p. 507). Especially due to the results of international comparative studies like TIMSS and PISA empirical research on the quality of instruction has taken on greater importance all over the world. Most models for quality of instruction include teachers' classroom management as one important precondition for successful teaching and learning (e.g., Brophy, 1999; Helmke, 2009; Slavin, 1994). In this respect "it is remarkable how few teacher education programmes explicitly address the topic" (Wubbels, 2006, p. 268). This is also true for educational research on classroom management. Authors often focus on "the aims that classroom management pursues rather than its techniques" (Wubbels, 2006, p. 268). There is still little quantitative research on the current status of classroom management in classrooms and on students' appraisal of teachers' practices. Nevertheless, as early as in 1970 Kounin did highlight the significance of students' perceptions in classroom management. He pointed out that when students perceive their teacher to be an efficient manager, they are more likely to work diligently and less likely to act disruptively (Kounin, 1970). "Both students and teachers have strong beliefs about what it takes to be an effective manager" (Woolfolk Hoy & Weinstein, 2006, p. 181). Former studies investigating the quality of instruction confirm these statements; they indicate that students' impressions of a lesson correlate with their achievements (Clausen, 2002).

T. Wubbels et al. (eds.), Interpersonal Relationships in Education, 167–185.

This study has developed instruments for investigating classroom management from different perspectives. First, a fairly high amount of students was asked how their teacher managed the lessons. Second, the study linked the perceptions of students to their outcomes.[i] This chapter thus focuses on the development and the validity of an instrument assessing students' perceptions of their teachers' classroom management (SPCM) and presents results of 2680 students. The sample is subdivided into students from elementary (n = 1326) and secondary (n = 1354) schools, as research indicates that elementary and secondary school teachers' managerial skills vary substantially between the two types of education (Weinert, 1996), which can (to some degree) be explained from their different educational backgrounds. After the description of the development process of the SPCM, its results will be linked to student outcomes.

THEORETICAL FRAMEWORK

Background of the Study

Changes in student outcomes after the transition from one school stage to another is an international problem and focus of research all over the world (Jindal-Snape, 2009). Regarding Germany, large-scale assessments like PISA 2003, for example, indicate that German secondary school students (grades 5 to 10) show lower performance in physics than the OECD average. In TIMSS 2007, however, German elementary students (grades 1 to 4) performed above the average of the participating countries (OECD 2004; Bos et al., 2008; for a detailed description of the German education system see KMK, 2010). Additionally, studies show a decrease in student motivation and interest up to grade 10 of secondary education (Gardner, 1998; Jenkins & Pell, 2006). Possible explanations, such as a general decline of interest during adolescent development, have been supported with empirical evidence for the middle and last years of secondary schooling in Germany (e.g., Hoffmann, Häussler, & Lehrke, 1997). Yet, the first years after transitioning to secondary education remain an important desideratum for research, including expected differences between instructional quality in elementary and secondary schools.

Research on Classroom Management

In the 1970s, specialists on teacher effectiveness research began to include classroom management in their investigations (e.g., Anderson, Evertson, & Brophy, 1979; Brophy & Evertson, 1976; Good & Grouws, 1975; as reported by Doyle, 1986), and first studies indicated correlations between classroom management and student achievements. It was at that time that research on classroom management was introduced to broader educational research in Anglo-American countries, though it remained less prominent in continental European states (Van Ackeren & Kühn, 2010). Research on classroom management is still part of more general pedagogical studies, although it has been recognized that "classroom management is not context-free, but rather is dependent upon the level of schooling" (Evertson & Weinstein, 2006, p. 7). Also, different subjects require specific managerial skills: Conducting experiments without spending too much time on organizing materials, for example, requires subject-specific managing competences (Kircher, Girwidz, & Häußler, 2007, p. 231) that every physics teacher should possess.

Wang, Haertel, and Walberg (1993) conducted a meta-analysis about conditional variables on school performance and found classroom management to rank second. They concluded their analyses by recognizing the fact that those who wish to facilitate academic performance should recognize proximal variables such as psychological determinants of learning (especially metacognition and cognition) and influential social and emotional aspects, including classroom management and student-teacher social interactions. Successful teachers ensure that lessons have as few disruptions as possible so that students can be engaged in learning activities as much as possible (Kounin, 2006). Also, recent studies confirm that effective classroom management increases student engagement, keeps students interested, helps to prevent discipline problems, enhances instructional and learning time, and finally, affects student achievement (cf. Emmer & Stough, 2001; Gruehn, 2000; Helmke, 2009; Rakoczy, 2006; Wang, et al., 1993; Wubbels, 2006). A high amount of 'time on task' not only advances students' school performance and improvement (cf. Evertson & Harris, 1992; Good & Brophy, 2003), but also seems relevant for the perceived motivational encouragement of students (Rakoczy, 2006).

The presented studies, however, have their shortcomings. All of them study classroom management either as a broad construct with multiple facets or, more narrowly, as a control variable within a larger set of variables. Both perspectives lead to difficulties in interpreting results: A narrower view misses the range of the large construct; a broad view – including social aspects like classroom atmosphere – makes it almost impossible to develop and conduct quantitative studies needed for the generalization of results. The idea of this study is to condense the existing framework into a measurable (physics-lesson-specific) definition and, therefore, be able to consider different perspectives of classroom management. Also, it investigates correlations of classroom management elements with student achievements with a sample of 2680 elementary and secondary students.

Definition of Classroom Management

Many present definitions of classroom management convey a broad, multifaceted view. To cite Kounin (2006) as an example, efficient classroom management creates effective lesson ecology with a learning-focussed milieu. This notion suggests that teachers need to posses a broad range of skills, but it does not make clear how to achieve this. Similarly, Anderson, Evertson, and Emmer (1980, p. 343) define classroom management as "*anything* that the teacher did to organize students, space, time and materials [...]". Duke (1979, p. xii) describes classroom management as the "provisions and procedures necessary to establish and maintain an environment in which instruction and learning can occur". Doyle (1986) focuses on the guidance of student behaviour: "classroom management refers to the actions and strategies teachers use to solve the problem of order in classrooms" (Doyle, 1986, p. 397). Emmer and Stough (2001) summarize the four main aspects of classroom management as a skill set that includes creating order in the sense of discipline and creating motivation by offering as much 'time on task' as possible.

The definitions above show that there is no coherent usage of the term 'classroom management' (Emmer & Stough, 2001). Different authors cite aspects they consider to be important in the sense of effective classroom management. Anderson and colleagues (1980) remark that the complex construct is difficult to account "adequately for all aspects" (Anderson et al., 1980, p. 345).

In order to be able to measure the impact of efficient classroom management on student achievement, an operationalized, measurable definition of the term is needed. For this study, the definition is concretized as a teacher's leading strategies in the classroom: The efficient management of a class includes reactive, preventive and proactive elements (Helmke, 2009). Based on these parameters, the three main constructs of classroom management within this study are *discipline*, *rule clarity and prevention of disruptions*.

AIMS AND RESEARCH QUESTIONS

The aim of the study is to clarify the relation between students' perceptions of teachers' classroom management and student achievement in a series of physics lessons. It is hypothesised that classroom management has a significant influence on lesson outcomes. The influence of students' perception of classroom management on students' knowledge gain and students' changing interest over a unit of three 90-minute-lessons can be modelled as presented in Figure 1.

Classroom management consists of various aspects that can influence lesson outcomes differently. In an individual's view, it specifies expectations, clarifies duties, and establishes possibilities in a specific situation. According to theories about the development of interest, learning-related interactions and the individually perceived quality of classroom management can evoke and foster topic-related interest (Krapp, 1998).

In a more general view, classroom management is aimed at giving an entire class the boundary conditions for learning-oriented interaction. This is a necessary prerequisite for ensuring time-on-task, which is again closely related to students' knowledge gains. This interpersonal view can be expressed as aggregated students' perceptions (class perceptions). Thus, the aggregated student perception of classroom management can be related to the gain of students' knowledge.

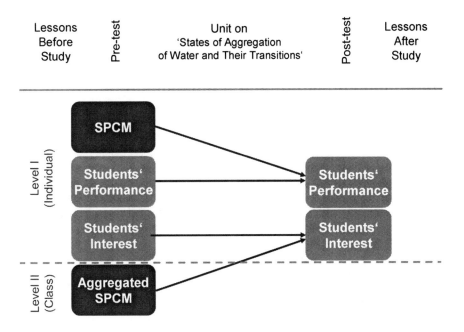

Figure 1. Classroom management and student outcomes in physics.

The lesson outcomes are described by interest and knowledge gain, the latter of which is operationalized by the residuals from pre- and post-scores on student performance tests. In this study, both the differential effects of elementary versus secondary school levels and the role of classroom management within the framework of this relation are studied. Additional variables such as students' general cognitive abilities, students' socioeconomic backgrounds, the duration of instruction and teachers' experience in teaching are used as control variables.

The following section introduces the instrument used to assess students' appraisals of teachers' classroom management: the questionnaire about students' perceptions of their teachers' classroom management (SPCM). To sum up, the leading research questions in this paper are:

(Q1) How do students at different school levels perceive their science teacher's classroom management?

(Q2) How is their perception related to their performance and interest in physics lessons?

METHOD

Development of the Questionnaire

In April 2008, a pilot study was conducted with 278 students from eleven classes of eleven teachers. Ninety of these 278 students were in elementary school (grade 4) while 188 were in secondary school (grade 6). The secondary school sample was subdivided into 78 students from *Hauptschule* (German secondary school for basic general education of low achievers), teachers with diverse training backgrounds and 110 students from *Gymnasium* (German secondary school for intensified general education on an advanced level). The pilot questionnaire on students' perceptions of their teacher's classroom management ($SPCM_{ps}$) consisted of three scales with nine items each: discipline (scale I), rule clarity (scale II) and prevention of disruptions (scale III). Discipline referred to questions about how disruptive the students' perceived their physics lessons to be and how often the teacher had to remind students to work quietly. The scale about rules and rituals referred to whether the teacher had *set up* a system of rules and rituals, and whether all of the students *knew, understood* and *adhered* to these. Scale III referred to questions about the students' perceptions of their teacher's 'omnipresence' and if they were able to notice and prevent disruptive behaviour, even when they were busy with individual students.

Rasch analysis confirmed the assumed three-dimensional structure of the data, as the three-dimensional partial credit model significantly fitted better than the one-dimensional model. Each dimension could be identified with one of the scales. Reliabilities were above $p > .776$ (EAP/PV Reliability) for all three scales (see Table 1). Moreover, based on the usual fit criteria ($-2.0 < T < 2.0$; $0.6 < MNSQ < 1.4$) Rasch analysis confirmed item fit for all except one item of each scale. Nevertheless, to ensure content validity, all items were kept. Descriptive results indicated that the rating scale was fully utilized (four point Likert scale: $0 =$ disagree to $3 =$ agree). Table 1 summarizes the quality parameters for the selected 17 items of the questionnaire on students' perceptions of their teachers' classroom management ($SPCM_{ms}$) that were used for the present study.

SPCM in the Present Study

Sample. Roughly 300 schools were asked to participate. For the main study, 2680 German students from 114 classes of 114 teachers participated voluntarily (convenience sample). The revised SPCM, consisting of five to six items per subscale for a total of 17 items, was administered to 60 elementary and 54 secondary school classes in Germany, comprising 1326 elementary and 1354 secondary school students.

Instrumentation. As previously mentioned, the questionnaire consists of three scales. Figure 2 shows an example of the questionnaire.

Table 1. Quality features of SPCM in the pilot phase.

Subscales	Discipline	Rule clarity	Prevention of Disruption
Amount of Items	6	5	6
# of items with MNSQ in acceptable range (-2.0 < T < 2.0; 0.6 < MNSQ < 1.4)	5	4	5
EAP/PV Reliability	.889	.777	.838
Minimum*	-84.01	-41.90	-.93.48
Maximum*	376.37	234.38	324.83
Mean*	112.91	115.53	106.30
Standard Dev.*	94.07	52.85	72.15

* Standardized Values: Mean is set to 100, standard deviation is set to 50.

Because the youngest participating students were only nine years old, the four point Likert scale was explained with an example. In order to prevent reading difficulties, every single item was presented by a university staff member. By completing the questionnaire with university staff instead of with their teacher, it was also guaranteed that the students would respond more honestly; without the fear that their teacher would know how they answered. Moreover, the meaning of the content in each scale was explained. For example, concerning the prevention of disruption construct (scale III) was as follows:

Now I would like to know whether your teacher tries to prevent in-class <u>disturbances</u> before they happen. That is, before a student is about to disrupt the lesson, the teacher gives him or her signals to be quiet. Such a signal could be a stern look.

The items of the SPCM were adapted from works of Gruehn (2000), PISA 2003 (OECD, 2004), Clausen (2002) and Schönbächler (2005). Nine of the 17 items were developed by the authors.

For other variables such as pre- and post-scores of students' performance, interest and control variables (see section 3) data were taken from the data set of the super ordinate project (see endnote i), in which this study was embedded and linked. All tests and questionnaires of the study were piloted and validated (Kauertz et al., 2010).

Please always and *only* think of your **science** lessons while responding to the questions.					
SPCM_P	Now I would like to know, whether your teacher tries to avoid the emergence of **disturbance** in the very beginning. Already before a student is about to begin to disrupt the lesson, the teacher gives him or her signals to be quiet. Such a signal could be a stern look.	Disagree	Partly agree	Mostly agree	Agree
SPCM_P13	Our teacher notices what the rest of the class is doing, even if he or she is busy with individual students.	☐	☐	☐	☐
SPCM_P06	Our teacher immediately notices students who mess about.	☐	☐	☐	☐
SPCM_P09	Our teacher notices everything we do.	☐	☐	☐	☐
...	...	☐	☐	☐	☐

Figure 2. Example of SPCM, selected items for the construct of prevention of disruptions.

RESULTS

Validity and Reliability of SPCM

Elementary and secondary students' responses to the 17 items of the SPCM were probabilistically analysed because probabilistic analyses enable the conversion of ordinal data into linear data, whereas parametric tests require linear data. In a rating scale, the 0, 1, 2 and 3 could be misleading in terms of the steps between the categories. It cannot necessarily be assumed that a student perceives boundaries to change from 'disagree' to 'partly agree' equally as from 'partly agree' to 'mostly agree'. Rasch allows one to convert this problematic data into data that can be used for statistical tests (Bond & Fox, 2007).

In the following section the quality of the questionnaire is shown by discussing Rasch models fit to data structure, the fit of the rating scale, differential functioning of the items, and reliability of the instrument. Descriptive results of the questionnaire regarding school levels and tracks are presented. Finally, the structure of interrelations is discussed based on multilevel analyses performed by means of MPlus.

Different partial credit models have been calculated in order to evaluate the dimensionality of the data, starting with a simple one-dimensional partial credit model. The significantly best fitting model is a three-dimensional partial credit model in which each dimension is formed by items from one scale. This indicates that the instrument represents the three expected components of discipline, rule clarity and prevention of disruptions. As Table 2 shows, correlations between the three subscales do exist, but as they are small it can still be assumed that the scales for rule clarity and prevention of disruption form different dimensions.

Table 2. Correlations between the three subscales of SPCM$_{ms.}$

	Discipline	Rule Clarity	Prevention of Disruption
Discipline	1	.051[*]	.143[**]
Rule Clarity	.051[*]	1	.472[**]
Prevention of Disruption	.143[**]	.472[**]	1

* Correlation is significant at the 0.05 level (2-tailed).
** Correlation is significant at the 0.01 level (2-tailed).

Within the three-dimensional partial credit model, item and person parameters indicated that the four-point Likert scale did not perfectly fit the participants' response pattern. Therefore, response categories were combined: category 0 (disagree) and 1 (partly agree) as well as 2 (mostly agree) and 3 (agree) were accumulated for the scale of rules and rituals.

In order to investigate if students from different school tracks responded differently to the items, the *type of school* was included into the three-dimensional partial credit model. The results indicated a medium size DIF for two items of the scale of rule clarity between elementary school students and students from *Hauptschule*. Therefore, it was decided to exclude these items one by one. This limited the scale of rule clarity to just three items, but therefore could guarantee corresponding response behaviour at all school levels.

All further analyses are thus based on 15 items with satisfying fit parameters (0.6 < MNSQ < 1.4) and the person parameters of a three-dimensional partial credit model without a DIF based on the type of school.
Reliability was computed for each dimension (scale).[ii] The internal consistency of the SPCM (EAP/PV reliability) was .805 for *discipline*, .593 for *rule clarity* and .762 for *prevention of disruption*.

Students' Perceptions of Teachers' Classroom Management

The means for each scale were computed separately for each school type. Table 3 shows the resulting measures based on the estimated person measures by Rasch (Warm likelihood estimates, *wle*).

Table 3. Standardized minima, maxima, means and standard deviations of each scale according to school type.

	Minimum	Maximum	Mean	SD
Elementary School (*n* = 1326 participating students, valid = 1260)				
Discipline	-99.27	326.50	103.55	81.15
Rule Clarity	2.32	197.68	162.04	52.94
Prevention of Disruption	-75.91	281.24	160.93	64.40
Secondary School for Lower Achievers (*n* = 601 participating students, valid = 543)				
Discipline	-99.27	326.50	95.58	91.70
Rule Clarity	2.32	197.68	170.18	49.68
Prevention of Disruption	-75.91	281.24	144.92	58.80
Secondary School for Higher Achievers (*n* = 753 participating students, valid = 717)				
Discipline	-99.27	326.50	109.62	89.26
Rule Clarity	2.32	197.68	131.66	68.85
Prevention of Disruption	-75.91	281.24	110.92	70.25

Descriptive results showed that students' answers to rule clarity tend to agree. Within a questionnaire, this means that the items were not able to represent the students' concerns about their rules and rituals in class. The same was somewhat true for prevention of disruption, but not as strong as for rule clarity. For the following interpretation, these weaknesses of the questionnaire need to be kept in mind.

Based on the estimated person measures, a multivariate analysis of variance (MANOVA) showed significant main effects for classroom management between all types of schools (F (2, 2517) = 59.43, $p < .001$, partial $\eta^2 = .07$). Since there are three dimensions within the questionnaire about classroom management, the following paragraphs will discuss more detailed results of subsequent univariate analyses of variance (ANOVA).

A subsequent ANOVA showed a significant main effects for discipline at the different school levels (F (2, 2517) = 4.13, $p < .05$, partial $\eta^2 = .003$; see Figure 3).

There were no significant differences in perceived discipline in physics lessons between elementary and secondary school students. Within the secondary school students' sample, there were disparities. Students who attended schools for higher achievers described the discipline in their science lessons significantly more positively than students who attended secondary schools for lower achievers (Δ = 14.04; $p < .05$).

The subsequent ANOVA for rule clarity showed a significant main effect for the different school levels (F (2, 2517) = 88.10, $p < .001$, partial $\eta^2 = .07$; see Figure 4).

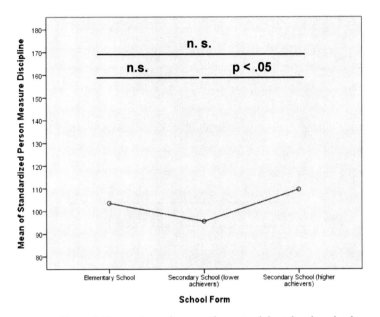

Figure 3. Comparison of means of perceived discipline by school type.

There were significant differences in the perception of rule clarity between all types of schools. Elementary school students described rule clarity as present and understandable in a significantly more positive way than secondary school students did (Δ = -8.14; p < .05 and Δ = 30.39; p < .001, respectively). Secondary school students who attended schools for lower achievers described rule clarity in their science lessons significantly more positively than students who attend secondary schools for higher achievers (Δ = 38.52; p < .001).

Subsequent univariate analyses of variance showed a significant main effect for prevention of disruption at the different school levels (F (2, 2517) = 135.53, p < .001, partial η^2 = .10; see Figure 5).

For the scale concerning prevention of disruptions, significant differences were once again found between all types of schools. Elementary school students described the preventive behaviour of their science teachers significantly more positively than students from secondary school (Δ = 16.01; p < .001 and Δ = 50.01; p < .001). The difference between the perceived prevention of disruptions in the two different types of secondary schools was also significant (Δ = 34.00; p < .001). Students from secondary school type I (lower achievers) perceived the prevention of disruptions in their science lessons significantly more positively than students from secondary school type II did.

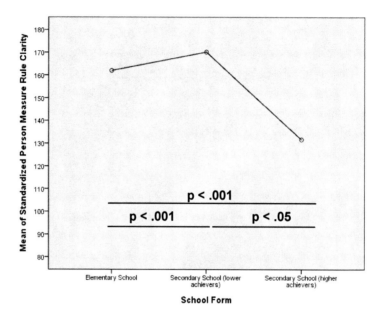

Figure 4. Comparison of means of perceived rule clarity by school type.

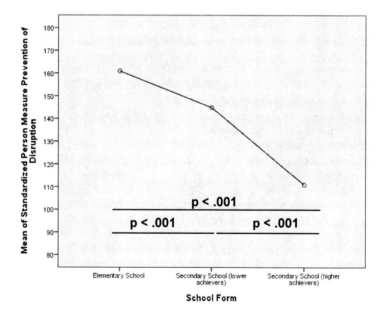

Figure 5. Comparison of means of perceived prevention of disruption by school type.

Classroom Management and Student Outcomes

In this section, results of multilevel analyses concerning the impact of (aggregated) student perceptions of their teacher's classroom management on students' knowledge gain and interest development will be presented. Since there were no significant correlations between the studied outcomes ($p = .167$), for each of the multilevel analysis, it was not necessary to include the other variable.

Due to differences in students' perceptions according to different school levels, it can be assumed that the impact of perceived classroom management on student achievement is moderated by the type of school. According to research question II, two main multilevel analyses were thus conducted. First, the impact of aggregated student perceptions on the students' knowledge gain over a unit on states of aggregation of water and its transitions was established. Then, the impact of individual perceived classroom management on the development of students' individual topic-related interest was determined.

As stated above, it is expected that the teachers' classroom management, measured by aggregated student perception of it, is a necessary prerequisite for time-on-task, which in turn is closely related to the students' knowledge gain. Thus, multilevel analyses were conducted controlling for the students' pre-knowledge, their socioeconomic status, gender and age on the individual level. At the class level, teachers' experience, their classroom management and the duration of instruction on the given topic was considered. Table 4 shows the results for the impact of teachers' classroom management on student knowledge gain in elementary school physics.

Results confirmed the expected influence of classroom management on student knowledge gain ($\beta = .131$; $p < .001$) at the elementary school level. In secondary schools, classroom management seemed to play only a subordinated role since no significant effects were found ($\beta = .021$; $p = .700$ and $\beta = .018$; $p = .675$, respectively).

The second aspect of research question II focuses on the individual's view of classroom management, which is assumed to be related to the individual's development of interest. Tables 5 to 7 show the results of multilevel analyses for all three investigated school tracks.

Results confirmed that individually perceived classroom management influenced students' development of topic-related interest. This effect seemed to be strongest at the elementary school level ($\beta = .202$; $p < .001$), followed by the secondary school for higher achievers level ($\beta = .189$; $p < .001$) and secondary school for lower achievers level ($\beta = .182$; $p < .001$).

Table 4. Impact of aggregated student perceptions of classroom management on knowledge gain in elementary school physics.

Students' Performance (SP) *postscore*: Elementary School

Predictors	Criterion: SP (post) β	P
Individual Level (L1)		
SP-Prescore	.482	.000
Age	-.085	.030
Gender	-.053	.143
Socioeconomic Status	.046	.047
General Cognitive Abilities	.124	.000
Class Level (L2)		
Classroom Management	.131	.023
Duration of Instruction	.106	.013
Job Experience	.058	.190
R^2 (predictors on class level)	.238	.034

Table 5. Impact of individual student perceptions of classroom management on topic-related interest in elementary school physics.

Students' Content Related Interest (SCRI) *postscore:* Elementary School

Predictors	Criterion: SCRI (post) β	P
Individual Level (L1)		
SCRI-Prescore	.375	.000
Age	-.039	.367
Gender	-.084	.032
Socioeconomic Status	-.020	.423
General Cognitive Abilities	.013	.597
Perceived Classroom Management	.202	.000
Class Level (L2)		
Classroom Management	.082	.125
Duration of Instruction	-.029	.427
Job Experience	-0.76	.052
R^2 (predictors on class level)	.154	.139

Table 6. Impact of individual student perceptions of classroom management on topic-related interest in secondary school (lower achievers) physics.

Students' Content Related Interest (SCRI) *postscore:* Secondary School (lower achievers)

Predictors	Criterion: SCRI (post)	
	β	P
Individual Level (L1)		
SCRI-Prescore	.466	.000
Age	.035	.518
Gender	.138	.039
Socioeconomic Status	.041	.381
General Cognitive Abilities	.030	.410
Perceived Classroom Management	.182	.000
Class Level (L2)		
Classroom Management	.115	.060
Duration of Instruction	-.003	.969
Job Experience	.021	.619
R² (predictors on class level)	.266	.244

Table 7. Impact of individual student perceptions of classroom management on topic-related interest in secondary school (higher achievers) physics.

Students' Content Related Interest (SCRI) *postscore:* Secondary School (higher achievers)

Predictors	Criterion: SCRI (post)	
	β	P
Individual Level (L1)		
SCRI-Prescore	.395	.000
Age	-.012	.877
Gender	.075	.219
Socioeconomic Status	-.028	.388
General Cognitive Abilities	.018	.596
Perceived Classroom Management	.189	.000
Class Level (L2)		
Classroom Management	.066	.190
Duration of Instruction	.028	.816
Job Experience	.052	.434
R² (predictors on class level)	.125	.410

DISCUSSION

Data analyses showed that discipline, rule clarity and prevention of disruption represent three dimensions of the classroom management construct. Although students who attended a secondary school for higher achievers perceive their physics lessons as quiet, they did not have the impression that their teachers always knew what was happening in the classroom when they were busy with individual students, nor did they feel that their teachers appropriately reacted to disruptions when they occurred. They were also unclear about rules, rituals and consequences for breaking rules. The results support findings from previous studies that managerial skills vary between teachers in different school stages. The authors' assume that reasons for this can be found in their educational backgrounds and professionalization during teacher training, which is characterized by an age group-specific approach and a differing ratio of content and educational sciences. Still, in future studies the results need to be correlated with a more objective view of teachers' classroom management assessed via video analyses before interpretations can be more precisely drawn. This will be done in a further step within the overarching research project (PLUS Project, Kauertz & Kleickmann, 2009), where all participating students and their teachers have been videotaped during lessons on the specific physics topics.

Multilevel analyses of relations between student achievement and classroom management revealed that the connection did not depend on students' individual impressions of their teachers' classroom management. Instead, it proved to be an interpersonal impression of classroom management that impacted their knowledge gains within a specific topic. As this was only the case for elementary school students, an explanation might be found in the relevance of order and routines for younger age groups. Older students might be more familiar with lesson progression so that the significance of this kind of classroom management is not regarded as relevant as it is at the elementary school level.

Individual perceptions of how teachers manage the classroom did indeed impact students' individual development of interest. Since classroom management adjusts the amount of freedom and security of individuals in a class, a positive impression is in line with a good balance of freedom and security, which allows for engagement and creativity. This effect could be found at all school levels. Again, in the future the very detailed analyses of 114 videotaped physics lessons will draw precise insight into the most relevant aspects of teachers' managerial behaviour and will help to clarify the presented results as measured by students' perceptions. A subsequent step will then be to compute whether a teacher needs to have high positive measures on all three constructs simultaneously, or if single constructs can be substituted or compensated by others.

By identifying central, observable factors of classroom management, the findings of this study can be used as a basis for fostering further professional teacher development concerning effective (age group-specific) classroom management. This could contribute to ensuring students' learning success and to better facilitating and supporting teachers' work pressure. This includes, last but not least, the notion that balance is achieved by "giving attention to guidance and structure, but also focusing on the development of independent learners and young democratic citizens" (Metzger, 2005, p. 13).

NOTES

[i] In order to be able to compare students' perceptions with their teachers' management activities in the classroom, highly inferential video analyses were used to gain a more objective view of the latter. Clausen (2002) found that teacher questionnaires do not provide reliable information about how they actually behave in classroom situations. To correlate findings about student perceptions of classroom management with observations, the study was embedded in a larger project, the 'German PLUS Project' (professional knowledge, teaching and learning in science, and students' outcomes in the transition from elementary to secondary school). In this study, numerous teacher and student questionnaires and tests are applied in a pre/-post design (Kauertz et al., 2010).

[ii] Cronbach's alpha is commonly used for questionnaires, but since an alpha uses raw nonlinear data, reliability in this case was computed within Rasch analysis.

REFERENCES

Anderson, L. M., Evertson, C. M., & Brophy, J. (1979). An experimental study of effective teaching in first-grade reading groups. *Elementary School Journal, 79*, 193-223.

Anderson, L. M., Evertson, C. M., & Emmer, E. T. (1980). Dimensions in Classroom Management Derived from Recent Research. *Journal of Curriculum Studies, 12*(4), 343-356.

Bond, T. G. & Fox, C. M. (2007). *Applying the Rasch Model: Fundamental measurement in the human sciences* (2nd edition). Mahway, NJ: Lawrence Erlbaum Associates.

Bos, W., Bonsen, M., Baumert, J., Prenzel, M., Selter, C., & Walther, G. (Hrsg.). *TIMSS 2007. Mathematische und naturwissenschaftliche Kompetenz von Grundschülern in Deutschland im internationalen Vergleich (Mathematical and scientific competence of elementary students in Germany in an international comparison).* Münster: Waxmann.

Brophy, J. (1986). Teacher Influences on Student Achievement. *American Psychologist, 41*(10), 1069-1077.

Brophy, J. (1999). *Teaching.* Available on: http://www.ibe.unesco.org/fileadmin/user_upload/archive/publications/EducationalEducationalPractic/prac01e.pdf (27 July 2010).

Brophy, J. (2006). History of Research on Classroom Management. In C.M. Evertson & C.S. Weinstein (Eds.), *Handbook of Classroom Management. Research, Practice, and Contemporary Issues* (pp. 17-43). USA: Lawrence Erlbaum Associates.

Brophy, J. E. & Evertson, C. M. (1976). *Learning from teaching: A developmental perspective.* Boston: Allyn & Bacon.

Clausen, M. (2002). *Unterrichtsqualität: Eine Frage der Perspektive? Empirische Analysen zur Übereinstimmung, Konstrukt- und Kriteriumsvalidität* (Quality of instruction: A question of perspective? Empirical analysis of agreement). Münster: Waxmann.

Doyle, W. (1986). Classroom organization and management. In C. M. Wittrock (Eds.), *Handbook of research on teaching* (3rd edition) (pp. 392-431). New York: Macmillan Publishing.

Duke, D. L. (1979). Editor's Preface. In D. L. Duke (Ed.), *Classroom management* (78th Yearbook of the National Society for the Study of Education, Part 2). Chicago: University of Chicago Press.

Emmer, E. T. & Stough, L. M. (2001). Classroom management: A critical part of educational psychology, with implications for teacher education. *Educational Psychologist, 36*(1), 103-112.

Evertson, C. & Harris, A. (1992). What we know about managing classrooms. *Educational Leadership, 49*(7), 74.

Evertson, C. M. & Weinstein, C. S. (Eds.) (2006). *Handbook of classroom management. Research, practice, and contemporary issues.* USA: Lawrence Erlbaum Associates.

Gardner, P. L. (1998). The development of males' and females' interests in science and technology. In L. Hoffmann et al. (Eds.), *Interest and learning* (pp. 41-57). Kiel: IPN.

Good, T. & Brophy, J. (2003). *Looking in classrooms* (9th edition). Boston: Allyn and Bacon.

Good, T. L. & Grouws, D. A. (1975). *Process product relationships in fourth-grade mathematics classrooms* (Grant No. NEG-00-3-0123). Columbia: University of Missouri, College of Education.

Gruehn, S. (2000). *Unterricht und schulisches Lernen: Schüler als Quellen der Unterrichtsbeschreibung.* Münster: Waxmann.

Helmke, A. (2009). *Unterrichtsqulität und Lehrerprofessionalität. Diagnose, Evaluation und Verbesserung des Unterrichts* (Quality of instruction and teacher profession. Diagnostic, evaluation and improvement of instruction). Seelze: Knallmeyer.

Hoffmann, L., Häussler, P., & Lehrke, P. (1997). *Die IPN-Interessenstudie Physik.* IPN Leibniz-Institut, Kiel.

Jenkins, E. W. & Pell, R. G. (2006). *The relevance of science education project (ROSE) in England: A summary of findings.* Leeds, UK: Centre for Studies in Science and Mathematics Education, University of Leeds.

Jindal-Snape, D. (Ed.). (2009). *Educational Transitions: Moving Stories from Around the World.* New York & London: Routledge.

Jones, V. (1996). Classroom Management. In J. Sikula (Ed.), *Handbook of research on teacher education* (2nd edition, pp. 503-521). New York: Simon & Schuster.

Kauertz, A. & Kleickmann, T. (2009). Postersymposium Professionswissen von Lehrkräften, verständnisorientierter naturwissenschaftlicher Unterricht und Zielerreichung im Übergang von der Primar- zur Sekundarstufe (PLUS) [Poster presentation on teachers' professional knowledge, implementation of understanding in science lessons and student achievements in the transition from elementary to secondary school]. In D. Höttecke (Eds.), *Gesellschaft für Didaktik der Chemie und Physik* (pp. 395-397). Berlin: Lit.

Kauertz, A., Kleickmann, T., Ewerhardy, A., Fricke, K., Fischer, H. E., Lange, K., Möller, K., & Ohle, A. (2010). Different perspectives on science teaching and learning in the transition from primary to secondary level. In M. F. Taşar & G. Çakmakcı (Eds.), *Contemporary science education research: Teaching* (pp. 419-436). Ankara, Turkey: Pegem Akademi.

Kircher, E., Girwidz, R., & Häußler, P. (2007). *Physikdidaktik: Theorie und praxis* [Teaching physics: Theory and practice]. Berlin: Springer.

KMK (2010). *The education system in the Federal Republic of Germany 2008. A description of the responsibilities, structures and developments in education policy for the exchange of information in Europe.* Bonn: Standing Conference of the Ministers of Education and Cultural Affairs of the Länder in the Federal Republic of Germany.

Kounin, J. S. (1970). *Discipline and group management in classrooms.* Holt; Rinehart and Winston: New York.

Kounin, J. S. (2006). *Techniken der Klassenführung* [Techniques of classroom management]. Standardwerke aus Psychologie und Pädagogik. Reprints. München: Waxmann.

Krapp, A. (1998). Entwicklung und Förderung von Interessen im Unterricht. *Psychologie in Erziehung und Unterricht, 44,* 185-201.

Metzger, D. (2005). Rethinking classroom management: Teaching and learning with students. *Social Studies and the Young Learner, 17*(2), 13-15.

OECD (2004). *Education at a glance.* Paris: OECD.

Rakoczy, K. (2006). Motivationsunterstützung im Mathematikunterricht [Supporting motivation in math lessons]. *Zeitschrift für Pädagogik, 52*(6), 822-843.

Schönbächler, M.-T. (2005). *Klassenmanagement auf der Primarstufe – Dokumentation zur Datenerhebung bei den Lehrpersonen und bei den Schülerinnen und Schülern* [Classroom management on elementary level – Data documentation of teachers and students]. Bern: Druckerei der Universität.

Slavin, R. E. (1994). Quality, appropriateness, incentive and time: A model of instructional effectiveness. *International Journal of Educational Research, 21,* 141-157.

Van Ackeren, I. & Kühn, S. M. (2010). Zwischen Anspruch und Realität. Die Diskussion um Unterrichtsstile und Klassenführung in Kanada und Finnland [Between rhetoric and reality. Teaching styles and classroom management in Canada and Finland]. In T. Bohl, K. Kansteiner-Schänzlin, M. Kleinknecht, B. Kohler, & A. Nold (Eds.), *Selbstbestimmung und Classroom-Management. Empirische Befunde und Entwicklungsstrategien zum guten Unterricht* (pp. 31-48). Bad Heilbrunn: Klinkhardt.

Wang, M. C., Haertel, G. D., & Walberg, H. J. (1993). Toward a knowledge base for school learning. *Review of Educational Research, 63,* 249-294.

Weinert, F. E. (1996). *Psychologie des Lernens und der Instruktion* [Psychology of learning and instruction]. Göttingen: Hogrefe.

Woolfolk Hoy, A. E. & Weinstein, C. S. (2006). Student and teacher perspectives on classroom management. In C. M. Evertson & C. S. Weinstein (Eds.), *Handbook of classroom management. Research, practice, and contemporary issues* (pp. 685-709). USA: Lawrence Erlbaum Associates.

Wubbels, T. (2006). Classroom management around the world. In M. Hayden, J. Levy, & J. Thompson (Eds.), *The Sage handbook of research in international education* (pp. 267-280). London: Sage Publications.

SIBEL TELLI AND PERRY DEN BROK[i]

12. TEACHER-STUDENT INTERPERSONAL BEHAVIOUR IN THE TURKISH PRIMARY TO HIGHER EDUCATION CONTEXT

INTRODUCTION

Teacher- student interactions are relevant in many teaching and learning processes in the classroom. The literature consistently provides support for the premise that high-quality teacher-student relationships are an important factor in effective teaching. Teachers' behaviours as perceived by students from an interpersonal perspective have an effect on students' achievement, motivation and attitudes (e.g., Martin & Dowson, 2009; Reid, 2007). The teacher-student relationship is also important because it directly relates to order in the classroom, one of the most common problem areas in education for both inexperienced and experienced teachers (Veenman, 1984). Furthermore, classroom misbehaviour may arise due to inconsistency in teacher interactions and unstable relationships between students and teachers are among the reasons for high teacher attrition, teacher mobility out of the profession and alternative career choices (Smithers & Robinson, 2003). Thus, the interpersonal relationship in the classroom is a vital element of teaching and the teaching profession.

Researchers have pointed out that teacher professional development can play a crucial role in improving teacher-student relationships (Becker & Luthar, 2002; Créton & Wubbels, 1984). In professional development activities, feedback on practice can form an important source of reflection (Darling-Hammond & McLaughlin, 1995; Guskey, 2002). The Questionnaire on Teacher Interaction (QTI) is such a feedback instrument with potential for teachers and for teacher education programs. The QTI provides teachers, teacher educators and researchers with feedback on teacher-student relationships via results as collected through students' perceptions, teachers' self-perceptions and teachers' ideal perceptions (Den Brok, Brekelmans, Levy, & Wubbels, 2002). While teacher-student interpersonal behaviour has been studied with the QTI in Turkey – the country of interest here –, present studies have mainly focused on the creation and use of a version for secondary education (e.g., Telli, 2006). This study adds to the field by mapping teacher-student interpersonal behaviour across educational levels, whereas most prior studies with the QTI only focused at one level at a time. For this purpose, next to the already existing Turkish secondary education version of the QTI, in this study versions were developed and tested for primary and higher education as well. As such, the purpose of this study was not to improve teacher interpersonal behaviour via a professional development program, but to create the

T. Wubbels et al. (eds.), Interpersonal Relationships in Education, 187–206.

(feedback) tools that might be used in such programs. In addition, comparison of the results of students' and teachers' perceptions of the three levels can learn us more about the degree to which interpersonal behaviours might be perceived differently or similarly across different education levels.

THEORETICAL FRAMEWORK

To describe students' perceptions of the interpersonal behaviour of a teacher, Wubbels, with the collaboration of colleagues Créton and Hooymayers (1992), adapted the model for interpersonal diagnosis of personality of Leary (1957) to the educational context and transformed it into the *Model for Interpersonal Teacher Behaviour* (MITB, see Figure 1). In this model, interpersonal behaviour is described along two dimensions, *Influence* (Dominance/Submission) and *Proximity* (Cooperation/Opposition). The two dimensions are depicted in a two-dimensional plane that is further subdivided into eight categories of behaviour: leadership, helpful/friendly, understanding, student freedom, uncertain, dissatisfied, admonishing, and strictness. In this model, each quadrant of the coordinate system encapsulates two sectors of behaviour.[ii] The position of these two sectors in the model varies, according to the amount of Influence and Proximity. In Figure 1, for example, DC (leadership) is a sector that refers to behaviour with high dominance and some cooperativeness; CD (helpful/friendly) represents behaviour that is highly cooperative and somewhat dominant.

Based on the MITB, Wubbels and his colleagues (1985) developed an instrument, *the Questionnaire on Teacher Interaction (QTI)*. The items of the questionnaire are connected to eight scales, representing the eight sectors, which in turn are related to the two dimensions in Figure 1.

The (original) QTI consisted of 77 items and was developed for the Dutch context via the modification, rewording and reduction of the 128 items of the *Interpersonal Adjective Checklist* (ICL) (Wubbels et al., 1992). Its development between 1978 and 1984 (Wubbels et al., 1985) included four rounds of testing using different sets of items, interviews with teachers, students and teacher educators, and researchers judging the face validity of items. Later, a 64-items American version was constructed by translating the set of 77 items from the Dutch version, adding several items (since several items could be translated in more than one way), and adjusting this set of items based on three rounds of testing (Wubbels & Levy, 1991). This form of the QTI was also used in the first Australian studies on teacher-student interpersonal relationships, but later a more economical 48-items Australian version followed (Fisher, Fraser, & Wubbels, 1993). The 64-items American version formed the basis for the development of the Turkish QTI for secondary education (Telli, Den Brok, & Cakiroglu, 2007).

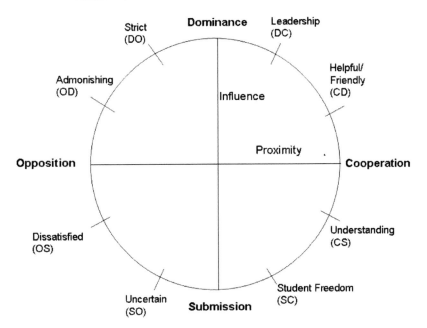

Figure 1. The Interpersonal teacher behaviour circumplex (Den Brok et al., 2006a).

Internationally, versions of the questionnaire have been constructed for different school levels, school types, languages and countries (e.g., Maulana, Opdenakker, Den Brok, & Bosker, 2011; Wubbels, Brekelmans, Den Brok, & Van Tartwijk, 2006). Research with the QTI has been conducted on topics such as teacher-student interpersonal relationships in multicultural classrooms (Van Tartwijk, Den Brok, Veldman, & Wubbels, 2009), the development of interpersonal relationships during the school year (Mainhard, 2009), the measurement and investigation of perceptions of psychosocial characteristics (Fraser, 1998), the effect of teacher-student interpersonal relationships on cognitive and affective outcomes (Den Brok, Brekelmans & Mainhard, 2010; Den Brok, Brekelmans, & Wubbels, 2004), the development of interpersonal behaviour during the teaching career and the importance of non-verbal behaviour for students' perceptions of teacher-student interpersonal relationships (Van Tartwijk, 1993). Additionally, data gathered with the QTI has led to the development of a teacher interpersonal behaviour style typology (Wubbels, Brekelmans, Créton, & Hooymayers, 1990). Furthermore, several studies have been conducted on the reliability and validity of the QTI (e.g., Den Brok, Fisher, Wubbels, Brekelmans, & Rickards, 2006).

Communication and perceptions obviously are under the influence of participants' ethnic backgrounds (e.g., Gay, 2002; Jacobs, 2003). The relationship atmosphere of the classroom, verbal and nonverbal behaviours are under the clear influence of these cultural factors (e.g., Gumperz, 1982; Ogbu, 1992). Because the QTI has been used in many different countries and contexts, it gives us the opportunity to compare findings from different countries in order to uncover some of these differences. For example, in one study in Turkey (Telli, 2006), Turkish science teachers were perceived as moderately dominant and very cooperative. They were rated .38 on the Influence dimension,[iii] which is comparable to science teachers from the Netherlands and Brunei, but lower than teachers from the United States, Australia, India, Indonesia, and Singapore (Den Brok, Fisher, & Koul, 2005; Den Brok et al., 2006; Maulana et al., 2011; Wubbels & Levy, 1993). In the same study, Turkish science teachers scored 1.00 on the Proximity dimension, which is similar to teachers from Singapore and some American studies, but much higher than the amount of Proximity reported in other countries (e.g., Den Brok et al., 2006; Wubbels & Levy, 1993).

Despite the international popularity of the QTI and reported outcomes, comparisons between different educational levels for the same country have – as far as the authors can oversee – not (yet) been conducted. So, what lacks is a general overview of student perceptions of teacher-student interpersonal relationships from primary to higher education within one country. This study attempts to do so for the Turkish context.

Research on teacher-student interpersonal behaviour with the QTI is quite recent in Turkey. The instrument drew the attention of teachers and researchers during the second half of the 2002 academic year in the master and PhD program in Middle East Technical University (METU), Ankara. It seemed a (systematic) solution to questions that kept researchers at this institute occupied, such as "How can a profile of a teacher in the classroom be determined from the students' point of view?" and "How is it possible that teachers are perceived differently by students in two different classes?". Studies on teacher-student interpersonal behaviour started in 2003 with a pilot study to adapt and develop the QTI to the Turkish context (Telli, 2006).

Outside Turkey, studies with the QTI have largely been conducted in secondary education (Wubbels et al., 2006) and there are not many examples at the tertiary (e.g., Mainhard, Van der Rijst, Van Tartwijk, & Wubbels, 2009) and primary education levels (e.g., Zijlstra, Wubbels, & Brekelmans, 2010). Similarly, up to this point studies in Turkey have mainly been conducted in secondary school classes (e.g., Telli, 2006).

Hence, most QTI studies bring us information on the teacher-student relationship for one particular school type or moment in the educational career of students and do not allow for systematic evaluation of perceptions throughout the educational life of students. This prevents us from forming a comprehensive (e.g., student age-related) overview, or from explaining or interpreting changes throughout crucial phases, such as the transition from primary to secondary education. To obtain a complete understanding of teacher-student relationships, there is a need to study interpersonal relationships from very low grades through higher education grades.

In short, the present study may provide us with an opportunity to analyse QTI scale and dimension scores from the primary to the higher education level and to see how the validity and reliability of students' perceptions of their teachers' interpersonal behaviour differ between these educational levels. With this in mind, this study aimed to investigate the following research questions:

- To what degree were valid and reliable versions of the Turkish QTI developed for the three forms of education (primary, secondary and higher education)?
- How do students' perceptions of their teachers' interpersonal behaviour as measured within the three versions compare in terms of the scale and dimension scores?

THE TURKISH CONTEXT

Focusing on the three educational levels that are the focus of this study, the educational system in Turkey can be outlined as follows.[iv]

Primary education is compulsory for every child between the ages of seven to fourteen (grade 1-8), and enrolment of children at the nearest school to their home is the general rule. Student achievement in the first three grades of primary education is evaluated on the basis of classroom performance. The number of lessons (40-minute) in a week is 30 and 1080 in a year in primary education, so that the average number of lessons a day is 6. The official maximum number of pupils per class is 30 students. However, in practice the size of classes differs between 20 and 40 students. For grades 1 to 5, general classroom teachers are individually responsible for their classes. However, lessons in grades 6 to 8 and some subjects (e.g., physical training, music, art, foreign language) in grade 4 and 5 are delivered by subject teachers (field specialists). Pupils receive the primary education diploma upon successful completion of eight years of compulsory education. Repetition is possible for underachieving students.

Secondary education is provided in general, vocational and technical education institutions offering four years of education.

General secondary education is provided at Anatolian, science, multi-programs, foreign language-based, Anatolian teacher preparation, Anatolian fine arts, social science, and sports high schools (data for the secondary educational level of this study was collected at general secondary education institutions). Each school type has some key characteristics. Admission requirements for secondary schools depend on the particular type of school to which a student is applying. In the case of some privileged schools (they are generally categorized as Anatolian schools with more foreign language lessons, limited numbers of students in classrooms, etc.), students have to pass a centrally administrated entrance examination, the *Level Determination Examination (SBS)*. In general in secondary education schools the average number of weekly lessons in each grade ranges from a minimum of 30 hours to a maximum of 45. Progression to the next grade is based on students' performance in all courses or on the students' average annual level of attainment. Transfers between schools and programs from vocational to technical secondary education schools are possible. Students who have more than two report card grades for subjects below the required level for a sufficient score repeat the same grade. There is no national examination requirement to complete secondary education.

Higher Education institutions consist of universities, higher technology institutes and independent private (foundation) vocational higher education schools. For admission to undergraduate programs at a university, a secondary school diploma and a minimum set level of performance in the entrance exam (named Yükseköğretime Giriş Sınavı, YGS) is needed. The entrance examination is administered in a single session at the same time throughout Turkey (Eurydice, 2010). The Turkish university system consists of a bachelor and master phase, each consisting of a maximum of four years. After the master phase, a selected group of students might enter a PhD program. Universities in Turkey can range widely in size, while some are fairly small, other reach a population of over 50,000 students, depending on their location and the number of studies they offer.

Obviously, teaching in Turkey has some particular characteristics specific to the country (Telli, 2006). Turkish teachers generally enjoy a high status in Turkish society. Turkish teachers demonstrate strong leadership behaviour in the classroom and they are usually well prepared. Although conflicts and arguments are common from time to time, especially with older students and inexperienced teachers, teachers usually (are expected to) have the last word. Moreover, while maintaining high control and strength in their classrooms, teachers are expected to behave in a calm manner. Additionally, arguments are mostly concluded with an agreement between teacher and student(s) without taking much time. Teachers are expected to manage their classroom in a way that reduces disorder and the risk of burn-out (teachers) or school-leaving (students), to be well prepared for instruction and to evaluate students as neutrally as possible. Turkish teachers are usually the first person to be aware of the personal problems of their students. Students might directly ask for help, guidance or explain their problems to their teachers.

METHOD

Sample

The sample consisted of 1,751 students of 62 classes, ranging from grade 2 through the last grade in the Bachelor of Science in Bursa.[v] A total number of 626 (36%) students from primary education participated in the study, 875 (50%) students from secondary education (only from general high schools) and 250 (14%) students from higher education. Classes were distributed over the three educational levels as follows: 20 classes (32%) in primary education, 33 classes (53%) in secondary education and 9 classes (15%) in higher education. There were 905 female (52%) and 809 (46%) male students in the sample (37 students or 2% did not indicate their gender). Moreover, 17 primary school teachers (10 female), 16 secondary school teachers (8 female) and 4 instructors (2 female) participated. The samples chosen from the accessible population was a sample of convenience. Teacher participation was voluntary and teachers themselves selected the participating classes. School subjects varied between the subsamples. In primary education most teachers taught either all subjects (47%) or (just) language (26%); in secondary education data was collected in science classes (physics, chemistry, and biology); in higher education data was collected in one teacher education institute with several teacher education programs, namely pre-primary (12%), primary (62%) and science teacher education (26%). The data was collected between the academic years 2005 and 2008. For more detailed information about the sample, please see Table 1.

Instrumentation

All students responded to the *Questionnaire on Teacher Interaction* (QTI) administered at their educational level. The Turkish version of the QTI for secondary education was the first version developed (Telli, 2006). The development was a process involving several steps, such as translation and back-translation of the American version of the QTI by two experienced researchers, one English-as-a-Foreign Language (EFL) teacher educator and two EFL university experts; piloting the translated version with a small sample of teachers and students; adapting this piloted version by adding new items, based on interviews with teachers and students and piloting the adapted version in two subsequent rounds with groups of teachers and students (for a detailed description, see Telli et al., 2007).

The secondary education version of the QTI for the Turkish context formed the starting point for the development of the primary (Telli & Den Brok, 2008) and higher education versions (Telli & Den Brok, 2009) of the QTI. Adaptations of the instrument involved some similar steps for the primary (47 items) and higher education versions (60 items), such as adapting item language, piloting subsequent versions while refining the items, inserting expert ideas, conducting interviews with students and teachers or instructors. Students answered the questionnaire on a Likert-type 5-point scale. For the primary education version, a Likert-type 3-point scale with images (smilies) was used. Item distribution over the scales per version is given in Table 2, with the same sample items presented for the three versions.

Table 1. Students' distribution over gender, grade level, school and subjects in terms of percentages for the present study (n = 1751).

	Primary Education	Secondary Education (General high schools)	Higher Education
	$n = 626$ (36%)	$n = 875$ (50%)	$n = 250$ (14%)
Gender	-Female (49.7%) -Male (48.6%) -Missing (1.8%)	-Female (50,2%) -Male (47,2%) -Missing (2.6%)	-Female (62.0%) -Male (36.8%) -Missing (1.2%)
*School/ Institution	3 Schools 1st (28.1%) 2nd (36.7%) 3rd (35.1%)	5 Schools 1st (35.4%) 2nd (19.5%) 3rd (12.7%) 4th (21.5%) 5th (10.9%)	1 University 1 Education Faculty (100.0%)
No of Classes Class size	20 classes -Min 22 students -Max 41 students Mean=31.30; SD=1.43	33 classes -Min 12 students -Max 38 students Mean=26.52; SD=1.00	9 classes -Min 11 students -Max 40 students Mean=27.78; SD=3.50
*Grade level	-Grade2 (6.1%) -Grade4 (23.2%) -Grade5 (21.6%) -Grade6 (28.0%) -Grade7 (3.8%) -Grade8 (17.4%)	-Grade 9 (45.4%) -Grade10 (24.0%) -Grade11 (30.6%)	2nd year (61.2%) 3rd year (27.2%) 4th year (11.6%)

* Percentages given are within the educational level.

Analysis

To answer the research questions, a number of analyses were performed with SPSS. For the study, Cronbach's alpha coefficients were computed and established at the class level, since the QTI measures construct positioned at the class level, and QTI data is only included in subsequent analyses at this level (e.g., De Jong & Westerhof, 2001; Den Brok et al., 2006). In order to measure the ability of the QTI to differentiate between classes, Eta squared values (Eta^2) were computed. This statistic represents the ratio of 'between' to 'total' variance and is the proportion of variance in scale scores accounted for by class membership. To investigate construct validity of the three QTI versions, *exploratory* factor analyses were conducted on the (class-aggregated) scale scores in order to see if two dimensions were present and to check the structure of the data (Den Brok et al., 2006). Also, scale inter-correlation was computed (see Appendix 1). The MITB is theoretically linked to a particular branch of models named *Circumplex Models* and based on a specific set of assumptions. In this circular structure each scale has the highest correlation with its adjacent scale, yet this correlation gradually decreases as the scales move further away and has the strongest negative correlation with the opposing scale (Khine & Fisher, 2002).

Table 2. Number of items per scale and sample items for three versions of the QTI in the Turkish context.

Label	Scale	Sample item (examples are from secondary education version)	Number of items per scale		
			Primary	Secondary	Higher
DC	Leadership	This teacher talks enthusiastically about his/her subject.	5	8	8
CD	Helpful/ Friendly	This teacher is someone we can depend on.	6	8	8
CS	Understan- ding	If we have something to say, this teacher will listen.	7	8	8
SC	Student Freedom	This teacher lets us make jokes in the classroom.	7	6	6
SO	Uncertain	This teacher does not know what to do when we break a rule.	5	7	7
OS	Dissatisfied	This teacher thinks we do not know anything.	7	9	9
OD	Admonishing	This teacher is impatient.	4	8	8
DO	Strict	We are afraid of this teacher.	6	8	6
		Total number of items	47	62	60

As for the second research question, scale and dimension scores in terms of students (average) perceptions of their teachers' interpersonal behaviour were determined with descriptive analyses and graphical profiles (spider plots) were created with the Excel package from Microsoft Office. For this purpose, scale scores were linearly transformed to a score between 0 and 1. The data from three educational levels were then merged into one data file and the dimension scores (Influence and Proximity) were subjected to an analysis of variance (ANOVA) with a Scheffé-test for post-hoc differences to check whether there were statistical differences among the educational types or not. It should be taken into account that while the scales and dimensions scores were transformed such that they fitted the same range, the actual scores themselves were based on different numbers of items for each version (see Table 2). This can obviously in itself have led to (small) differences between versions.

RESULTS

Validity and Reliability of the Primary, Secondary and Higher Educational Turkish Versions of the QTI

The first research question concerned the degree of validity and reliability of the versions developed for primary, secondary and higher education. Table 3 provides the reliability of the QTI scales and the variance at the class level (Eta^2). As can be seen, Cronbach's alpha coefficient for the different QTI scales ranged from .76 to .92 for the primary education version, from .67 to .92 for the secondary education version, and from .69 to .95 for the higher education version. Cronbach's alpha was lowest for the student freedom scale for the three versions, which is in alignment with prior studies, where mostly the lowest reliability is reported for this scale (Den Brok et al., 2003). The results indicated that the different versions can be considered reliable, since all reliability coefficients were above the .60 level suggested by Nunnally (1978) and the .65 level suggested acceptable for research purposes by Wubbels, Créton, Levy, & Hooymayers, (1993). Nevertheless, the results from the student freedom scale should be interpreted with care. Percentages of variance (Eta^2) at the class level ranged between 0.16 and 0.31 for the primary education level; between 0.25.and 0.45 for secondary education; and between 0.06 and 0.20 for higher education. In all cases, the percentages of variance found at the class level were statistically significant. This suggests that the versions of the questionnaire were able to discriminate between classes.

An *exploratory* factor analysis was conducted on the (class-aggregated) scale scores in order to see if two dimensions were present in the data (Den Brok et al., 2006; Rickards, Den Brock, & Fisher, 2005). Inspection of the factor loadings (Table 4) suggested two dimensions that could be labelled in terms of Influence (Factor 2) and Proximity (Factor 1) for the secondary and higher education versions, but for the primary education version, 3 dimensions were found at the class level (Table 4). The first factor in the primary education set could be interpreted as a Proximity-like dimension, but factors 2 and 3 were less interpretable and seemed a mixture of Influence and Proximity.

Table 3. Reliability (alpha) of QTI scales at the class level and variance at the class level (Eta^2).

Label	Scale	Primary Alpha	Primary Eta^2	Secondary Alpha	Secondary Eta^2	Higher Alpha	Higher Eta^2
DC	Leadership	.83	.20	.83	.37	.84	.14
CD	Helpful/Friendly	.90	.18	.92	.29	.85	.09
CS	Understanding	.90	.20	.90	.25	.92	.10
SC	Student Freedom	.76	.26	.67	.33	.69	.17
SO	Uncertain	.90	.20	.93	.36	.95	.20
OS	Dissatisfied	.86	.16	.89	.30	.92	.13
OD	Admonishing	.92	.28	.87	.31	.87	.12
DO	Strict	.87	.31	.86	.45	.77	.06

Table 4. Exploratory factor loadings for three versions at class level.

Scale	Primary Factor 1	Primary Factor 2	Primary Factor 3	Secondary Factor 1	Secondary Factor 2	Higher Factor 1	Higher Factor 2
DC	.15	.41	.06	.21	.18	-.24	-.22
CD	.11	.32	-.17	.21	-.06	-.14	.11
CS	.08	.38	.09	.20	-.10	-.13	.13
SC	-.08	.04	.86	-.01	-.38	.18	.58
SO	.34	.01	-.29	-.20	-.21	.23	.20
OS	.26	-.07	-.14	-.20	.01	.20	.04
OD	.33	.12	.07	-.15	.19	.16	-.06
DO	.38	.22	.19	-.01	.39	-.04	-.45

Second, the assumption of two, independent interpersonal dimensions was tested by computing a correlation between the two dimension scores.[vi] No statistically significant correlation was found for the secondary education (0.20) and higher (0.55) education versions – although correlations were thus certainly not close to zero – but a statistically significant correlation was found for the primary education data (0.49), indicating association between the two dimensions. This finding does not converge with the theoretical assumptions behind the model.

Third, assumptions for the circumplex structure were studied by inspecting inter-scale correlations. Correlations between opposing scales should be most negative, while correlations between adjacent scales should be most positive and correlations should decrease in (equal) steps when moving from adjacent scales towards opposing scales (e.g., Gurtman & Pincus, 2000; Tracey, 1994). Correlation analyses showed that the circumplex assumption was violated most often with the primary education version. This disrupted pattern led to an uneven distribution of the scales over the circle (see the factor loadings in Table 4 for a confirmation of this process). Inter-scale correlations for the three versions are given in Appendix 1.

Students' Perceptions of Their Teachers' Interpersonal Behaviour in Terms of Scale and Dimension Scores

For the second research question, a descriptive analysis was performed to obtain the average scale scores in the sample (n = 1,751; classes = 62). The means for each of the QTI scales are provided in Table 5, while a graphical display is presented in Figure 2 (only for dimension scores). The results indicated that students generally perceived that their teachers displayed cooperative behaviours (leadership, helping/friendly, and understanding). The scores on these scales were similar to those found in other international studies and previous studies in Turkey (see Telli et al., 2007; Wubbels & Levy, 1993). Overall, the strict scale generally got a higher mean score compared to other countries, but it was similar to that in previous studies in Turkey (e.g., Telli, 2006). In general, Turkish students perceived their teachers as displaying both cooperative and dominant behaviours.

Table 5. Mean scores and standard deviations (SD) for the QTI scales and dimensions for the primary, secondary and higher educational level in the Turkish context (class level).

Label	Scale	Primary	Secondary	Higher
DC	Leadership	.94 (.03)	.75 (.09)	.73 (.06)
CD	Helpful/Friendly	.91 (.03)	.73 (0.8)	.75 (.05)
CS	Understanding	.95 (.03)	.77 (.07)	.79 (.05)
SC	Student Freedom	.68 (.05)	.55 (.07)	.69 (.05)
SO	Uncertain	.43 (.05)	.34 (.08)	.42 (.07)
OS	Dissatisfied	.47 (.05)	.41 (.07)	.42 (.05)
OD	Admonishing	.49 (.06)	.45 (.07)	.47 (.05)
DO	Strict	.65 (.05)	.59 (.10)	.49 (.03)
DS	Influence	.44 (.07)	.42 (.25)	.11 (.13)
CO	Proximity	1.03 (.16)	.74 (.31)	.79 (.23)

Scale scores can range between 0 and 1, dimension scores between –3 and +3.

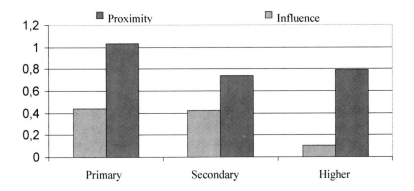

Figure 2. Graphical average of the interpersonal dimension scores for primary, secondary and higher education.

A test of differences (ANOVA) for the dimensions showed a statistically significant difference between groups for both the Influence (DS) dimension (F (2, 20) = 26,107; p = .00) and the Proximity (CO) dimension (F (2, 22) = 11,756, p = 0.00). A post-hoc Scheffé-test revealed that higher education students (Mean = .11) rated their teachers different from both primary (Mean = .44) and secondary (Mean = .42) education students (effect size 0.26) on the Influence dimension, while no differences existed between the latter two. As for Proximity, the post-hoc test also indicated that primary education students (Mean = 1.03) rated their teachers different than the other two educational levels, whilst there were no statistically significant differences between secondary (Mean = 0.74) and higher (Mean = 0.79) education students (effect size 0.22). For Proximity, primary education students thus rated their teachers higher than students from the other two education types, while for Influence the higher education students rated their teachers lower than students from the other two education types.

DISCUSSION

In this study the validity and reliability of the QTI versions for the primary, secondary and higher education context in Turkey were established. Besides this, students' perceptions of their teachers' interpersonal behaviour on the QTI scales and dimensions were described.

The outcomes of the first research question indicated that all QTI versions had satisfying reliability. Cronbach's alpha of the scales at the class level was close to .80 in all versions. Cronbach's alpha was the lowest for the student freedom scale for the three versions. Moreover, in the construction process of questionnaires (adaptation and development process), this scale took particular effort and attention; items were revised considerably during the pilots, especially for the primary education version. In other QTI studies the strict and student freedom scales are usually reported as having the lowest reliability (Den Brok et al., 2006), so our reported problems with reliability, but also those with validity are in that respect no surprise. It seems as if in particular these items and scales are culturally and context sensitive. In future studies particular attention should be given to item development for these scales and more qualitative studies could be conducted as to why these scales and items are so context and culture specific and why they have the inclination to disrupt the circumplex validity of the QTI. A comparison of the Eta-squared statistics of the three version of the QTI indicated that the instruments were able to distinguish between classes but that the primary and higher educational versions can be improved in this respect. However, considering the small sample size for the higher educational level (9 classes), outcomes for this level need to be interpreted with caution.

The QTI represented the MITB reasonably well in the secondary education and higher versions (two uncorrelated dimensions, factor analyses showing two factors that could be interpreted as Influence and Proximity). As for the primary education version, 3 instead of 2 factors (dimensions) were found in exploratory factor analyses, and factor loadings could not be interpreted in a straightforward manner. Only a Proximity dimension was clearly recognizable from the data. In addition, dimension scores were heavily correlated and scale correlation patterns violated the circumplex assumptions on several occasions for this version. Similar validity problems have been reported in other studies for lower age groups with the QTI as well (e.g., Kokkinos, Charalambous, & Davazoglou, 2009). These problems might arise due to young students' difficulties in distinguishing adults' behaviour (Dubow & Ullman, 1989; Lenske, Praetorious, & Helmke, 2010) or due to problems in mapping students' perceptions via questionnaires for students of this young age (Chambers & Johnston, 2002; Pianta, 1999; Pianta & Steinberg, 1992). It seems as if primary education students answer most of the QTI questions in terms of liking or disliking their teachers, and do not go much further. That is why future studies in primary education should collect more qualitative data, which might help researchers to understand what types of behaviours younger students may have difficulty with to perceive. The reliability and validity problems may have been connected to the answering scale, it may be that the three-point scale does not lead to sufficient differentiation in the primary school version as well, resulting in unexpected correlations. For the higher education version, an unexpected (high) correlation between the two dimensions was found as well. However, this correlation was not statistically significant, probably as a result of the small number of groups involved. Hence, it is unclear whether the correlation was a result of the wording of the items or the specific (small) sample in which it was tested. Future research on larger numbers of student groups could verify whether the higher education version is plagued by validity problems or not.

The results of the second research question suggest that students perceived their teachers in all educational contexts as *somewhat dominant* and *highly cooperative.* Especially primary school students perceived their teachers much more intensively on the Proximity dimension. Apart from the noted validity and reliability problems as well as the different numbers of items for the scales in the different versions, it is possible that younger students need more emotional and instructional support from their teachers and project these needs onto their perceptions. Obviously, this interpretation is highly speculative and further research could help to uncover this.

Primary school students perceived their teachers higher than secondary and higher education students on Proximity, while higher education students perceived their teachers lowest on Influence. One may wonder if these differences are age-based or if they are also associated with gender distribution of both teachers and students (which differs between levels) and the nature of the subject taught. Prior research has suggested that these variables also have an effect on students' perceptions (Levy, Den Brok, Wubbels, & Brekelmans, 2003).

In this study, all Turkish teachers were perceived higher on Influence and especially on Proximity compared to other countries. The findings were comparable to previous studies in Turkey, however (Telli, 2006). This highly cooperative rating for Turkish teachers can be a reflection of the fact that Turkey is a highly collective culture (Hofstede, 1991). This may have led to a stronger focus of Turkish students on their teachers' cooperative behaviours, but perhaps teachers may have also displayed more cooperative behaviours in their classrooms.

This study was subject to a number of limitations, which create new avenues for research. The first limitation is that background variables such as subject taught, class composition (like girl/boy ratio), student and teacher background characteristics (e.g., age, gender, etc.) were not included in the study. The second limitation of the study concerns the sampling process: in secondary education only science classes were included and in higher education only one educational faculty was included. In addition, all participating classes were chosen by the teachers or instructors. The third limitation of the study lies in measuring differences between levels; we do not know how teachers adapt their behaviour to student age across the educational levels. Future studies focusing on different age groups and allowing for more complex analyses are needed in this respect. Last, the validity and reliability issues mentioned with respect to the three versions make it difficult to actually compare the findings of the three versions (in addition to the use of different answering scales). It is not unlikely that these issues have affected the actual scale scores and variance within and between the three school types. It seems that (much) more work is needed in constructing valid and reliable versions of the QTI, in particular for the primary education context.

No other studies are known by the researchers describing students' perceptions on the QTI scales and dimensions throughout the entire educational career of students. The outcomes of this study only provide a preliminary picture. However, the study shows some interesting results and has brought forward new questions that deserve attention. Such as: "To what degree are differences in perceptions between schools levels/types age-based, context-based or instruction-based?"; "Is there a need to calibrate MITB for the different educational levels ?"; and "To what degree can younger students distinguish between interpersonal sectors and behaviours (as displayed in items) and what are the factors causing these difficulties?". Hence there is still a world open to explore!

APPENDIX 1

Scale-inter correlations of the QTI versions

Primary education

Scale* **	DC	CD	CS	SC	SO	OS	OD	DO
DC	1							
CD	.758**	1						
CS	.851**	.787**	1					
SC	-.212	-.423	-.214	1				
SO	-.408	-.490*	-.504*	.025	1			
OS	-.568**	-.572**	-.659**	.164	.686**	1		
OD	-.332	-.400	-.446*	.341	.695**	.722**	1	
DO	-.181	-.321	-.239	.373	.618**	.672**	.660**	1

Secondary education

Scale* **	DC	CD	CS	SC	SO	OS	OD	DO
DC	1							
CD	.735**	1						
CS	.689**	.918**	1					
SC	-.214	.287	.355*	1				
SO	-.853**	-.599**	-.566**	.363*	1			
OS	-.703**	-.761**	-.807**	-.041	.618**	1		
OD	-.321	-.664**	-.711**	-.351*	.465**	.642**	1	
DO	.335	-.168	-.257	-.741**	-.341	.144	.502**	1

Higher education Scale***	DC	CD	CS	SC	SO	OS	OD	DO
DC	1							
CD	.738*	1						
CS	.695*	.909**	1					
SC	-.032	.191	.259	1				
SO	-.885**	-.674*	-.714*	-.072	1			
OS	-.899**	-.901**	-.913**	-.151	.910**	1		
OD	-.740*	-.970**	-.949**	-.177	.725*	.921**	1	
DO	-.356	-.756*	-.729*	-.521	.284	.590	.650	1

* Correlations are significant at the 0.05 level (2-tailed).
** Correlations are significant at the 0.01 level (2-tailed).
*** DC (Leadership), CD (Helpful/Friendly), CS (Understanding),
SC (Student Freedom), SO (Uncertain), OS (Dissatisfied),
OD (Admonishing), DO (Strict).

NOTES

[i] The authors would like to thank the two anonymous reviewers of this chapter for their constructive comments. The authors would like to thank Ayfer Kaya for her support with collecting the data for this research over the years.

[ii] Recently, the wording of the dimensions and sectors has become focus of discussion. For a recent status on this issue, see the contribution by Wubbels et al., elsewhere in this book.

[iii] Dimension scores in most studies are reported on a range between -3 and + 3 and lie in most countries between 0 and .50.

[iv] More information about the educational system in Turkey can be assessed via Information on Education System and Policies in Europe (EURYDICE) web page.

[v] Bursa is the fourth largest city in Turkey (population over 2.5 million) and has 600 primary schools (321.920 students), 176 high schools (92 general high schools; 121.235 students), one university (42.443 students) is located in the city (Bursa Province, 2011).

[vi] Dimension scores were computed using theoretical (factor) values. The specific locations of sectors or scales on the two dimensions are as follows (the weights in the next two formulae represent goniometric positions): Influence = $(.92*DC) + (.38*CD) - (.38*CS) - (.92*SC) - (.92*SO) - (.38*OS) + (.38*OD) + (.92.*DO)$; Proximity = $(.38*DC) + (.92*CD) + (.92*CS) + (.38*SC) - (.38*SO) - (.92*OS) - (.92*OD) - (.38*DO)$.

REFERENCES

Becker, B. E. & Luthar, S. S. (2002). Social-emotional factors affecting achievement outcomes among disadvantaged students: Closing the achievement gap. *Educational Psychologist, 37*, 197-214.

Bursa Province (2011). Retrieved, March 13, 2011 from http://www.bursa.gov.tr/?sayfa=mymenu&-pid=59.

Chambers, C. T. & Johnston, C. (2002). Developmental differences in children's use of rating skills. *Journal Pediatric Psychology, 27*(1), 27-36.

Créton, H. & Wubbels, Th. (1984). *Order problems of beginning teachers* [in Dutch]. Utrecht: W. C. C.

Darling-Hammond, L. & McLaughlin, M. W. (1995). Policies that support professional development in an era of reform. *Phi Delta Kappan, 76*(8), 597-604.

De Jong, R. & Westerhof, K. J. (2001). The quality of student ratings of teacher behaviors. *Learning Environment* Research, *4*, 51-85.

Den Brok, P. J., Brekelmans, M., Levy, J., & Wubbels, Th. (2002). Diagnosing and improving the quality of teachers' interpersonal behaviour. *International journal of educational management, 16*(4), 176-184.

Den Brok, P., Fisher, D., Brekelmans, M., Rickards, T., Wubbels, Th., Levy, J., & Waldrip, B. (2003). *Students' perceptions of secondary teachers' interpersonal style in six countries: a study on the validity of the Questionnaire on Teacher Interaction.* Paper presented at the annual meeting of the American Educational Research Association, Chicago. ERIC document: ED475164.

Den Brok, P., Brekelmans, M., & Wubbels, Th. (2004). Interpersonal teacher behaviour and student outcomes. *School Effectiveness and School Improvement, 15*, 407-442.

Den Brok, P., Fisher, D., & Koul, R. (2005). The importance of teacher interpersonal behaviour for secondary science students in Kashmir. *Journal of Classroom Interaction, 40*, 5-19.

Den Brok, P., Brekelmans, M., & Wubbels, T. (2006a). Multilevel issues in studies using students' perceptions of learning environments: The case of the Questionnaire on Teacher Interaction. *Learning Environments Research, 9*(3), 199-213.

Den Brok, P., Fisher, D., Wubbels, T., Brekelmans, M., & Rickards, T. (2006b). Secondary teachers' interpersonal behaviour in Singapore, Brunei and Australia: A cross-national comparison. *Asia Pacific Journal of Education, 26*, 79-95.

Den Brok, P. J., Brekelmans, M., & Mainhard, T. (2010). The efect of students' perceptions of their teachers' interpersonal behaviour on their educational outcomes: A meta analysis of research with the Questionnaire on Teacher Interaction (QTI). *The International Conference on Interpersonal Relationships in Education (ICIRE)* (p. 21), April 28-29, 2010, Boulder, Colorado, USA.

Dubow, E. F. & Ullman, D. G. (1989). Assessing social support in elementary school children: The survey of children's social support. *Journal of Clinical Child Psychology, 18*, 52-64.

EURYDICE 2010 (The information network on education in Europe), *National Summary Sheets on Education Systems in Europe and ongoing reforms.* Retrieved, March 13, 2011 from http://eacea.ec.europa.eu/education/eurydice/eurybase_en.php#turkey.

Fisher, D. L., Fraser, B. J., & Wubbels, T. (1993). Interpersonal teacher behaviour and school climate. In T. Wubbels & J. Levy (Eds.), *Do you know what you look like? Interpersonal relationship in Education (*pp. 103-112). London: The Falmer Press.

Fraser, B. J. (1998). Science learning environments: Assessment, effects and determinants. In B. J. Fraser & K. G. Tobin (Eds.), *The international handbook of science education* (pp. 527-564). Dordrecht, The Netherlands: Kluwer Academic Publishers.

Gay, G. (2002). Culturally responsive teaching in special education for ethnically diverse students: Setting the stage. *Qualitative Studies in Education, 15*, 613-629.

Gumperz, J. J. (1982). *Discourse strategies.* London: Cambridge University Press.

Gurtman, M. B. & Pincus, A. L. (2000). Interpersonal adjective scales: confirmation of circumplex structure from multiple perspectives. *Personality and Social Psychology Bulletin, 26*, 374-384.

Guskey, T. R. (2002). Professional development and teacher change. *Teachers and Teaching: Theory and Practice, 8*(3), 381-391.

Hofstede, G. (1991). *Cultures and organizations: Software of the mind.* London: McGraw-Hill.

Jacobs, D. T. (2003). *Shifting attention from "discipline problems" to "virtue awareness" in American Indian and Alaska native education.* ERIC Document No. ED480732.

Khine, M. S. & Fisher, D. L. (2002). *Classroom environments, student attitudes and cultural background of teachers in Brunei.* Paper presented at the Annual Meeting of the American Educational Research Association, New Orleans, USA.

Kokkinos, M. C., Charalambous, K., & Davazoglou, A. (2009). Interpersonal teacher behaviour in primary school classrooms: A cross-cultural validation of a Greek translation of the Questionnaire on Teacher Interaction. *Learning Environment Research.* DOI 10.1007/s10984-009-9056-9, pp. 101-114.

Leary, T. (1957). *An interpersonal diagnosis of personality.* New York: Ronald-Press.

Levy, J., Den Brok, P., Wubbels, Th., & Brekelmans, M. (2003). Students' perceptions of interpersonal aspects of the learning environment. *Learning Environments Research, 6*, 5-36.

Lenske, G., Praetorious, A., & Helmke, A. (2010). Zur Validität von Schülerfeedback in der Primarstufe. Paper presented at *74. Tagung der Arbeitsgruppe für Empirische Pädagogische Forschung* (AEPF), 13-15. September 2010, am Institut für Erziehungswissenschaft der Friedrich-Schiller-Universität Jena, Jena, Germany.

Mainhard, T. (2009). *Time consistency in teacher-class relationships.* Utrecht: W.C.C.

Mainhard, T., Van der Rijst, R., Van Tartwijk, J., & Wubbels, T. (2009). A model for the supervisor-doctoral student relationship. *Higher education, 58,* 359-373.

Martin, A. J. & Dowson, M. (2009). Interpersonal relationships, motivation, engagement and achievement: Yields for theory, current issues and educational practice. *Review of Educational Research, 79*(1), 327-365.

Maulana, R., Opdenakker, M-C., Den Brok, P., & Bosker, R. (2011). Teacher-student interpersonal relationships in Indonesian secondary education: Profiles and importance to student motivation. *Asia Pacific Journal of Education, 31*(1), 22-49.

Nunnally, J. C. (1978). *Psychometric theory.* (2nd ed.). New York: McGraw Hill.

Ogbu, J. U. (1992). Understanding cultural diversity and learning. *Educational Researcher, 21,* 5-14.

Pianta, R. C. (1999). *Enhancing relationships between children and teachers.* Washington, DC: American Psychological Association.

Pianta, R. C. & Steinberg. M. S. (1992). Relationships between children and kindergarten teachers from the teachers' perspective. In R. C. Pianta (Ed.), *Beyond the parent: The role of other adults in children's lives* (pp. 61-80). San Francisco: Jossey-Bass.

Rickards, T., Den Brok, P., & Fisher, D. (2005). The Australian science teacher: A typology of teacher-student interpersonal behaviour in Australian science classes. *Learning Environments Research, 8,* 267-287.

Reid, A. C. (2007). *Teacher interpersonal behaviour: Its' influence on student motivation, self-efficacy and attitude towards science.* Unpublished doctoral dissertation, Curtin University of Technology, Perth, Australia.

Smithers, A. & Robinson, P. (2003). *Factors affecting teachers' decisions to leave the profession* (Research Report PR430). UK: Department of Education and Skills.

Tracey, T. J. (1994). An examination of complementarity of interpersonal behaviour. *Journal of Personality and Social Psychology, 67,* 864-878.

Telli, S. (2006). *Students' perceptions of their science teachers' interpersonal behaviour in two countries: Turkey and the Netherlands.* Unpublished doctoral dissertation, Middle East Technical University, Ankara, Turkey.

Telli, S. & Den Brok, P. J. (2008) *Primary school students' perceptions of their teacher's behaviour and Questionnaire on Teacher Interaction* [in Turkish]. Paper presented at VII. National Primary School Teaching Symposium, Çanakkale Onsekiz Mart University, Çanakkale, Turkey.

Telli, S. & Den Brok, P. J. (2009) *Turkish university students' perceptions of their lecturers' interpersonal behaviour.* Paper presented at the Biannual Meeting of European Association for Research on Learning and Instruction (EARLI), Amsterdam, The Netherlands.

Telli, S., Den Brok, P. J., & Cakiroglu, J. (2007). Students' perceptions of science teachers' interpersonal behaviour in secondary schools: Development of the Turkish version of the Questionnaire on Teacher Interaction. *Learning Environment Research, 10*(2), 115-129.

Van Tartwijk, J. (1993). *Sketches of teacher behaviour: The interpersonal meaning of non-verbal teacher behaviour in the classroom* [in Dutch]. Utrecht: W. C. C.

Van Tartwijk, J,. Den Brok, P., Veldman, I., & Wubbels, T. (2009). Teachers' practical knowledge about classroom management in multicultural classrooms. *Teaching and Teacher Education, 25,* 453-460.

Veenman, S. (1984). Problems of beginning teachers. *Review of Educational Research, 54,* 143-178.

Wubbels, Th. & Levy, J. (1991). A comparison of interpersonal behaviour of Dutch and American teachers. *International Journal of Intercultural Relationships, 15,* 1-18.

Wubbels, Th. & Levy, J. (1993). *Do you know what you look like?* London: The Falmer Press.

Wubbels, T., Créton, H., & Hooymayers, H. (1985). *Discipline problems of beginning teachers, interactional teacher behaviour mapped out.* Paper presented at the annual meeting of the American Educational Research Association, Chicago, IL.

Wubbels, T., Brekelmans, M., Créton, H., & Hooymayers, H. P. (1990). Teacher behaviour style and learning environment. In H. C. Waxman & C. D. Ellett (Eds.), *The study of learning environments, Volume 4* (pp. 1-12). Houston: University of Houston.

Wubbels, Th., Créton, H. A., & Hooymayers, H. P. (1992). Review of research on teacher communication styles with the use of the Leary model. *Journal of Classroom Interaction, 17*(1), 1-11.

Wubbels, Th., Créton, H. A., Levy J., & Hooymayers, H. P. (1993). The model for interpersonal teacher behaviour. In T. Wubbels & J. Levy (Eds.), *Do you know what you look like? Interpersonal relationships in education* (pp.13-28). London: The Falmer Press.

Wubbels, Th., Brekelmans, M., Den Brok, P., & Van Tartwijk, J. (2006). An interpersonal perspective on classroom management in secondary classrooms in the Netherlands. In C. Evertson & C. S. Weinstein (Eds.), *Handbook of classroom management: Research, practice and contemporary issues* (pp. 1161-1191). New York: Lawrence Erlbaum Associates.

Zijlstra, H., Wubbels, T., & Brekelmans, M. (2010). *Child perceptions of the child-teacher relationship and mathematical achievement: An interpersonal perspective on teaching early grade classrooms.* Paper presented at the International Conference on Interpersonal Relationships in Education (ICIRE), April 28-29, 2010, Boulder, Colorado, USA.

RIDWAN MAULANA, MARIE-CHRISTINE OPDENAKKER,
PERRY DEN BROK AND ROEL J. BOSKER[i]

13. TEACHER-STUDENT INTERPERSONAL RELATIONSHIPS DURING THE FIRST YEAR OF SECONDARY EDUCATION

A Multilevel Growth Curve Analysis

INTRODUCTION

Problems regarding absenteeism, school failure, disobedience and misbehaviour in the early years of secondary education are often associated with the drastic changes occurring in everyday's life of students during the critical transition from primary to secondary school (Hargreaves, Earl, & Ryan, 1996; Howard & Johnson, 2004). The culture of primary school focuses on providing caring and hospitable environments, offering a sense of belonging and sustaining cohesion to collective young individuals. In contrast, secondary school culture is directed to teaching specific subjects and differentiation of students based upon academic achievement leading to the construction of fragmented and isolated experiences (Howard & Johnson, 2004). Therefore, the two cultures set different expectations that should be met by students. Unfortunately, not all students can meet the expectations when entering the secondary school due to various reasons such as having low inhibitory control, externalizing problems, academic underachieving and experiencing harsher parents (Hughes, 2010).

Many students display a drop in motivation and engagement in learning after the transition from primary to secondary education (Opdenakker & Maulana, 2010) because transitions seem to facilitate stressful, yet excited moments for them (Johnstone, 2002). In effect, students' level of anxiety, emotional stability, confusion, hostility and disengagement during this transition may boost to a great extent (Howard & Johnson, 2004). In addition, students' enjoyment and pride tend to decrease (Ahmed, 2010) while students' boredom and anxiety tend to increase over time (Hill & Sarason, 1966; Zeidner, 1998). Differences in the culture of primary and secondary education are sometimes called in as a plausible explanation. There is also evidence for further decrease of motivation during the first year of secondary education (Opdenakker & Maulana, 2010) as well as for changes during the whole period of secondary education (Van der Werf, Kuyper, & Opdenakker, 2008). Although there is evidence that motivational and learning engagement problems are reported most frequently in vocational secondary education (e.g., Byrne, 1991; Creten, Lens, & Simons, 2001; Hastings, 1994;

T. Wubbels et al. (eds.), Interpersonal Relationships in Education, 207–224.

Olweus, 1993), this does not imply that higher ability tracks of secondary education do not suffer from student emotional and behavioural problems.

There are multiple factors determining students' performance. Teacher and student characteristics, together with other contextual aspects (e.g., school, parents, home, etc.) play roles in constructing unique and complex events during school periods. Nevertheless, research shows clearly that teacher variables, amongst other factors, are the most significant predictor of students' attitudes (Osborne, Simon, & Collins, 2003). Amidst other teacher characteristics, teacher-students relationships are argued to be one of the major factors determining students' success at schools (Anderman & Maehr, 1994; Guthrie & Wigfield, 2000; Speering & Rennie, 1996).

Previous studies have shown the importance of healthy teacher-student interpersonal relationships (TSIR) for student outcomes (e.g., Den Brok, Brekelmans, & Wubbels, 2004; Henderson, Fisher, & Fraser, 2000). However, little is known about the development of the TSIR during a school year. More in particular, developmental trends of the TSIR after the transition to secondary school have been neglected. In this study, the first year of secondary school is considered as the transitional year between primary and secondary education due to the fact that it is the initial year when students experience secondary education environments, which based on the literature reviewed above, are different from primary education environments.

Teacher-Student Interpersonal Relationships (TSIR)

Two basic approaches underlying the interpersonal perspective on teacher-student relationships are the Communication Systems Theory (Watzlawick, Beavin, & Jackson, 1967) and the Personality Theory of Leary (1957). According to the first approach, the teacher and students form a system in which actions of one part influence the others within the system in a reciprocal manner. The Personality Theory of Leary provides a base for studying interpersonal relationships of those involved in the system. Leary developed a circumplex model representing the most apparent traits of human nature. This circumplex model is a circular continuum of personality. It is formed from the intersection of two base axes called Power and Love, and offers a map of interpersonal traits. These two perspectives facilitated the construction of a diagnostic measure to study the TSIR based upon students' and teachers' perceptions throughout the world (see Wubbels & Brekelmans, 2005 for a review).

Derived from the theoretical frameworks mentioned, a Model for Interpersonal Teacher Behavior (MITB) was constructed. This model follows a circumplex model applying two orthogonal dimensions as identifiers of interpersonal behaviours called Influence and Proximity. These dimensions are independent to each other and assume that every individual's interpersonal behaviour shares the characteristics of both dimensions. Influence refers to behaviours that emphasize control relative to others, while Proximity represents behaviours underlining one's interpersonal bonds with others.

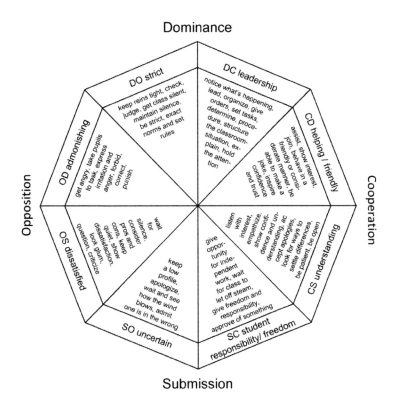

Figure 1. Model for Interpersonal Teacher Behaviour (Wubbels & Levy 1991).

For example, students having a drudging teacher are likely to experience chaotic and disorganized learning atmospheres in which the teacher is struggling really hard yet ineffectively to manage the classroom. In this case, students will perceive the teacher low on both Influence and Proximity dimensions. Teacher interpersonal behaviours differ considerably across cultures and are associated positively with student outcomes (see Brekelmans, Levy, & Rodriguez, 1993 for a review).

In the light of the importance of the TSIR for learning outcomes, it is essential to understand how the TSIR, particularly during and after the 'critical' transition moments, change and develop throughout time. Previous studies in secondary education have revealed that the quality[ii] of the TSIR decreases across school years (Brekelmans, 1989; Evertson & Veldman, 1981; Mainhard, 2009). However, we know very little concerning the development of the TSIR during the first year of secondary education. The present longitudinal study was conducted to add to the knowledge base by providing evidence from a specific context after the transition from primary to secondary education at the beginning of secondary education.

The general question is: How do the TSIR develop during the first year of secondary education? Particularly, how do class means of teacher Influence and Proximity develop across the first year of secondary education in mathematics and English as Foreign Language (EFL) classes? Based upon the literature reviewed above, we expect that there will be a general decline in teacher Influence and Proximity over time.

METHOD

Participants and Procedure

Participants were 566 students (310 boys, 250 girls, 6 unknown; age 11-13 years) from 20 mathematics and EFL classes of three schools in the Netherlands. The students were taught by eight mathematics and seven EFL teachers. A total of 458 students completed the questionnaires on all occasions; the rest completed the questionnaires on some of the four occasions because they were removed to other classes or were absent on the dates of data collection. 109 students of one school completed the questionnaires in the first and the last occasions only. About 60% of the classes were high ability tracks classes and 40% heterogeneous mixed ability classes.

The surveys were conducted during a school year. The research period lasted from the start of the new school year between September 2008 (after six weeks) and June 2009 (after 40 weeks). During this period, the QTI was repeatedly completed by students on four different occasions. Each questionnaire was put in an envelope and was distributed to the students in each class. Written instruction was provided and students were instructed by their mentors (homeroom teacher) to complete the questionnaires during mentor hours.

Measure

Teacher-student interpersonal relationships. A short version of the *Questionnaire on Teacher Interaction* (QTI; Den Brok, Brekelmans, & Wubbels, 2006) was used to examine students' perceptions of the TSIR. The measure consists of eight scales of 50-items provided on a *never* (1) to *always* (5) response.

In this study, reliabilities of the QTI ranged between .60 (Student Freedom) and .89 (Understanding) at the student level and .80 (Student freedom) and .97 (Uncertain) at the class level (Table 1). *Exploratory* factor analyses (PCA with varimax rotation) on one of the data gathering occasions revealed that two factors with an eigenvalue larger than one could be extracted. These two factors explained 87% of the variance in sector scores. Interpretation of the factor loadings suggested the existence of the two dimensions: Influence and Proximity.

The validity of the circular structure of the eight subscales of the four measurements was tested using a *confirmatory factor analysis* (with Mplus; Muthen & Muthen, 1999). Results of these analyses show that a perfect circumplex model (two dimensions with circular ordering of the scales) fits the data reasonably well (^{2}/df = 182.91/26 with p < .00). The Comparative Fit Index (CFI = .99) and Tucker Lewis Index (TLI = .97) show good fit. In addition, the Root Mean Square Error of Approximation (RMSEA = .06) and Standardized Root Mean Square Residual (SRMR = .003) suggest good fit between the data and the model. Unfortunately, it was not possible to establish validity across measurements, nor to compare differences between measurements due to the limited sample at the class level. However, we argue that because this perfect circumplex model fits the total data set reasonably well, it may also fit with each of the separate measurements within the data (if one or more than one measurements would be different in terms of validity or not fit to the data, overall model fit would not be good).

Table 1. Reliability of the QTI scales across measurements and mean scores.

Scale (sectors)	Time 1			Time 2		
	Student	Class	M	Student	Class	M
DC Leadership	.79	.93	.61	.81	.91	.61
CD Helpful/Friendly	.80	.89	.73	.86	.95	.68
CS Understanding	.85	.95	.70	.88	.96	.68
SC Student Freedom	.61	.83	.46	.60	.81	.47
SO Uncertain	.75	.91	.22	.84	.97	.28
OS Dissatisfied	.82	.95	.20	.88	.94	.26
OD Admonishing	.83	.94	.25	.85	.93	.32
DO Strict	.73	.87	.38	.70	.86	.39
DS Influence			.32			.25
CO Proximity			1.10			.89

Scale (sectors)	Time 3			Time 4		
	Student	Class	M	Student	Class	M
DC Leadership	.79	.94	.59	.81	.89	.53
CD Helpful/Friendly	.84	.95	.66	.87	.93	.59
CS Understanding	.87	.94	.64	.89	.95	.59
SC Student Freedom	.62	.89	.47	.60	.80	.49
SO Uncertain	.86	.98	.32	.82	.86	.38
OS Dissatisfied	.88	.96	.32	.85	.96	.37
OD Admonishing	.85	.95	.35	.85	.91	.40
DO Strict	.75	.91	.41	.72	.91	.43
DS Influence			.20			.10
CO Proximity			.70			.46

M = Mean. Dimension scores (DS, CO) are computed as follows (with the numbers before the scale labels representing the factor loadings): Influence = 0.92DC + 0.38CD – 0.38CS – 0.92SC – 0.92SO – 0.38OS + 0.38OD + 0.92DO; Proximity = 0.38DC + 0.92CD + 0.92CS + 0.38SC – 0.38SO – 0.92OS – 0.92OD – 0.38DO.

Results of descriptive analyses of both interpersonal dimensions show that, in general, teachers are moderately dominant and friendly/cooperative (Table 2). This finding is in line with previous findings of larger studies (e.g., Den Brok, 2001; Den Brok et al., 2004).

Table 2. *Descriptive statistics of teacher Influence and Proximity across measurements.*

	M	SD	Min	Max
Influence (DS)	.21	.24	-.28	1.08
Proximity (CO)	.77	.53	-.59	1.97
Measurements per class (Weeks)	16.75	13.11	0	35

Possible dimension scores were set to range between -3 and +3. The score ranges were given a meaning as follows: 0 – .5 (moderately positive), .5 – 1 (positive) and > 1 (very positive) (Den Brok et al., 2004)

Personal and contextual characteristics. Time was coded in accordance with the survey intervals (in weeks) as follows: 6 weeks, 16 weeks, 28 weeks, and 40 weeks. Class type was divided into two categories: Homogeneous and heterogeneous classes. A score of '0' was assigned to homogeneous classes (correspond to high ability tracks) in which all the students follow the same track. A score of '1' was assigned to heterogeneous classes (correspond to mixed ability tracks) in which the students follow a curriculum which does not differentiate yet between two tracks. Teacher and student gender were included in the analyses as dummy variables with '0' for males and '1' for females, and '0' for boys and '1' for girls respectively. In addition, subject taught was dummy coded with math as a baseline (= 0).

Data Analysis

Preliminary analyses were conducted to analyse general developmental trends of the TSIR and covariance stability over time. For these purposes, mean scores of each interpersonal dimension (at class level) were computed and average correlations between occasions were estimated. Furthermore, multilevel growth curve analyses (with MLwiN; Rasbash, Charlton, Browne, Healy, & Cameron, 2005) were applied to the data. The models were built based on two-level hierarchical data with measurement occasions as level 1 and class as level 2. Subsequently, two models consisting of Influence and Proximity were estimated with maximum likelihood estimation. As suggested by Rasbash, Steele, Browne and Goldstein (2009), we tested several models in a stepwise manner in order to find the most representative description of the data. Accordingly, components representing linear (a model describing steady positive or negative growth) and polynomial (a model illustrating de- or accelerated growth) terms were examined. Additional components describing changes across time that might improve the fit between model and data were investigated. Finally, personal and contextual characteristics were added to the model. In the final model, only significant predictors at $p < .05$ (personal characteristics) and $p < .10$ (contextual characteristics) were retained. Non-significant predictors were removed stepwise from the model starting from the highest to the lowest p values. The fixed effects in the model were tested by using t-ratio coefficients, considering that an absolute t-value should be greater than 1.96 ($p < .05$, personal characteristics) or 1.64 ($p < .10$, contextual characteristics) for a significant effect of a variable (Snijders & Bosker, 1999).

RESULTS

Preliminary Analyses

The description of the development of teacher Influence and Proximity at class, student and subject levels are provided. Figure 2 describes the general raw trajectories of both interpersonal dimensions based on student perceptions throughout the school year.

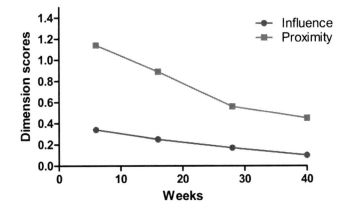

Figure 2. General trajectories of Influence and Proximity based on student perceptions (raw scores) over time.

After six weeks of the school year, students generally perceive their teachers as moderately dominant and very friendly/cooperative. During a school year, students' scores on both dimensions show considerable decrease and continue to decline until the end of the school year. Noticeably, the decrease for Proximity is more remarkable than that for Influence, placing the teachers from very friendly/cooperative to moderately friendly/cooperative. In general, there seems to be a continuous decrease in teacher Influence and Proximity across the school year.

To get an idea of the changes in both dimensions of individual classes, see Figure 3. The figure shows that the intercepts (e.g., initial class perceptions of teacher Influence and Proximity after six weeks) differ clearly across classes for both dimensions.

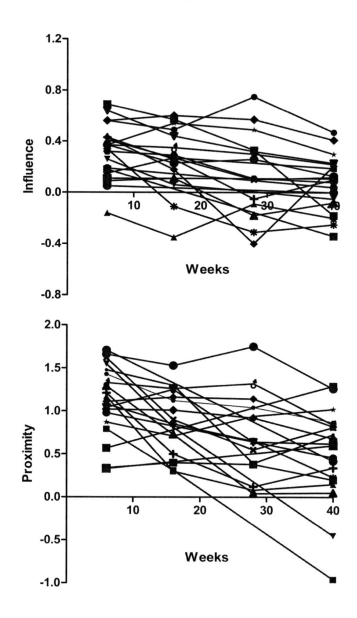

Figure 3. General trajectories of Influence and Proximity based on class perceptions (raw scores) over time.

The differences in trajectories are also noticeable. The trajectories for proximity show a more dispersed pattern than those for Influence. Nevertheless, the paths of the development for both dimensions at this stage are not clear yet; some classes show decreasing trajectories, while others fluctuate.

Regarding the two subjects, the results show that there are general declining patterns across the school year for both dimensions (see Figure 4). Furthermore, there are some small differences between the trajectories of both subjects, while for Proximity the decline is most pronounced for all teachers. With regard to Influence, mathematics teachers display a slightly lower degree of dominance than EFL teachers after six weeks of the school year, then start to increase after 15 weeks and decrease at the end of the school year.

In terms of covariance stability, moderate correlations across measurements for both dimensions are found (mean r Influence = .36; mean r Proximity = .46; Table 3). These rather moderate correlations indicate differences regarding students' perceptions of their teacher interpersonal behaviour across measurement occasions; the smaller the r values are, the more students perceive their teachers different from time to time. In this study, the correlations between measurement occasions are relatively heterogeneous. The longer the distance between the measurement occasions, the lower the correlations are.

Overall, the results of the preliminary analyses suggest that there seem to be systematic changes with respect to mean scores of both Influence and Proximity, with declining trends, throughout the school year. In addition, the covariance stability of students' ratings is moderate across measurements, indicating that students' perceptions of teacher interpersonal behaviour seem to change from time to time during their interactions with their teachers.

Multilevel Growth Curve Analyses

Results of multilevel analyses, including class at level 2 and time at level 1, are presented in Table 4. Normality and linearity assumptions were checked with plots of the standardized residuals against normal score: These plots conform closely to straight lines. Hence, the assumptions are adequately met.

The development of teacher Influence and Proximity across time for class data is adequately represented by linear growth terms. Additional analyses revealed that it was not necessary to include polynomial terms in the model. This suggests that there is no evidence regarding de- or acceleration of growth in both dimensions. Although the effect of time on both dimensions is rather modest, it is statistically significant (Influence: -.01; Proximity: -.02 on a score running from -3 to 3), which is most pronounced for Proximity. It seems that both dimensions are relatively stable, but show a continuous linear declining trend over time. Class type can explain differences between classes in both Influence and Proximity, but gender of the teacher and the subject taught cannot. On average, students in homogeneous classes (high ability track) tend to rate teachers lower on both dimensions than heterogeneous classes (mixed ability track). The interaction effect

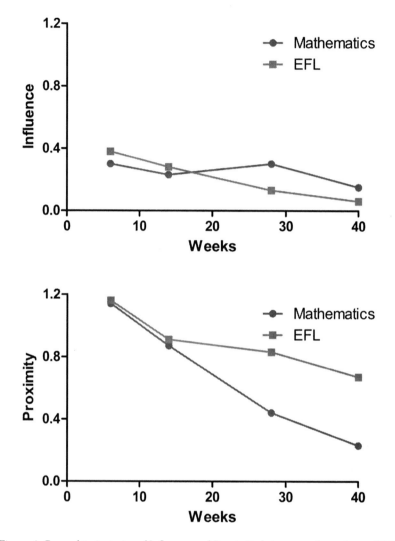

Figure 4. General trajectories of Influence and Proximity between mathematics and EFL classes (raw scores) over time.

Table 3. Correlations between ratings for Influence (upper right part) and Proximity (lower left part) over time (student perceptions).

Week	6	16	28	40
6	-	.42	.37	.16
16	.56	-	.50	.29
28	.39	.68	-	.40
40	.22	.33	.60	-

Table 4. Best fitting multilevel models of the growths of teacher Influence and Proximity based on class perceptions over time.

Variable	Influence ($n = 67$)		Proximity ($n = 67$)	
	Coefficient	SE	Coefficient	SE
Fixed effect				
Intercept	-.1973	.2379	.9941	.3674
Time (line)	-.0070*	.0014	-.0145*	.0035
Class type	.2520*	.0894	.2740*	.1381
Subject taught	.0137	.0841	-.1442	.1299
Teacher gender	.0766	.0901	-.1026	.1391
Time x Class type	-.0052*	.0026	.0020	.0071
Random effect				
Level 2 variance (Class)				
Intercept	.0183	.0118	.0857	.0406
Time (line)	.0009	.0016	.0002	.0001
Intercept x Time (line)	-.0003	.0003	-.0013	.0015
Level 1 variance (Time)				
Residual	.0221	.0058	.0539	.0139
Deviance (-2 x loglikelihood)	-30.3719		45.6077	
Decrease in deviance compared to model with time as fixed effect.	2.7; $df = 2$; $p < .273$		26.01; $df = 2$; $p < .011$	

* $p < 0.05.$

between time and class type for Influence is significant but not for Proximity. This implies that the effect of time in Influence is different between class types. In heterogeneous classes, the decline in Influence is more pronounced compared to homogeneous classes. Across the school year (40 weeks), the decrease in Influence score is about half a range (-.28), while the decrease in Proximity is more than a range (-.60).[iii] This means that, in general, the score in the Influence dimension drops from moderately positive to neutral or moderately negative and the score on Proximity from positive to moderately positive.

Concerning the random effect of time, the results show that the decrease in deviance for Influence is not significant. This suggests that there seem to be very small systematic variations between the linear growth of Influence associated with different classes. Hence, the strength of the decline seems to be about similar for all classes. This can be seen in the between class variation in the linear effect of time (*SD* Influence is almost close to zero). In contrast, variances in intercept and slope for Proximity are significant. This means that there are systematic variations between the linear growth of Proximity in different classes. Thus, the strength of the decrease over time differs between classes.

The covariance term (reflecting the association between the intercept of each class and slope) indicates a weak correlation for Proximity ($r = -.32$). Adding a random linear model has absorbed residual related to time in both dimensions, reducing from .03 to .02 for Influence, and from .11 to .06 for Proximity. These changes are rather small. Hence, there seems to be no indication that variation in the slope of random linear growth components accounts for some of the within-classes variation in times. This suggests that introducing the linear effect of time to vary across classes in the model is not necessary. The best-fitted model shows that the proportion of variance explained at the class level is 9% (Influence) and 16% (Proximity), while the proportion of variance located at the occasion level is 13% (Influence) and 16% (Proximity).

In Figure 5, intercepts (class perceptions after six weeks of secondary education) and linear growths of all classes across the first school year are provided based on the best-fitted multilevel models for Influence and Proximity. All 20 classes are ranked concerning the extent to which they deviate from the average means of Influence and Proximity. Every vertical line refers to the deviation of each class with an error bar ($\pm$ 1.96 standard errors). Overall, classes differ more in their intercept than in their growth curve for Influence, while for Proximity, there seems to be no clear differences between class intercepts and their linear growth across the school year.

In terms of Influence, 13 out of 20 classes are located within the confidence interval of the mean intercept. The remaining classes lie at the opposite ends of the plot for which the 95% confidence interval does not include the mean intercept of the sample. One class begins with lower than average values of Influence, whilst five classes start with higher than average values of the same dimension. Therefore, there are differences between classes with regard to their TSIR at the moment of the first measurement. The average decrease of the linear growth in Influence comprises the confidence interval of all classes, since all class values are all in the range of the overall mean. This means that classes differ not that much with regard to the change of the quality of TSIR in terms of Influence.

For Proximity, the mean intercept of the total sample is included for about 18 out of the 20 classes. Only one class is located at each opposite ends of the graph. This means that most of the classes do not differ much with regard to the initial Proximity level of their teachers, but some of the them do: One class scored significantly higher and one class significantly lower than most of the classes. The

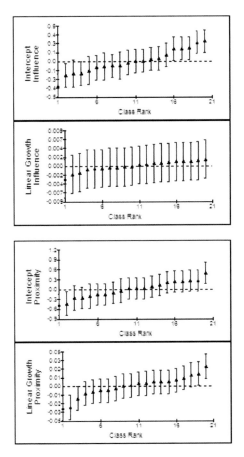

Figure 5. Classes rank regarding differences of Influence and Proximity; vertical lines refer to the deviation from the overall mean of a single class with 80% confidence interval. Intercept reflects between class variation in intercept and Linear Growth represents the between class variation in the linear growth of Influence and Proximity.

average linear growth (e.g., the decrease) consists of the confidence interval of 17 classes. One class shows a significantly more negative decline than the average sample, while two classes display a significantly smaller trend than the average decline. Hence, a relatively moderate decline seems to be the prevailing tendency for both Influence and Proximity.

DISCUSSION

In the present study, the development of the TSIR throughout the first year of secondary education was investigated. Multilevel growth curve modelling was applied to four repeated measures data in mathematics and EFL classes. The

219

developmental trends of teacher Influence and Proximity were examined. Interpersonal teacher behaviour was assessed through estimating student perceptions of teacher Influence and Proximity.

Consistent with our expectation, the present study showed that the level of teacher Influence and Proximity decreased during the first grade of secondary school. There was an indication that students perceived their teachers rather differently at start of the first grade than at the end of the first grade, with a deteriorating pattern over time. It seemed that the quality of the TSIR was more favourable at the beginning of the school year, and became systematically less positive towards the end of the school year. This finding is in accordance with previous studies regarding the development of classroom environments (e.g., Brekelmans, 1989; Evertson & Veldman, 1981; Mainhard, 2009). This study also showed that there is a weak relationship between the class perceptions of teacher Proximity and the decrease of Proximity over time. Since the literature shows that the higher the degree of teacher Influence and Proximity, the better the classroom quality seems to be (Brekelmans & Wubbels, 1991; Den Brok et al., 2004; Wubbels & Brekelmans, 2005) and the more supportive teachers are, the more confident students will likely to be (Ahmed, 2010), the findings of the present study can be seen as a caveat for current classroom environments, since current classroom environments tend to loose quality and, perhaps, that has a baleful influence on the confidence of students.

This study also revealed that being in homogeneous and heterogeneous classes could predict part of the class perceptions on the TSIR across the school year. In general, homogeneous classes rated the TSIR lower on both dimensions than did heterogeneous classes. Additional analyses revealed that student gender could also explain differences in the TSIR.[iv]

The fact that the quality of the TSIR declined over time needs further attention. Why does the level of Influence and Proximity decrease over time? In addition, our data showed that there is a week tendency that the higher the students rated teacher Proximity in the beginning of the school year, the faster the subsequent decrease was. This suggests that the tension between teacher and class seems to increase over time, resulting in systematic negative changes in student perceptions. Mainhard (2009) argued that all negative events (e.g., conflicts), as well as positive events, happening during interactions might be a determinant for students' perceptions that can be self-escalated across time. Hence, it seems possible that students experienced conflicts during the school year that determined their response subsequently. One example is when a teacher had high expectations that could be shown by the tendency of giving students difficult tests, and subsequently giving low grades. Quite frequently, giving low grades is associated with teacher hostility. Hence, the tendency of giving low grades may explain why the decrease in teacher Proximity already appeared after more than six weeks of interaction because during this period, exams or tests already took place.

In addition, it is noteworthy to mention the possibility of a 'favourite teacher' effect on student responses. This effect seems to appear when students have sufficient experience with multiple teachers. Once students decide the most favourite teacher for themselves, the ratings for other teachers are likely to be underestimated. This is related to the nature of secondary education context which facilitates fragmented and isolated experiences. Patrick, Turner, Meyer, and Midgley (2003) asserted that the first impression a teacher makes can greatly determine the subsequent student perceptions. However, this argument seemed to be ruled out in our findings.

Hughes (2010) argued that predictors of positive teacher-student relationships can be seen from student characteristics such as academic competence and self regulation as well as teacher characteristics such as confidence and level of stress/depression. When negative trends of teacher-student relationships are found, it might be due to the deterioration of teacher provision of autonomy, structure and involvement supports across the school year (Skinner & Belmont, 1993). However, future research is needed to shed lights on this issue.

Although there is no ground to suggest that students' report on both dimensions at the beginning of the year is erroneous, we may argue the assumption that it is accurate. It seems reasonable to argue that students' ratings during the initial school year might not exactly be truthful because their ratings were heavily influenced by their elementary school experience. Thus, students tended to 'judge a book from its cover'. Besides, the initial interaction moments could be considered as 'getting to know each other' period where teachers might not show their actual behaviour (yet). Hence, students' ratings at the beginning might have resulted from their unrealistic perceptions in connection with prior elementary school experience.

Interestingly, the more students experienced interactions with teachers, the worse they rated their teacher's Influence and Proximity. This implies that across the school year, there were (problematic) events occurring in the classroom that affected changes in students' perceptions of the TSIR. It is a challenge for future research to identify various events in the classroom that might explain negative (and positive) changes in students' perceptions of the TSIR. However, it might also be that students were influenced by 'gut feelings' phenomena; students may have tended to rate their teachers less positive based upon their common sense or intuitive feelings instead of realistic observed behaviour.

The present study suffers from several limitations. First, this study is limited to the domain of mathematics and EFL, which prevents direct generalization to other subjects. Nonetheless, given the assumption that interpersonal behaviours are more person- than subject-specific related, our focus on these particular subjects is legitimate.[v] In addition, the average ratings on both dimensions found in this study were comparable to previous large-scale studies (e.g., Den Brok et al., 2006).

Second, Singer and Willet (2003) argued that the more measurement occasions we include, the more accurate the power to detect the effects is likely to be. Hence, the inclusion of merely 20 classes and four measurement occasions within a year may hamper the functional form of growth that can be investigated. Future research should incorporate more time points and a more year-to-year developmental investigation to capture changes at a more micro level and to obtain more representative estimates of changes of Influence and Proximity over time. In addition, incorporating teacher perceptions can be of value-added to the knowledge base. However, given the idea that student perceptions tend to stabilize after a few months of interactions (e.g., Brekelmans, 1989; Neill, 1991; Skinner & Belmont, 1993), our study has contributed to adding the knowledge base that a systematic decline is noticeable across the first school year.

Third, testing effects might have appeared in the present study. This implies that the repeated measures design might have affected students' responses across times. Nevertheless, this can be expected considering the longitudinal design we employed and thus distributing the same questionnaires every three months in a year might impose a moderate degree of students' response stability. The relatively small values of estimated correlation coefficients may reveal a problematic predictive validity of the measure over time, indicating that the developmental trends over time may also be attributed to the fact that students were not completely able to generate valid data about the interpersonal relationship of their teachers. However, there is a clear tendency that ratings with closer time intervals correlate stronger than ratings with higher time intervals. This suggests evidence for systematic changes over time. Furthermore, the fact that the highest scores decrease most could be, to some extent, caused by a regression toward the mean effect. However, we should remember that this tendency was only found with regard to Proximity. In addition, if the trajectories of the TSIR suggest a regression to the mean, then we might expect that the standard deviation would be much smaller at a later moment in time. Nevertheless, we warn against broader generalizations of the findings, before replications of similar studies are available.

The present research adds to the knowledge base by providing the finding from the first year of secondary education context that the quality of teacher-student relationships seemed to decrease over time. Even more striking, this finding was drawn from schools offering higher levels of academic tracks rather than more vocational loads. We could expect that because of the level of the students, the TSIR stayed at a higher level. Research has established that personal characteristics of student groups have also an influence on the teacher (and his/her behaviour). For example, Skinner and Belmont (1993) discovered that students who showed higher initial behavioural engagement received subsequently more of autonomy support, structure and involvement of the teacher. In addition, Opdenakker and Van Damme (2006) found that the average cognitive level of the students in the classroom and the achievement motivation level of the class affect the learning climate in the class.

The described developmental trend helps us identify the critical moments of interactions that need to be focused on for further investigation and intervention studies. Moreover, this study provides a starting point to shed light on what is happening in first grade classrooms after the transition from primary to secondary education; why do teacher-student interpersonal relationships tend to decrease over time? What are factors triggering these changes to happen and what are effects of this deteriorating quality of the TSIR on student motivation and academic achievement across the school year? The answers to these questions are worth-investigating to inform schools and educators for improving the quality of learning environments for better student outcomes.

NOTES

[i] The authors would like to thank the editors and the two anonymous reviewers for their constructive feedback on the previous draft of this article. This study was part of the PhD project of the first author, while the second author received a grant from Rosalind Franklin Fellowships (University of Groningen, The Netherlands).

[ii] The quality of interpersonal relationships refers to the degree of teacher Influence and Proximity based on previous studies: The higher the Influence and Proximity, the better the student outcomes, suggesting a better quality of interpersonal relationships (e.g., Brekelmans, 1989; Evertson & Veldman, 1981).

[iii] According to possible range of dimension scores given by Den Brok et al. (2006; one range equals to 0.5 interval, see Table 2).

[iv] The effect of student gender on the TSIR was found when analysing the TSIR at the student level data. Since the focus of this article is on class level data, readers interested more in depth in student data can contact the first author for further information.

[v] We found no differences regarding the direction of developmental trends in both subjects.

REFERENCES

Ahmed, W. (2010). *Expectancy-value antecedents and cognitive consequences of students' emotions in mathematics.* Unpublished doctoral dissertation, Groningen University, Groningen.

Anderman, E. M. & Maehr, M. L. (1994). Motivation and schooling in the middle grades. *Review of Educational Research, 64,* 287-309.

Brekelmans, M. (1989). *Interpersonal teacher behavior in the classroom* [in Dutch]. Utrecht: W. C. C.

Brekelmans, M. & Wubbels, T. (1991). Student and teacher perceptions of interpersonal teacher behavior: A Dutch perspective. *The Study of Learning Environments, 5,* 19-30.

Brekelmans, M., Levy, J., & Rodriguez, R. (1993). A typology of teacher communication style. In T. Wubbels & J. Levy (Eds.), *Do you know what you look like?* (pp. 46-55). London: The Falmer Press.

Byrne, B. M. (1991). Burnout: Investigating the impact of background variables for elementary, intermediate, secondary and university educators. *Teaching and Teacher Education, 7*(2), 197-209.

Creten, H., Lens, W., & Simons, J. (2001). The role of perceived instrumentality in student motivation. In A. Efklidees et al. (Eds.), *Trends and prospects in motivation research,* (pp. 37-45). Dordrecht: Kluwer Academic Publishers.

Den Brok, P. (2001). *Teaching and student outcomes. A study on teachers' thoughts and actions from an interpersonal and a learning activities perspective.* Utrecht: W.C.C.

Den Brok, P., Brekelmans, M., & Wubbels, T. (2004). Interpersonal teacher behavior and student outcomes. *School Effectiveness and School Improvement, 15,* 407-442.

Den Brok, P., Brekelmans, M., & Wubbels, T. (2006). Multilevel issues in studies using students' perceptions of learning environments: The case of the Questionnaire on Teacher Interaction. *Learning Environment Research, 9,* 199-213.

Evertson, C. M. & Veldman, D. J. (1981). Changes over time in process measures of classroom behavior. *Journal of Educational Psychology, 73*(2), 156-163.

Guthrie, J. T. & Wigfield, A. (2000). Engagement and motivation in reading. In M. L. Kamil, P. B. Mosenthal, P. D. Pearson, & R. Barr (Eds.), *Handbook of reading research, Volume III* (pp. 403-422). New York: Erlbaum.

Hargreaves, A., Earl, L., & Ryan, J. (1996). *Schooling for change: Reinventing education for early adolescents.* London: Falmer Press.

Hasting, N. (1994). Enhancing motivation in the classroom: Strategies for intervention. *Educational and Child Psychology, 11*(2), 48-55.

Henderson, D., Fisher, D. L., & Fraser, B. J. (2000). Interpersonal behavior, laboratory learning environments, and student outcomes in senior biology classes. *Journal of Research in Science Teaching, 37,* 26-43.

Hill, K. T. & Sarason, S. B. (1966). The relation of test anxiety and defensiveness to test and school performance over the elementary-school years. *Monographs of the Society for Research in Child Development, 31*(2), 1-76.

Howard, S. & Johnson, B. (2004, November). *Transition from primary to secondary school: Possibilities and paradoxes.* Paper presented at AARE International Education Research Conference, Melbourne.

Hughes, J. N. (2010, March). *Students' social and academic lives: Related spheres of influence.* Paper presented at ISED Caring and Teaching Symposium, Amsterdam.

Johnstone, K. (2002, December). *The transition to high school: A journey of uncertainty.* Paper presented at the Association for Active Educational Researchers, Australia.

Leary, T. (1957). *An interpersonal diagnosis of personality.* New York: Ronald-Press.

Mainhard, T. (2009). *Time consistency in teacher-class relationships.* Unpublished doctoral dissertation. Utrecht University, Utrecht.

Muthen, L. K. & Muthen, B. O. (1999). *Mplus users' guide: The comprehensive modeling program for applied researchers.* Los Angeles: Muthen and Muthen.

Neill, S. (1991). *Classroom nonverbal communication.* London: Routledge.

Olweus, D. (1993). *Bullying at school.* Cambridge, UK: Blackwell.

Opdenakker, M.-C. & Van Damme, J. (2006). Teacher characteristics and teaching styles as effectiveness enhancing factors of classroom practice. *Teaching and Teacher Education, 22*(1), 1-21.

Opdenakker, M.-C. & Maulana, R. (2010, April). *Teacher-student relationships and academic engagement: How do they develop and link?* Paper presented at the International Conference on Interpersonal Relationships in Education, Boulder, Colorado.

Osborne, J., Simon, S., & Collins, S. (2003). Attitudes towards science: A review of the literature and its implications. *International Journal of Science Education, 25*(9), 1049-1079.

Patrick, H., Turner, J. C., Meyer, D. K., & Midgley, C. (2003). How teachers establish psychological environments during the first days of school: Associations with avoidance in mathematics. *Teachers College Record, 105*(8), 1521-1528.

Rasbash, J., Charlton, C., Browne, W. J., Healy, M., & Cameron, B. (2005). *MLwiN Version 2.0.* Centre for Multilevel Modeling, University of Bristol.

Rasbash, J., Steele, F., Browne, W. J., & Goldstein, H. (2009). *A users' guide to MLwiN (Version 2.10).* Centre for Multilevel Modeling, University of Bristol.

Singer, J. D. & Willet, J. B. (2003). *Applied longitudinal data analysis.* Oxford: Oxford University Press.

Skinner, E. A., & Belmont, M. J. (1993). Motivation in the classroom: Reciprocal effects of teacher behavior and student engagement across the school year. *Journal of Educational Psychology, 85*(4), 571-581.

Snijders, T. A. B., & Bosker, R. J. (1999). *Multilevel analysis: An introduction to basic and advanced multilevel modeling.* London: Sage Publishers.

Speering, W. & Renie, L (1996). Students' perceptions about science: The impact of transition from primary to secondary school. *Research in Science Education, 26,* 283-289.

Van der Werf, M. P. C., Kuyper, H. & Opdenakker, M. C. (2008). Testing a dynamic model of student and school effectiveness with a multilevel growth curve approach. *School Effectiveness and School Improvement, 19*(4), 447-462.

Watzlawick, P., Beavin, J. H., & Jackson, D. (1967). *The pragmatics of human communication.* New York: Norton.

Wubbels, T. & Brekelmans, M. (2005). Two decades of research on teacher-student relationships in class. *International Journal of Educational Research, 43,* 6-24.

Wubbels, T. & Levy, J. (1991). A comparison of interpersonal behavior of Dutch and American teachers. *International Journal of Intercultural Relations, 15,* 1-18.

Zeidner, M. (1998). *Test anxiety: The state of the art.* New York, USA: Plenum Press.

THEO WUBBELS, MIEKE BREKELMANS, PERRY DEN BROK,
JACK LEVY, TIM MAINHARD AND JAN VAN TARTWIJK

14. LET'S MAKE THINGS BETTER

Developments in Research on Interpersonal Relationships in Education

INTRODUCTION

Philips, the Dutch multinational, had as its mission until 2004 "Let's make things better". We chose this sentence as the title of our contribution to this book because despite considerable progress in the study of interpersonal relationships in education during the last two decades, a great deal of work remains. Two topics are particularly relevant. First, further development is needed on the theoretical basis of the Model for Interpersonal Teacher Behaviour and the instrument based on this model, the Questionnaire for Teacher Interaction (QTI; Wubbels, Brekelmans, Den Brok & Van Tartwijk, 2006). Second, attention is needed for the search for (causal) relationships between moment-to-moment interactions in the classroom and the patterns of interpersonal relationships between teacher and students. The first is a *sine qua non* for sustainable progress in the field and the development towards a more parsimonious model. The second will advance progress in providing formative guidance and professional development to teachers in pre and in-service programmes.

This chapter will first summarise the original presentation of the Model for Interpersonal Teacher Behaviour and the QTI. It reflects on some problematic issues, including: the use of eight scales of the QTI versus the two dimensions underlying the model, the model's graphic representation, the names for its dimensions and scales, and the difficulties when translating the QTI to different languages. The chapter then analyses our research on moment-to-moment interactions and teacher-students relationships. Recommendations for improvement and future research as well as references to other chapters in this volume are provided.

THE MODEL FOR INTERPERSONAL TEACHER BEHAVIOUR

An Interpersonal Perspective on Teaching

Throughout the past three decades our overriding aim has been to improve teacher education by building a knowledge base about effective learning environments. Within this domain we have focused our research on the role of the teacher in the classroom social climate. Naturally, a variety of perspectives have been employed in the study of teaching, including views of effectiveness based on methodology,

T. Wubbels et al. (eds.), Interpersonal Relationships in Education, 225–249.

discourse, moral positions and orientations toward gender and ethnic diversity. Because of our belief in the importance of human relationships we have chosen to analyse the field from an interpersonal perspective that describes and analyses teaching in terms of the relationship between teacher and students.

This outlook analyses the perceptions of students and teachers regarding their interpersonal relationships according to the Model for Interpersonal Teacher Behaviour (MITB). Starting in the Netherlands in the 1980s, this line of research has now expanded to many other countries, including Australia, Canada, Greece, Israel, Slovenia, Serbia, Turkey, Korea, Taiwan, Indonesia, Singapore, and the US.

The Model for Interpersonal Teacher Behaviour is based on Timothy Leary's research on the interpersonal diagnosis of personality (1957) and its application to teaching (Wubbels, Créton, & Hooymayers, 1985). The Leary model has been investigated extensively among others in clinical psychology and psychotherapeutic settings (Strack, 1996) and has proven effective in describing human interactions (Foa, 1961; Lonner, 1980). While not conclusive, there is evidence that the Leary model is cross-culturally generalizable (Abele & Wojciszke, 2007; Brown, 1965; Dunkin & Biddle, 1974; Kiesler, 1983; Lonner, 1980; Segall, Dasen, Berry, & Poortinga, 1990). Two significant dimensions emerged from Leary's research, which he named 'Dominance-Submission' and 'Hostility-Affection'. Although these two dimensions have occasionally been given other names – Brown (1965) used 'Status and Solidarity', and Dunkin and Biddle (1974) called them 'Warmth and Directivity' – they have generally been accepted as universal descriptors of human interaction. According to interpersonal theory (Fiske, Cuddy, & Glick, 2007; Judd, James-Hawkins, Yzerbyt, & Kashima, 2005) these two dimensions are primary to all interpersonal perceptions.

The two dimensions have also been applied to education. Slater (1962) used them to describe pedagogical relationships, and Dunkin and Biddle (1974) demonstrated their importance in teachers' efforts to influence classroom events. Robertson (2002) employed two similar dimensions – assertiveness and cooperation – to describe classroom management behaviour. In the original MITB the two dimensions were Influence (Dominance-Submission) and Proximity (Opposition-Cooperation), represented in an orthogonal coordinate system depicted in Figure 1. The two dimensions, represented as two axes, underlie eight types of teacher behaviour: Leadership, Helpful/Friendliness, Understanding, Student Freedom and Responsibility, Uncertainty, Dissatisfaction, Admonishing, and Strictness (see Figure 2).

The sectors are labelled DC, CD, etc., according to their position in the coordinate system (much like the directions in a compass). For example, the sectors Leadership and Helpful/Friendly are both characterized by Dominance and Cooperation. In the DC-sector, Dominance prevails over Cooperation and includes behaviours such as teacher enthusiasm, motivating strategies, and the like. The adjacent CD-sector includes more cooperative and less dominant perceptions in which the teacher demonstrates helpful, friendly and considerate behaviour.

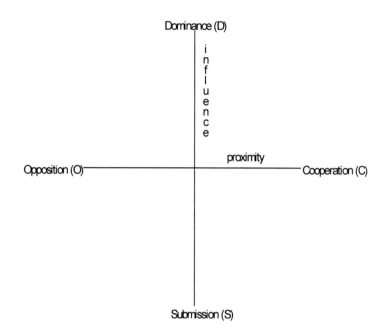

Figure 1. Two-dimensional coordinate system of the Model for Interpersonal Teacher Behaviour (Wubbels et al., 1985).

Figure 2 presents an overview of typical teacher behaviours that relate to each of the eight sectors of the Model.

The MITB (as well as the Leary model) is a unique entity within a branch of models characterized by their circumplex structure. Circumplex models are based on a specific set of assumptions that describe interpersonal constructs (Tracey, 1994). The following assumptions undergird the MITB: (Fabrigar, Visser, & Browne, 1997; Gurtman & Pincus, 2000; Tracey, 1994)
(1) the eight behavioural sectors of the model are represented by two dimensions;
(2) the two dimensions are uncorrelated;
(3) the sectors can be evenly distributed in a circular structure.
The implications of these assumptions are that a sector correlates highest with its adjacent sectors and lowest with the sector opposite in the model.

The Questionnaire on Teacher Interaction

The perceptions of teachers and students of the teacher-students relationship can be measured with the Questionnaire on Teacher Interaction (QTI). To map interpersonal teacher behaviour, the QTI was designed according to the two-

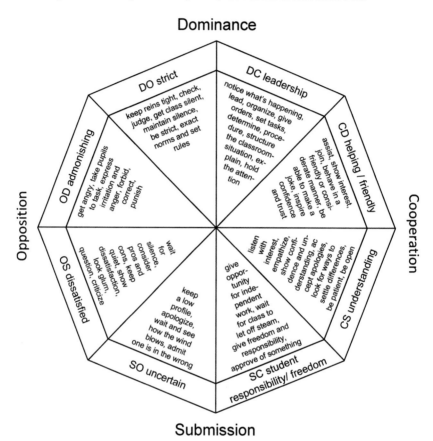

Figure 2. Model for Interpersonal Teacher Behaviour (Wubbels & Levy 1991).

dimensional Leary model and the eight sectors (Wubbels et al., 1985, 2006). It was originally developed in the Netherlands, and a 64-item American version was constructed in 1988 (Wubbels & Levy, 1991). The original Dutch version consists of 77 items that are answered on a five-point Likert scale ranging from 'Never/Not at all' to 'Always/Very'. The items are divided into eight scales corresponding with the eight behaviour types. Since its development the QTI has been translated, revised and administered in a number of countries, including Australia (Fisher, Waldrip, & Den Brok, 2005), Brunei (Den Brok, Fisher, & Scott, 2005b; Khine, 2002), Canada (Lapointe, Legault, & Batiste, 2005), China (Wei, Den Brok, & Zhou, 2009), Cyprus (Kyriakides, 2005), India (Den Brok, Fisher, & Koul, 2005a), Indonesia (Margianti, 2002), Israel (Kremer-Hayon & Wubbels, 1993a, 1993b), Korea (Lee, Fraser, & Fisher, 2003), the Netherlands (e.g., Brekelmans, Wubbels, & Créton 1990; Den Brok, Brekelmans, & Wubbels, 2004), Poland (Sztejnberg,

Den Brok, & Hurek, 2004), Singapore (Goh & Fraser, 1998), Turkey (Telli, Den Brok, & Cakiroglu, 2007), Thailand (Wei & Onsawad, 2007), the UK (Wales; Van Oord & Den Brok, 2004), and the US (Wubbels & Levy, 1991, 1993), among others.[i]

As noted above, in *circumplex models* such as the one on which the QTI is based, scales representing the octants are expected to be ordered in a circular structure and be represented by two uncorrelated factors or dimensions. The factor loadings of a factor analysis on the eight scales represent coordinates within the circular structure, and each scale is expected to load on both factors at the same time, even though different in magnitude. For example, the *leadership* subscale loads stronger on Influence than on Proximity. This is different from regular factor models, in which scales (or items) are constructed so as to load on only one factor. Thus, Influence and Proximity scores are calculated by linearly transforming the eight scale scores from the QTI on the basis of their position on the interpersonal circle.[ii]

Several studies have been conducted on the reliability and validity of the QTI. They have included research on Dutch (e.g., Brekelmans et al., 1990; Den Brok, 2001; Den Brok, Brekelmans, & Wubbels, 2006a; Wubbels et al., 1985), American (Wubbels & Levy, 1991) and Australasian (Den Brok, Fisher, Brekelmans, Wubbels, & Rickards, 2006b; Fisher, Fraser, & Wubbels, 1992; Fisher, Henderson, & Fraser, 1995) samples, among others.

REFLECTIONS ON THE PAST

Dimensions or Scales

Circumplex models are a way to combine two dimensions in an orthogonal framework (see e.g., Leary, 1957; Wiggins, 1991). Though Leary (1957) often used 16 (and occasionally 32) sectors, we decided to use eight in our circular structure in order to operationalise the two underlying dimensions. In research, for most analyses, use of the two dimensions has advantages over the eight scales because the latter are mutually correlated whereas (ideally) the two dimensions are not and their scores are sufficient (and necessary) to describe the interpersonal relationships. We have not identified any studies outside our own research group that used dimension scores in their analyses, and therefore we want to emphasise the need for this type of analysis. These scores can be based on the ideal formula mentioned in note 2 or can be calculated from actual factor scores derived from a two-factor analysis, either confirmatory or exploratory.

One might wonder why we still want to use scale scores at all. In many teacher education institutes and secondary schools both in the Netherlands and abroad teachers reflect on sector results to develop more productive relationships with their students. For these pre- and in-service teachers the eight sector profiles are more understandable than points on a dimension. A comparison of Figures 3 and 4 clarifies the difference between reporting in terms of scales versus dimensions (Wubbels et al., 2006).

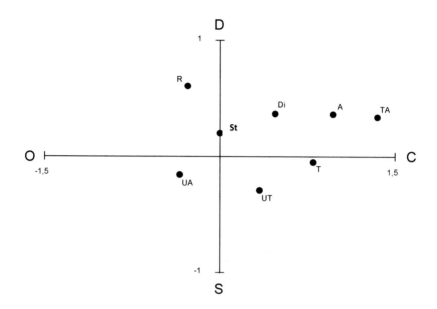

A = Authoritative, Di = Directive, St = Struggling ,T = Tolerant, R = Repressive, TA = Tolerant/Authoritative, UA = Uncertain/Aggressive, UT = Uncertain/Tolerant.

Figure 3. Main points of the eight types of patterns of interpersonal relationships.

Circle, Dimension and Sector Labels

For technical reasons the model has until recently been presented as an octagon. A possible drawback to this presentation is that the two dimensions seem less important than the sectors (see Figure 2). This is unintended, since – as noted – in a circumplex model the underlying dimensions are crucial for statistical analyses. To be more loyal to its circumplex nature, we began to present the model as a circle rather than an octagon. (e.g., Den Brok et al., 2006a, 2009; Telli, Den Brok, & Cakiroglu, 2010; Wei et al., 2009) (Figure 5).

We now propose some other adaptations (see Figure 6). The first will better align the dimension names with those used in other studies on interpersonal relationships. In addition, we will adjust sector labels to improve clarity and consistency.

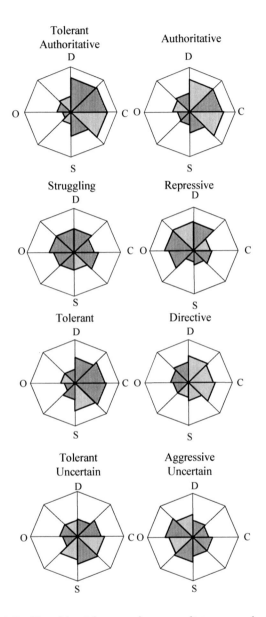

Figure 4. Profiles of the eight types of patterns of interpersonal relationships.

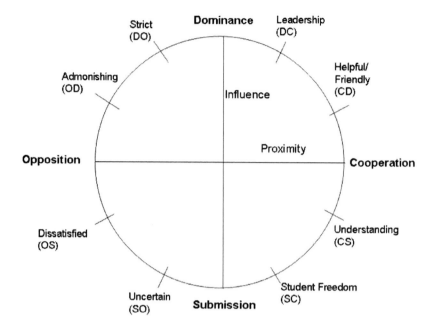

Figure 5. The Interpersonal teacher behaviour circumplex (Den Brok et al., 2006a).

In psychological research on interpersonal relationships the terms 'Affiliation' and 'Control' have been widely used as dimension labels. (e.g., Kiesler, 1983; Tiedens & Jimenez, 2003). Interpersonal theory assumes these factors to be primary to all social interaction (Fiske et al., 2007; Gurtman & Pincus, 2000; Judd et al., 2005). Control and Affiliation can therefore be considered equivalent to Dominance-Submission (Influence) and Cooperation-Opposition (Proximity). As a result, we will now use Control and Affiliation to designate the two dimensions of the Model for Interpersonal Teacher Behaviour.

We have also noted some inconsistencies in our sector labels. First, while most referred to the teacher's behaviour, one sector (Student Responsibility and Freedom) describes the effects on students. The term 'Student Responsibility and Freedom' inaccurately leads readers to imagine a broad range of teacher behaviours that might help students bear responsibility. Instead the label should reflect the particular combination of low teacher Control and medium teacher Affiliation. We have therefore changed the label to 'Accommodating' to describe teacher behaviour that is in between the interpersonal meaning of Understanding and Uncertain.

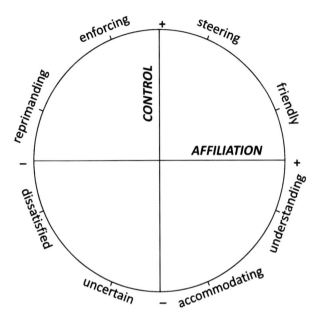

Figure 6. Adapted Interpersonal teacher behaviour circumplex.

Second, 'Leadership' was conceived by many readers as a broad term that can in fact refer to behaviours in many sectors, including friendliness, understanding or dissatisfaction. Thus, the term 'Leadership', was intended to specify a particular combination of a high amount of teacher Control and medium amount of teacher Affiliation rather than a mix of broad categories. We therefore propose to change the label to 'Steering'.

Third, two sectors ('Helpful/Friendly' and 'Student Responsibility and Freedom') included two terms each, whereas the other six labels only used one term. The revised sector labels will only include one word. Finally, the definitions of some of the labels were misunderstood. We changed the label for the 'Admonishing' sector to 'Reprimanding', primarily because admonishing appeared to be used infrequently in English and was not understood by many readers. Finally, we replaced 'Strict' by 'Enforcing', which better describes teacher actions.

Figure 6 presents the best current representation, a circle with eight titles placed equidistantly on the circumference that represent the original sectors as measured by the eight scales of the QTI.

Translation of the QTI

The Dutch and US/Australian versions of the QTI were developed after several pilot administrations and analyses (see Wubbels & Levy, 1993). Extensive interviews with students and teachers were conducted and items were repeatedly revised in pursuit of satisfactory psychometric properties. The goal was to produce an instrument with high alpha reliabilities for each scale, as well as a pattern of scale correlations that represented the circumplex nature of the model. Employing a similar comprehensive process, Telli, Den Brok, and Cakiroglu (2007) developed a Turkish QTI version and Wei, Den Brok, and Zhou (2009) a Chinese version. The design procedure for these newer versions were noteworthy in that the authors did not simply translate the items from one language to another, but rather adapted them to the cultural environment as well. Most QTI adaptations, however, were not as thorough and usually involved translation and occasional back translation. This heightened the risk of misunderstanding caused by variation in the interpretation of similar words in different languages.

In addition to the limited attention to the circumplex framework of the model in translating the QTI, two characteristics of the Dutch QTI and later the US version hindered adequate development of adaptations in other languages. Translators were not aware of these problems because they had only been published in Dutch (Créton & Wubbels, 1984). Wubbels and Levy (1991) provided an indication of these challenges in their comparison of the Dutch and US versions. First, the correlations between scales deviated from that expected of an ideal circumplex: in terms of the original scale labels, the correlation between the Leadership and Strict scales was not strong enough, whereas the correlation between Friendliness and Understanding was too strong. This led to an uneven distribution of the scales in the circle (see Wubbels & Levy, 1991, 1993). Unless the translators were aware of these weaknesses, adaptations of the QTI to other languages risked exacerbating them. Next, in the Student Freedom and Responsibility scale some items had deliberately been chosen because they tended to correlate higher with Understanding and others with Uncertain. Taken together this resulted in adequate correlations with the two adjacent scales, but a translation might distort the importance of one item over another, thus further distorting the relationship between scales. Finally, misunderstandings caused by the sector titles (described above) might have further hindered the development of sound versions in other languages. As a result of these difficulties, psychometric qualities of translated versions are usually lower than those of the Dutch, US/Australian and Turkish versions (see Den Brok et al., 2005b, 2006a, 2006b; Kokkinos, Charalambous, & Davazoglou, 2009; Telli et al., 2007).

CHALLENGE FOR THE FUTURE

From previous research we know that teacher-students relationships that are characterized by a combination of high levels of teacher control and affiliation are conducive to learning. Several studies have shown that students who attend classes with relatively high average levels of teacher control and affiliation show greater cognitive achievement and more positive subject-related attitudes than those whose teachers are rated lower on these dimensions (See, for example, overviews of studies with the QTI Den Brok et al., 2004; Wubbels et al., 2006, and Fraser in this volume, and for other studies Allen, Witt, & Wheeless, 2006; Cornelius-White, 2007). In this volume several chapters have added to the knowledge base on positive teacher-students relationships. For example, Georgiou and Kyriakides confirmed the relationships between control and affiliation and student achievement in the Cypriotic setting. In addition, Wentzel provided extensive evidence for the association between teacher-students relationships and student motivation. She describes effective teachers as those who develop relationships with students that are emotionally close, safe, and trusting; that provide access to instrumental help; and that foster a more general ethos of community and caring in classrooms. In their study of kindergarten teachers, Roorda, Koomen, and Oort reported that the amount of teacher affiliation was negatively related to conflicts and student external problem behaviour. In another study of kindergarten classrooms Spilt and Koomen found that effective management and sensitivity on the part of teachers led to lower levels of conflict for boys experiencing external problem behaviour. The results of these studies are consistent with the conclusion that teachers who demonstrate high control and affiliation behaviour form more positive relationships with their students and experience greater success in learning outcomes. It should be noted, however, that the studies provided more support for the effects of affiliation than of control.

The challenge for future research is to determine how teachers can create such positive relationships. Teacher-students relationships can be understood as the generalized interpersonal meaning students and teachers attach to their interactions with each other. However, the exact moment-to-moment interactions of teachers and students that add up to the more general conceptual level remain unknown. Dynamic systems theory (e.g., Thelen & Smith, 1994) can provide a framework for analysis of the relationship between these two levels in communication by connecting two separate time scales of development: a micro-social or moment-to-moment scale (i.e., teacher-students interaction) and a macro-social or outcome[iii] scale (i.e., the teacher-students relationship). The theory aims to understand the changing patterns of moment-to-moment interactions in relation to changes in outcome patterns. For example, Bronfenbrenner and Morris's (1998) bio-ecological theory posits that the moment-to-moment time scale (teacher-students interaction) is the primary engine of development and outcomes (e.g., teacher-students relationships). Thus, moment-to-moment interactions may be regarded as building blocks of patterns and habits of interaction within a social system (Hollenstein, 2007). Self-stabilizing feedback is the mechanism by which moment-to-moment processes determine macro-level outcomes. In turn, macro-level factors feed back on and restrict moment-to-moment interactions, thus serving both as outcomes (of previous processes) and as constraints (for subsequent processes). In terms of the dynamic systems theory the challenge for future research is to learn the type of moment-to-moment interactions that lead to profitable teacher-students relationships at the macro-social level.

Some outcomes in this domain have already been realized. In 1989, Créton, Wubbels, and Hooymayers (1989) reported findings regarding the relationship between undesirable teacher-students relationships and everyday teacher-students interactions. In a case study they found that teacher-students relationships that were low on both Control and Affiliation had been reinforced by such behaviours as overresponding aggressively or not at all to student disruptive behaviour. The sections to follow will elaborate on future challenges building on what already has been achieved.

Measurement

A prerequisite for progress in the research on teacher-students interactions is the ability to measure the interpersonal valence[iv] of teacher and student behaviour at the moment-to-moment level. Building on earlier work of Van Tartwijk, Brekelmans, Wubbels, Fisher, and Fraser (1998), Mainhard, Brekelmans, and Wubbels (2011a) developed coding schemes for observation of both teacher and student behaviour (Figure 7). Observers used videotaped lessons, and the interpersonal valence was coded in real-time following an event-sampling procedure. Each change in interpersonal valence of teacher or student behaviour was separately recorded. The coding process was consistently dyadic, with teacher and student behaviour each coded for valence. A specific combination of students

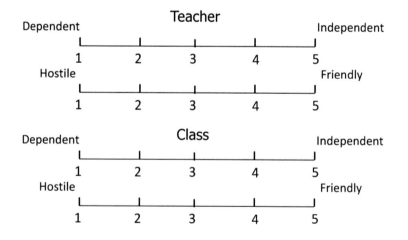

Figure 7. Coding scheme for observation of teacher and class behaviour at the micro level of interactions.[v]

and teacher behaviour was considered an *interpersonal state* of the classroom social system.[vi] An example would be a teacher lecturing and the students listening. The class interpersonal standing was conceived as a generalized aggregate of all students in a class. Acceptable inter-rater reliability in terms of concordance and Cohen's kappa was established (Mainhard et al., 2011a).

Non-verbal Behaviour and Relationships

Van Tartwijk et al. (1998) investigated associations between judges' perceptions of the interpersonal aspect of teachers' messages (micro level) and the students' perceptions of the teacher-students relationship (macro level). Strong significant correlations were established between students' and judges' control perceptions during lecturing whereas no significant correlations were found during individual seatwork. These findings suggest that the teacher control behaviour during whole class teaching (which normally takes place in front of the class) is more important for the development of the teacher-students relationship than during seatwork.

Given these relationships between the interpersonal meaning of teacher behaviour at the micro level and the teacher-students relationship at the macro level, it is important to examine specific features of teacher behaviour that are systematically related to the interpersonal meaning at the message level. Van Tartwijk (1993) described strong relationships between teachers' non-verbal behaviour of the teacher and students' perceptions of the interpersonal valence of the teacher's messages. The latter were measured by observers as proxies whose ratings correlated significantly with student scores (Van Tartwijk et al., 1998). Five channels of behaviour were investigated: space (the teacher's use of the space in the classroom); body (position and movement of the trunk, the arms and the head), face (various expressions), visual behaviour (duration of the teacher looking at the students), and voice (the non-content aspects of speech). All channels explained variance in the perceived degree of Control at the message level, with voice being the most important channel. Only Face and Voice significantly explained the Affiliation variance, with facial expression most strongly related. Figure 8 presents a summary of Control behaviours across all channels. It describes behaviours that occurred together often and were linked with high control perceptions (left) and low score control perceptions (right). For example, teachers who continuously look at students and speak loud and emphatically generally were perceived as strong in Control by students.

Interactions in Different Classes

In Mainhard et al. (2011a) we reported on a first study in which the moment-to-moment interactions of two teachers – one with favourable ratings (a Tolerant and Authoritative profile, Figures 3 and 4) and another with unfavourable ratings (a Struggling profile, Figures 3 and 4) were coded during three consecutive lessons for each. Results were displayed with State Space Grids (Lewis, Lamey, & Douglas, 1999), one for Control and one for Affiliation.

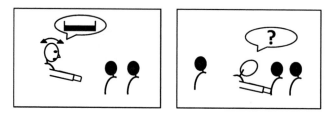

Figure 8. Combinations of behaviour with a relatively high (left) and low (right) control perception. In the left position the teacher is relatively far from the student, with his or her head in upright position, scanning and talking extensively in a low voice. In the right position the teacher is close to the students with head down so that his/her facial expression cannot be seen and the message content cannot be heard.

Figure 9 presents an example of a State Space Grid representing a few minutes of teacher-students interaction for the Control dimension. Twenty-five combinations of teacher and student scores are possible. Each time the combination of the interpersonal valence of teacher or student behaviour changes, a new point is plotted. The recorded interaction in the example starts in cell 42 (xy convention), and represents moderately high teacher control and intermittently dependent class behaviour. The observation was made during a lecture in which students listened quietly for a while and then began to chat with each other. Since their interaction did not interfere with the teacher's presentation the class behaviour was rated as less dependent than the initial 42 rating and thus the Control rating changed to cell 43. The teacher then asked students to work on an assignment, and though they began the task they were not silent. At this point the teacher began to grade papers at his desk, and his Control behaviour was represented by cell 33 (i.e., both teacher and class are assigned a moderate degree of interpersonal Control), and so on. Next, when students started to chat and engage in more off-task behaviour the teacher rose and walked through the classroom. He again asked the students work on their assignments, but without a great deal of success. Thus, the students' behaviour became more independent, while the teacher became more dependent on the class (cell 24). Finally, the teacher returned to the front of the room and loudly demanded that students stop talking and start working again. This interaction is once again represented by cell 43. In Figure 9 the resulting trajectory of interpersonal interaction is shown as it evolves over time.

The concept of complementarity is helpful in interpreting the results. Complementarity describes the behaviour in interactions that most probably invites specific reactions (De Jong, Van Tartwijk, Veldman, Verloop, & Wubbels, 2010). Research on human interactions has shown that Affiliation behaviour most probably invites similar responses. For example, friendly behaviour triggers a friendly reaction, and angry behaviour evokes anger (Tracey, 1994, 2004).

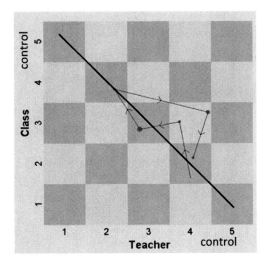

Figure 9. Example of a State Space Grid of teacher-class interaction in terms of interpersonal Control. The horizontal axis shows the control valence of the teacher's behaviour, the vertical axis represents the behaviour of students or the class. The arrowed line represents the change in the Control of teacher and class over the course of a few minutes, and the thickness of the dots indicates the duration of each interaction. The position of a dot in a cell is arbitrary. The bold line represents complementary interaction.

Behaviour on the Control dimension most probably invites contrasting responses: dominant behaviour, for instance, might invite a submissive reaction, and submissive behaviour can lead the recipient to try and take Control (Dryer & Horowitz, 1997). For example, a person might be talking (high Control), while the companion responds by listening (low Control). Sequences of communication are called complementary if they proceed according to these patterns. Complementarity is theorized to be the most probabilistic pattern, but other responses may occur (Estroff & Nowicki, 1992; Markey, Funder, & Ozer, 2003; Tiedens & Fragale, 2003; Tiedens & Jimenez, 2003; Tracey, 1994, 2004, 2005). Given these general trends it is interesting to analyse the degree to which the State Space Grids in our study demonstrate complementary interactions between teacher and students. Figure 9 includes three of the five combinations that represent complementarity.

Figure 10 presents the State Space Grids for Control and Affiliation for three consecutive lessons of the Struggling and Tolerant and Authoritative teacher. The grids for Control are similar in that the most frequent combination of teacher and student control can be seen in cell 42 which represents a complementary interaction of medium high teacher and low student control. A corresponding classroom situation is an orderly, teacher-guided discussion, where students raise their hands and wait their turns to speak. However, the grids for control differ in

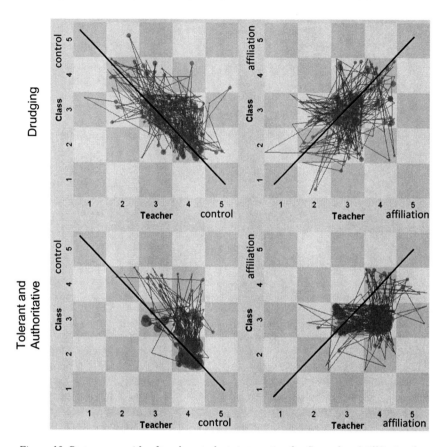

Figure 10. State space grids of teacher-students interaction for Control and Affiliation for three lessons for a Struggling teacher (unfavourable teacher-students relationships) and a Tolerant and Authoritative teacher (favourable teacher-students relationships). Bold lines represent complimentary interpersonal interactions.

the stability of the interactions: the Struggling classroom has a greater variety of interactions (as indicated by a larger number of cells) and does so more frequently than the Tolerant and Authoritative classroom. These cells deviate from complementary interaction in that they represent relatively more student control. The second most frequently occurring interaction for the Struggling teacher is cell 34. In this instance the teacher might be lecturing but is often interrupted by students, resulting in a disorderly atmosphere.

There is a greater difference in the Affiliation grids for the two teachers than in the Control grids. Again there is more variation for the Struggling teacher, but in addition the most frequently occurring type of interaction for Affiliation differs between the two classrooms. For the Struggling teacher, communication is mainly found in cell 33, which indicates complementarity in moderate Affiliation for both teacher and students. For example, the teacher might unenthusiastically present a homework assignment and then ask students to provide the answers. Students might cooperate but do not contribute voluntarily or spontaneously. For the Tolerant and Authoritative teacher, the most frequent interaction does not indicate complete complementarity, with medium high teacher Affiliation and moderate student affiliation.

The results initially indicate the range of communication in classes with more and less positive teacher-students relationships. A salient similarity between the two classrooms was that in both settings there was a higher Control valence for the teacher than for students (complementarity), and mutually positive Affiliation behaviours were most frequently observed. This might reflect the commonly-assumed social relationship in class in which a teacher exercises legitimate power and students are receptive and civil. Though the most frequent interactions in both classrooms were similar in terms of Control, in the more favourable Tolerant and Authoritative classroom these patterns were more stable. In the more positive classroom, Affiliation behaviours (ex: Friendly) occurred more frequently than in the less favourable setting. Strikingly, these interactions were not complementary: the students' affiliation towards the teacher was lower than would be expected based on the principle of complementarity. While the most frequently occurring interactions were comparable in the two classrooms, the differences at the start of the school year were especially apparent in terms of stability – especially in deviations of this most frequently occurring interaction and the number, duration, and kind of episodes. The Struggling teacher paid more and longer attention to call-outs and disruptions, and displayed both very strict (i.e., high Control) and moderately low Control behaviours. At times the Struggling teacher behaved with hostility towards the students (i.e., very low Affiliation). These types of teacher behaviours did not occur in the favourable classroom, where the communication was characterized by high teacher Affiliation indicated by friendliness from both teacher and class. These types of interactions did not occur in the less favourable classroom.

Coercive and Supportive Behaviour and Teacher-Students Relationship

A final study on the link between teacher-students relationships and moment-to-moment interactions employed students' perceptions of coercive and supportive teacher behaviour in one lesson. The students' views were gathered in 10 consecutive lessons of 48 teachers (Mainhard, Brekelmans & Wubbels, 2011b). Through multiple administrations of short versions of the QTI that assured that students did not have to answer the same questionnaire more often than once every three weeks, data were gathered on both teacher-students relationships and the occurrence of supportive and coercive incidents (the Teacher Behaviour Observation Checklist). For the latter instrument, an example of a coercive incident item is "In this lesson the teacher yelled at us", and an example of a supportive incident is "In this lesson the teacher said we were doing well". The student observations were very reliable and showed sufficient agreement between students of the same class. Supportive and coercive-behaviour-incident scores were negatively correlated (-.44; $p < .01$).

It appeared that coercive teacher behaviour incidents (e.g., using sarcasm, yelling at students, or punishing students during a classroom lesson) were associated with lower teacher Affiliation, both during the same lesson and in a lesson a week later. Thus, using coercive behaviour immediately disrupted the relationship between teacher and class, and unfortunately the effect remained for a week. However, if no new additional coercive behaviour occurred in the subsequent two weeks after the incident, the affiliation level was re-established.

There was not a straightforward link between coercive behaviour and teacher Control in the teacher-students relationship. The use of coercive behaviour in one lesson was associated with somewhat more Control in class, but acting coercively in two consecutive lessons appeared to diminish Control. This finding is in contrast to more general theories on interpersonal power (French & Raven, 1959; Schrodt et al., 2008) which assume that coercive behaviour strengthens interpersonal influence. It is, however, in agreement with some studies which show that coercive strategies are associated with more student misbehaviour (Lewis, Romi, Xing, & Katz, 2005; Miller, Ferguson, & Byrne, 2000). This result might be unpleasant for teachers, because it seems to highlight the unproductiveness of using coercion to establish greater control, whereas from the general theory on interpersonal power it is reasonable to expect positive results from coercion on Control. Although coercion seemed to work to some degree within a single lesson, teacher control seemed to decline in the long run. Further, coercive behaviour might also be viewed as unproductive given its effect on the Affiliation dimension. Teachers who engage in coercive behaviour may understand that this is not beneficial to their affiliation with students. However, these teachers may deliberately sacrifice affiliation in the belief that it will ultimately be re-established or be replaced by greater control. Disciplinary actions may be necessary at times, even though it might ruin the positive classroom atmosphere.

Teachers who exhibited supportive behaviour frequently were perceived by students as demonstrating greater Affiliation, an effect that was repeated in two lessons that spanned a week. Nonetheless, the effect faded after two weeks. Finally, frequent supportive behaviour was not significantly associated with teacher Control.

Overall, coercive and supportive teacher behaviour related more strongly to student perceptions of a teacher's affiliation than to control. In both cases (coercive and supportive) the effects did not last longer than one week. In addition, for supportive behavioural incidents the relationship improved and for coercive episodes it declined. The fact that teacher behaviour was less associated with teacher control than affiliation is in agreement with earlier findings. There are some indications that differences between classrooms of the same teacher are greater in Affiliation than Control (Wubbels et al., 2006). This may demonstrate that the Affiliation dimension is subject to more situational (i.e., classroom) influences than Control. It may also point to the need to account for additional situational factors. For example, yelling at students may be associated with more Control if students agree that they misbehaved, whereas if students disagree it might have the opposite effect.

CONCLUSION

Summary

The main messages of this chapter have been the need to focus on the QTI dimensions rather than the scales, and consideration of the model as circumplex in nature. We therefore propose a new name for the model: Teacher Interpersonal Circle (TIC). In addition we have offered some ideas to improve the circle's labels and alerted colleagues to the danger of straight translations of the QTI without contemplating unique language and cultural aspects. Such adaptations usually require several pilot rounds to acquire an understanding of the interpersonal meaning of words. From a strictly scientific point of view, the measurement of interpersonal relationships only requires a small number of items on the circle, and the original Dutch and US QTI versions were not very efficient. The 48-item Australian QTI (Wubbels, 1993) is an improvement in this respect, but unfortunately it is slightly less valid and reliable than the longer versions. For research purposes 8-16 well chosen items might be sufficient to map the teacher-students relationship. It is our experience, however, that teachers appreciate feedback on several scales regarding their relationships with students. Consequently, we are now developing 16-32 item versions of the QTI with eight scales distributed over the circle in which each scale would include 2-4. Thus, we hope to serve both practice and science, while using the time of respondents efficiently.

This chapter also offered initial results for what we believe to be the main challenge for future studies on the (causal) relationships between moment-to-moment interactions (the micro level) and the macro-level teacher-students relationship. Several studies (e.g., Lewis, 2001; Sava, 2002) had already shown the destructive effects of coercive teacher disciplinary actions. Our work highlights the way in which coercive and supportive behaviour associates with the teacher-students relationship and how these linkages appear across time. We can conclude that although consequences of teacher coercive actions do fade away, they nonetheless have negative effects when they repeatedly occur. Further, efforts to improve control through coercive actions do not seem effective.

In the two classes that featured high and low-quality teacher-students relationships, our work suggests that the most frequent interactions were similar in terms of Control. In the Tolerant and Authoritative classroom higher levels of Affiliation appeared in the favourable than in the less favourable setting. The favourable and less favourable classrooms differed at the start of the school year in the stability of and deviations from the most frequently occurring communications. The Struggling teacher paid more and longer attention to call-outs and disruptions, behaved with greater hostility towards the students at times, and displayed both very strict and very lenient behaviour. These types of teacher behaviours did not occur in the favourable classroom.

Implications

We have advocated elsewhere that teachers should create classroom environments where students perceive high teacher Control and Affiliation in the teacher-students relationship (Wubbels et al., 2006). In addition, we have now proposed some new ideas about creating such an atmosphere through moment-to-moment interactions. When, as we expect, the differences we found between the teachers with favourable and less favourable teacher-students relationships become generalizable, our results will send a clear message to teachers: they should try to keep classroom interactions consistent, make as few disciplinary interventions as possible, and reduce the number and duration of interactions that deviate from more favourable types. Our research results support the recommendation that teachers should use small rather than intense corrections, behave as unaggressively as possible (Evertson & Weinstein, 2006), and apply increased intensity of disciplinary actions only for seriously disruptive student behaviour (Créton et al., 1989).

For future research we suggest a greater focus on individual students – in terms of teacher behaviour and their perceptions. Until now, we have coded classroom interactions as a dyadic process between teacher and class. It may be argued that, especially on the level of moment-to-moment interaction, the teacher interacts not only with the whole class, but also with individual students. A fruitful avenue for future research might therefore be to focus in the teacher-class interaction on teacher contacts with individual students and/or specific groups of students. Some studies employing State Space Grids in other contexts have indeed chosen such an approach to study group level development from samples of individual interactions (cf., Martin, Fabes, Hanish, & Hollenstein, 2005). It might also be informative to differentiate between teacher-whole class interaction and interaction with individual students. A related issue is the conceptualization of the teacher-students relationship as a class-level construct. We analysed the association between teacher behaviour and the teacher-students relationship, rather than studying links with individual student perceptions. A drawback of this strategy is that processes relating to individual as opposed to collective aspects of student perceptions cannot be studied. Especially when studying effects on student learning outcomes, individual aspects of student perceptions, in addition to collective aspects, may be essential.

This section has summarized the main points of the chapter, presented implications for practice and mentioned issues for future research. The chapter has tried to facilitate further research that is simultaneously scientifically more productive, yet still useful for practice: as the title suggests, it hopes to "make things better".

NOTES

[i] The QTI was intended originally for use in Secondary Education and formed the basis of several new versions such as for Primary Education (e.g., Goh & Fraser, 1996), early primary education (Zijlstra, Wubbels, & Brekelmans, 2011), and for Higher Education teachers (e.g., Soerjaningsih, Fraser, & Alldridge, 2002), for supervisors of student teachers (Kremer-Hayon & Wubbels, 1993a), and one for teachers about school managers (the Questionnaire on Principal Interaction, e.g., Kremer-Hayon & Wubbels, 1993b; Fisher & Cresswell, 1998). The instrument also formed the starting point for adaptations that are being used in post-compulsory education (Hockley & Harkin, 2000) and in supervision of doctoral students (Mainhard, Van der Rijst, Van Tartwijk, & Wubbels, 2009).

[ii] To this end the eight scores are represented as vectors in a two-dimensional space, each dividing a section of the model of interpersonal behaviour in two and with a length corresponding to the height of the scale score. We then compute the two coordinates of the resultant of these eight vectors. Dimension scores are computed as follows: Influence = 0.92DC + 0.38CD – 0.38CS – 0.92SC –0.92SO – 0.38OS + 0.38OD + 0.92DO; Proximity = 0.38DC + 0.92CD + 0.92CS + 0.38SC – 0.38SO– 0.92OS – 0.92OD – 0.38DO.

[iii] This is often referred to as developmental outcome, but we avoid the term developmental because also at the micro-social level development occurs.

[iv] Interpersonal valence or standing refers to the meaning of the behaviour for the other party in the interaction.

[v] For the teacher, Affiliation ranged from level 1/very low (e.g., the teacher behaves hostile towards the students, is repulsive or uses sarcasm, the teacher is irritated or angry) to level 5/very high (e.g., the teacher is very responsive towards the students needs, he or she is very friendly, praises students for good work, makes students feel at ease, grabs the students' attention); Control ranged from level 1/very low (e.g., instead of guiding the general classroom process the teacher is forced to act in response to students call outs and interruptions, the teacher is uncertain or hardly intervening in what the students do) to level 5/very high (e.g., the teacher is strict or firmly leading the classroom processes). For students, Affiliation ranged from level 1/very low (e.g., students are hostile, quarrel with or make fun of the teacher, students are dissatisfied) to level 5/very high (e.g., students are enthusiastic, laugh, are grabbed by the classroom process in a positive way, or actively cooperate with the teacher); and Control ranged from level 1/very low (e.g., students obey the teacher, are submissive and hinge on the teacher in many ways, students are uncertain or anxious) to level 5/very high (e.g., students do what they want, show off –task behaviour in presence of the teacher, refuse to comply and ignore or violate rules the teacher had set, students ignore the teacher).

[vi] Observing a classroom group of students posited some specific challenges. An important issue was whether individual students or the group as a whole should be rated. Therefore, priority scores that followed two rules, were used to rate the valence of student behaviour: 1) whenever specific events occurred, for example, a call out or other interruption of the ongoing classroom process initiated by a specific student, or if the teacher interacted with a specific student, the interpersonal valence of the behaviour of this student was coded; and 2) the general tendency of the group was coded (e.g., students work quietly on an assignment, or actively participate in a classroom discussion). Note that the first rule had priority over the second rule.

REFERENCES

Abele, A. E. & Wojciszke, B. (2007). Agency and communion from the perspective of self versus others. *Journal of Personality and Social Psychology*, *93*(5), 751-763.

Allen, M., Witt, P. L., & Wheeless, L. R. (2006). The role of teacher immediacy as a motivational factor in student learning: a meta-analysis and causal model. *Communication Education*, *55*, 21-31.

Brekelmans, J. M. G., Wubbels, Th., & Créton, H. A. (1990). A study of students perceptions of Physics Teachers behavior. *Journal of Research in Science Teaching*, *27*, 335-350.

Bronfenbrenner, U. & Morris, P. A. (1998). The ecology of developmental processes. In W. Damon (series Ed.) & R. M. Lerner (Vol. Ed.) Handbook of child psychology: Vol. 1. *Theoretical models of human development* (5th ed., pp. 993-1028). New York: Wiley.

Brown, R. (1965). *Social psychology*. London: Collier-McMillan.

Cornelius-White, J. (2007). Learner-centered teacher-student relationships are effective: a meta-analysis. *Review of Educational Research*, *77*(1), 113-143.

Créton, H. A. & Wubbels, Th. (1984). *Discipline problems with beginning teachers* [in Dutch]. Utrecht: W.C.C.

Créton, H. A., Wubbels, T., & Hooymayers, H. P. (1989). Escalated disorderly situations in the classroom and the improvement of these situations. *Teaching and Teacher Education*, *5*(3), 205-215.

Den Brok, P. (2001). *Teaching and student outcomes: A study on teachers' thoughts and actions from an interpersonal and a learning activities perspective*. Utrecht, The Netherlands: W.C.C.

Den Brok, P., Brekelmans, M., & Wubbels, T. (2004). Interpersonal teacher behavior and student outcomes. *School Effectiveness and School Improvement*, *15*(3/4), 407-442.

Den Brok, P., Fisher, D., & Koul, R. (2005a). The importance of teacher interpersonal behaviour for secondary science students' attitudes in Kashmir. *Journal of Classroom Interaction*, *40*(2), 5-19.

Den Brok, P., Fisher, D., & Scott, R. (2005b). The importance of teacher interpersonal behaviour for student attitudes in Brunei primary science classes. *International Journal of Science Education*, *27*, 765-779.

Den Brok, P., Brekelmans, M., & Wubbels, T. (2006a). Multilevel issues in studies using students' perceptions of learning environments: The case of the Questionnaire on Teacher Interaction. *Learning Environments Research*, *9*(3), 199-213.

Den Brok, P., Fisher, D., Brekelmans, M., Wubbels, T., & Rickards, T. (2006b). Secondary teachers' interpersonal behaviour in Singapore, Brunei and Australia: A cross-national comparison. *Asia-Pacific Journal of Education*, *26*(1), 79-95.

De Jong, R., Van Tartwijk, J., Veldman, I., Verloop, N & Wubbels, Th. (2010). *Teachers' expectations about teacher-student interactions*. Paper presented at the 2010 Annual Meeting of the American Educational Research Association, Denver, April 30-May 4, 2010.

Dryer, D. C. & Horowitz, L. M. (1997). When do opposites attract? Interpersonal complementarity versus similarity. *Journal of Personality and Social Psychology*, *72*, 592-603.

Dunkin M. & Biddle, B. (1974). *The study of teaching*. New York: Holt, Rinehart & Winston.

Estroff, S. D. & Nowicki, S. (1992). Interpersonal complementarity, gender of interactants, and performance on word puzzles. *Personality and Social Psychology Bulletin*, *18*, 351-356.

Evertson, C. M. & Weinstein, C. S. (2006). Classroom management as a field of inquiry. In C.M. Evertson, & C.S. Weinstein (Eds.), *Handbook of classroom management: Research, practice, and contemporary issues* (pp. 3-16). Mahwah, NJ: Erlbaum.

Fabrigar, L. R., Visser, P. S., & Browne, M. W. (1997). Conceptual and methodological issues in testing the circumplex structure of data in personality and social psychology. *Personality and Social Psychology Review*, *1*, 184-203.

Fisher, D. & Cresswell, J. (1998), Actual and ideal principal interpersonal behaviour. *Learning Environments Research*, *1*, 231-247.

Fisher, D. L., Fraser, B. J. & Wubbels, Th. (1992) *Teacher communication style and school environment*.Paper presented at the 1992 ECER conference, Enschede.

Fisher, D., Henderson, D., & Fraser, B. (1995). Interpersonal behavior in senior high school biology classes. *Research in Science Education*, *25*, 125-133.

Fisher, D., Waldrip, B., & Den Brok, P. (2005). Students' perceptions of primary teachers' interpersonal behaviour and of cultural dimensions in the classroom environment. *International Journal of Educational Research, 43*, 25-38.

Fiske, S. T., Cuddy, A. J. C., & Glick, P. (2007). Universal dimensions of social cognition: warmth and competence. *Trends in Cognitive Sciences, 11*(2), 77-83.

Foa, U. G. (1961). Convergence in the analysis of the structure of interpersonal behavior. *Psychological Review, 68*, 341-353.

French, J. R. & Raven, B. (1959). The basis of social power. In D. Cartwright (Ed.), *Studies in social power* (pp. 150-167). Ann Arbor, MI: University of Michigan Press.

Goh, S. C. & Fraser, B. J. (1996). Validation of an elementary school version of the questionnaire on teacher interaction. *Psychological Reports, 79*, 515-522.

Goh, S. C. & Fraser, B. J. (1998). Teacher interpersonal behavior, classroom environment and student outcomes in primary mathematics in Singapore. *Learning Environments Research, 1*, 199-229.

Gurtman, M. B. & Pincus, A. L. (2000). Interpersonal adjective scales: Confirmation of circumplex structure from multiple perspectives. *Personality and Social Psychology Bulletin, 26*, 374-384.

Hockley, M. & Harkin, J. (2000), Communicating with students with learning difficulties in further education. *Educational Action Research, 8*(2), 341-360.

Hollenstein, T. (2007). State space grids: Analyzing dynamics across development. *International Journal of Behavioral Development, 31*(4), 384-396.

Judd, C. M., James-Hawkins, L., Yzerbyt, V., & Kashima, Y. (2005). Fundamental dimensions of social judgment: understanding the relations between judgments of competence and warmth. *Journal of Personality and Social Psychology, 89*(6), 899-913.

Khine, M. S. (2002). Study of learning environments for improving science education in Brunei. In M. S. Khine & S. C. Goh (Eds.), *Studies in educational learning environments* (pp. 131-152). Singapore: World Scientific.

Kiesler, D. J. (1983). The interpersonal transaction circle: a taxonomy for complementarity in human processes. *Psychological Bulletin, 77*, 421-430.

Kokkinos, C.M., Charalambous, K., & Davazoglou, A. (2009). Interpersonal teacher behaviour in primary school classrooms: A cross-cultural validation of a Greek translation of the Questionnaire on Teacher Interaction. *Learning Environments Research, 12*, 101-114.

Kremer-Hayon, L. & Wubbels, Th. (1993a). Supervisors' interpersonal behavior and student teachers' satisfaction. In T. Wubbels & J. Levy (Eds.), *Do you know what you look like?* (pp. 123-135) London: Falmer Press.

Kremer-Hayon, L. & Wubbels, Th. (1993b). Principals' interpersonal behavior and teachers' satisfaction. In T. Wubbels & J. Levy (Eds.), *Do you know what you look like?* (pp. 113-122) London: Falmer Press.

Kyriakides, L. (2005). Extending the comprehensive model of educational effectiveness by an empirical investigation. *School Effectiveness and School Improvement, 16*, 103-152.

Lapointe, J. M., Legault, F., & Batiste, S. J. (2005). Teacher interpersonal behavior and adolescents' motivation in mathematics: A comparison of learning disabled, average, and talented students. *International Journal of Educational Research, 43*(1-2), 39-54.

Leary, T. (1957). *An interpersonal diagnosis of personality.* New York: Ronald Press Company.

Lee, S. S. U., Fraser, B. J., & Fisher, D. L. (2003). Teacher-student interactions in Korean high school science classrooms. *International Journal of Science and Mathematics Education, 1*, 67-85.

Lewis, M. D., Lamey, A. V., & Douglas, L. (1999). A new dynamic systems method for analysis of early socioemotional development. *Developmental Science, 2*, 457-475.

Lewis, R. (2001). Classroom discipline and student responsibility: The students' view. *Teaching and Teacher Education, 17*(3), 307-319.

Lewis, R., Romi, S., Xing, Q., & Katz, Y. J. (2005). Teachers' classroom discipline and student misbehavior in Australia, China and Israel. *Teaching and Teacher Education, 21*(6), 729-741.

Lonner, W. J. (1980). The search for psychological universals. In H. C. Triandis & W. W. Lambert (Eds.), *Handbook of cross cultural psychology* (vol. 1, pp. 143-204). Boston: Allyn and Bacon.

Mainhard, T., Van der Rijst, R., Van Tartwijk, J., & Wubbels, T. (2009). A model for the supervisor-doctoral student relationship. *Higher Education, 58*(7), 359-373.

Mainhard, T., Brekelmans, M., & Wubbels, T. (2011a). Stability and variability in teacher-class interaction at the start of the school year: A comparison of two classrooms. (Submitted for publication.)

Mainhard, T., Brekelmans, M., & Wubbels, Th. (2011b, in press). Coercive and supportive teacher behaviour: Associations with the social climate within and across classroom lessons. *Learning and Instruction.*

Margianti, E. S. (2002). Learning environments research in Indonesia. In M.S. Khine & S.C. Goh (Eds.), *Studies in educational learning environments* (pp. 153-168). Singapore: World Scientific.

Markey, P. M., Funder, D. C., & Ozer, D. J. (2003). Complementarity of interpersonal behaviours in dyadic interactions. *Personality and Social Psychology Bulletin, 29,* 1082-1090.

Martin, C. L., Fabes, R. A., Hanish, L. D., & Hollenstein, T. (2005). Social dynamics in the preschool. *Developmental Review, 25,* 299-327.

Miller, A., Ferguson, E., & Byrne, I. (2000). Pupils' causal attributions for difficult classroom behaviour. *British Journal of Educational Psychology, 70*(1), 85-96.

Robertson, J. (2002). The boss, the manager and the leader: Approaches to dealing with disruption. In B. Rogers (Ed.) *Teacher leadership and behaviour management* (pp. 20-39) London: Sage.

Sava, F. A. (2002). Causes and effects of teacher conflict-inducing attitudes towards pupils: A path analysis model. *Teaching and Teacher Education, 18*(8), 1007-1027.

Schrodt, P., Witt, P. L., Myers, S. A., Turman, P. D., Barton, M., & Jernberg, K. (2008). Learner empowerment and students' ratings of instruction as functions of teacher power use in the college classroom. *Communication Education, 57,* 180-200.

Segall, M. H., Dasen, P. R., Berry, J. W., & Poortinga, Y. H. (Eds.). (1990). *Human behavior in global perspective: An introduction to cross-cultural psychology.* New York: Pergamon.

Slater, P. E. (1962). Parental behavior and the personality of the child. *Journal of Genetic Psychology, 101,* 53-68.

Soerjaningsih, W., Fraser, B. J., & Alldridge, J. M. (2002). *Instructor-student interpersonal behavior and student outcomes at the university level in Indonesia.* Paper presented at the annual meeting of the American Educational Research Association, April, New Orleans.

Strack, S. (1996). Introduction to the special series – Interpersonal theory and the interpersonal circumplex: Timothy Leary's legacy. *Journal of Personality Assessment, 66,* 212-216.

Sztejnberg, A., Den Brok, P., & Hurek, J. (2004). Preferred teacher-student interpersonal behaviour: Differences between Polish primary and higher education students' perceptions. *Journal of Classroom Interaction, 39*(2), 32-40.

Telli, S., Den Brok, P., & Cakiroglu, J. (2007). Students' perceptions of science teachers' interpersonal behaviour in secondary schools: Development of a Turkish version of the Questionnaire on Teacher Interaction. *Learning Environments Research, 10,* 115-129.

Telli, S., Den Brok, P., & Cakiroglu, J. (2010). The importance of teacher-student interpersonal relationships for students' subject-related attitudes in Turkey. *Research in Science and Technological Education, 28*(3), 261-276.

Thelen, E. & Smith, L. B. (1994). *A dynamic system approach to the development of cognition and action.* Cambridge, MA: Bradford/MIT Press.

Tiedens, L. Z. & Fragale, A. R. (2003). Power moves: Complementarity in dominant and submissive nonverbal behavior. *Journal of Personality and Social Psychology, 84,* 558-568.

Tiedens, L. Z. & Jimenez, M. C. (2003). Assimilation for affiliation and contrast for control: Complementary self-construals. *Journal of Personality and Social Psychology, 85*(6), 1049-1061.

Tracey, T. J. (1994). An examination of complementarity of interpersonal behavior. *Journal of Personality and Social Psychology, 67,* 864-878.

Tracey, T. J. G. (2004). Levels of interpersonal complementarity: A simplex representation. *Personality and Social Psychology Bulletin, 30,* 1211-1225.

Tracey, T. J. G. (2005). Interpersonal rigidity and complementarity. *Journal of Research in Personality, 39,* 592-614.

Van Oord, L. & Den Brok, P. (2004). The international teacher: Students' and teachers' perceptions of preferred teacher-student interpersonal behaviour in two United World Colleges. *Journal of Research in International Education, 3*(2), 131-155.

Van Tartwijk, J. (1993). *Sketches of teacher behavior: The interpersonal meaning of nonverbal teacher behavior in the classroom* [in Dutch]. Utrecht: W.C.C.

Van Tartwijk, J., Brekelmans, M., Wubbels, T., Fisher, D. L., & Fraser, B. J. (1998). Students perceptions of teacher interpersonal style: The front of the classroom as the teacher's stage. *Teaching and Teacher Education, 14*, 1-11.

Wei, M., & Onsawad, A. (2007). English teachers' actual and ideal interpersonal behaviour and students' outcomes in secondary schools of Thailand. *The Journal of Asia TEFL, 4*(2), 1-29.

Wei, M., Den Brok, P., & Zhou, Y. (2009). An investigation of teacher interpersonal behaviour and student achievement in English as a Foreign Language (EFL) classrooms in China. *Learning Environments Research, 12*(3), 157-174.

Wiggins, J. S. (1991). Agency and communion as conceptual coordinates for understanding and measurement of interpersonal behavior. In W. M. Grove & D. Cicchetti (Eds.), *Thinking clearly about psychology* (pp. 89-113). Minneapolis: University of Minnesota Press.

Wubbels, Th. (1993). *Teacher-student relationships in science and mathematics classes.* What Research Says to the Science and Mathematics, number 11.

Wubbels, T. & Levy, J. (1991). A *comparison* of interpersonal behavior of Dutch and American teachers. *International Journal of Intercultural Relations, 15*, 1-18.

Wubbels, T. & Levy, J. (Eds.) (1993). *Do you know what you look like? Interpersonal relationships in education.* London: Falmer.

Wubbels, T., Créton, H. A., & Hooymayers, H. P. (1985, March-April). *Discipline problems of beginning teachers, interactional teacher behavior mapped out.* Paper presented at the annual meeting of the American Educational Research Association, Chicago (ERIC document 260040).

Wubbels, T., Brekelmans, M., Den Brok, P., & Van Tartwijk, J. (2006). An interpersonal perspective on classroom management in secondary classrooms in the Netherlands. In C. Evertson & C. S. Weinstein (Eds.), *Handbook of classroom management: Research, practice and contemporary issues* (pp. 1161-1191). New York: Lawrence Erlbaum Associates.

Zijlstra, H., Wubbels, T., & Brekelmans, M. (2011). Child perceptions of the teacher-child relationship and mathematical achievement: An interpersonal perspective on teaching early grade classrooms. (Submitted for publication.)

NOTES ON CONTRIBUTORS

Roel J. Bosker, PhD, is professor of education and director of GION, Groningen Institute for Educational Research at the University of Groningen, The Netherlands. He has co-authored books on multilevel analysis and on educational effectiveness. His current research focuses on standard setting by teachers and its effects on student achievement, models for assessing schools' value added, professional learning communities and pre-school literacy programs. r.j.bosker@rug.nl

Mieke Brekelmans, PhD, is full professor at the Faculty of Social and Behavioural Sciences, Utrecht University, The Netherlands. She is director of the Research Centre Learning in Interaction. Her main research interest is the study of classroom social climate, in particular the development of the teacher student relationship. m.brekelmans@uu.nl

Alan J. Daly, PhD, is an assistant professor of Education Studies at the University of California, San Diego, USA. His research interests include leadership, educational policy and reform, and social network theory. He recently published a book on social networks entitled, Social Network Theory and Educational Change (2010). ajdaly@ucsd.edu

Nilusha De Alwis, MPsych, works as a research assistant in the Faculty of Education, Monash University, Melbourne, Australia, as well as a School Psychologist. She received Faculty and external awards for research presentations based on her Master of Psychology and Postgraduate Diploma of Psychology degrees, in the areas of teaching career motivations, wellbeing and burnout processes. nilusha.dealwis@monash.edu

Perry den Brok, PhD, is full professor and director of research at the Eindhoven School of Education, Eindhoven University of Technology, The Netherlands. He has published extensively on teacher-student interpersonal relationships in education, on topics such as teacher interpersonal behaviour and student outcomes, teacher interpersonal competence in multicultural classrooms and cross-national studies on teacher-student interpersonal relationships. p.j.d.brok@tue.nl

Walter Doyle, PhD, is a professor in the Department of Teaching, Learning, and Sociocultural Studies in the College of Education at The University of Arizona, Tucson, USA. His research has centered on classroom processes, curriculum

T. Wubbels et al. (eds.), Interpersonal Relationships in Education, 251–256.
© *2012 Sense Publishers. All rights reserved.*

theory, and, recently, the design of teacher education experiences that promote powerful practices in mathematics and science teaching for beginning elementary school teachers. wdoyle@email.arizona.edu

Hans E. Fischer, PhD, is a professor of Physics Education at the University of Duisburg-Essen, Germany, and head of the research group Teaching and Learning of Science. His main research interests are in the area of quality of instruction as a global framework for analysing effects of classroom interventions. hans.fischer@uni-due.de

Katharina Fricke is a PhD candidate at the University of Paderborn, Germany. At the University of Duisburg-Essen she worked on a research project focussing on science teaching and learning in the transition from elementary to secondary school. Her research interest is the impact of teachers' classroom management on student achievement in science lessons. katharina.fricke@uni-paderborn.de

Maria Georgiou, PhD, is a Deputy Head of the Secondary Education public schools of Cyprus. In June 2010 she received her doctorate from the Department of Education at the University of Cyprus. In her dissertation she examined the relationships between school effectiveness, interpersonal behaviour and job satisfaction. sepgmg1@ucy.ac.cy

Alexander Kauertz, PhD, is a professor of Physics Education, with a focus on elementary level education, at the University of Education of Weingarten, Germany. His main research interests are learning outcomes and learning processes of students in elementary and secondary schools. kauertz@ph-weingarten.de

Leonidas Kyriakides, PhD, is associate professor of Educational Research and Evaluation at the University of Cyprus. His main research interests are modelling educational effectiveness, research methods in educational effectiveness, and the application of effectiveness research to the improvement of educational practice. kyriakides@ucy.ac.cy

Helma M. Y. Koomen, PhD, is an assistant professor in Special Education at the Research Institute for Child Development and Education, University of Amsterdam, The Netherlands. Her research interests address student-teacher interactions and teachers' pedagogical practices in relation to student emotional well-being, social adjustment, and task behaviours. h.m.y.koomen@uva.nl

Jack Levy, PhD, is the Chair of the Department of Curriculum & Instruction at the University of Massachusetts, Boston, USA. His main research interests are in the areas of multicultural and international teacher education, and interpersonal teacher behaviour. jack.levy@umb.edu

Tim Mainhard, PhD, is an assistant professor in the Faculty of Social of Behavioural Sciences at Utrecht University, The Netherlands. His work focuses on how social relations in educational settings, and especially the classroom social climate, enhances or hampers student cognitive and social development. Furthermore, he is interested in how student perceptions should be analyzed by taking the specific multiple-membership and cross classification structure of educational settings into account. m.t.mainhard@uu.nl

Ridwan Maulana is a Postdoc researcher at the University Centre for Learning and Teaching, University of Groningen, The Netherlands. His dissertation explores changes in teacher-student relationships and links with motivational outcomes in secondary education in the Netherlands and Indonesia. His research interests involve developments of classroom social climates affecting student learning in cross-cultural contexts as well as statistics and methods associated with longitudinal multilevel analyses. r.maulana@rug.nl

Janet M. McGee, Ed.D., has been an educator for the last 37 years. She has experience as an elementary school teacher, elementary and middle school principal, four years as an assistant professor in the Educational Leadership Department at the University of Central Florida, Orlando, USA and recently opened a charter school focusing on STEM education. Her passion is with children and adolescents with a research focus on bullying, cyberbullying, and safety in schools. She was a crisis coordinator/instructor, trainer and coach for new and mentoring teachers. janmcgee2006@bellesouth.net; mcgeej@burnsscitech.org

Nienke M. Moolenaar, PhD, is a postdoctoral researcher at the Department of Educational Sciences at the University of Twente, Enschede, The Netherlands. Her research interests include social capital theory, social network analysis, school leadership, and organizational behaviour. Her chapter in this book is based on her PhD dissertation which she defended (cum laude) in 2010. n.m.moolenaar@utwente.nl

Frans J. Oort, PhD, is full professor of Methods and Statistics in Educational Research, director of the Graduate School of Child Development and Education, and program director of the Research Master Educational Sciences, University of

Amsterdam, The Netherlands. His research interests include measurement and statistical modelling. f.j.oort@uva.nl

Marie-Christine Opdenakker, PhD, is associate professor of Educational Science at the GION Groningen Institute for Educational Research, University of Groningen, The Netherlands. Her research focuses on the effectiveness of teachers and schools on student outcomes. Teacher-student interaction in relation to the development of student motivation, self-regulation and achievement is one of her main interests as well as methodological issues concerning educational effectiveness research. m.c.j.l.opdenakker@rug.nl

Heather E. Price is a PhD candidate at the University of Notre Dame, Indiana, USA, with an appointment in the Center for Research on Educational Opportunity in the Sociology Department. Her dissertation investigates the influence of school networks on school community and school effectiveness. Her research interests include sociology of education, urban and community sociology, statistics and methods, and educational policy. hprice@nd.edu

Paul W. Richardson, PhD, is an associate professor in the Faculty of Education, Monash University, Melbourne, Australia. He has held faculty positions at the University of Sydney, Gippsland Institute of Advanced Education, the University of Michigan, and Monash University. His research interests include teacher motivation, teacher education, teacher socialisation and professional development; as well as the interface between literacy practices and identity among youth and emerging adults. paul.richardson@monash.edu

Philip Riley, PhD, researches the overlapping space of psychology, education and leadership at Monash University, Melbourne, Australia. After a long career in schools, he previously served at La Trobe University. His work focuses on relationship formation and maintenance, principal development, health and wellbeing and classroom management through the application of attachment theory. philip.riley@monash.edu

Debora L. Roorda, MSc, is a PhD candidate at the Research Institute of Child Development and Education, University of Amsterdam, The Netherlands. Her research interests focus on teacher-student interactions and their influence on children's emotional well-being, school engagement, and achievement. d.l.roorda@uva.nl

Dennis Rosemartin is a PhD candidate in the Department of Teaching, Learning, and Sociocultural Studies in the College of Education at The University of Arizona, Tucson, USA. His area of specialization is teacher preparation and environmental education. His interests include curriculum theory, assessment practices, and the institutionalization of environmental education in pre-service teacher preparation programs. derosemar@email.arizona.edu

Peter J. C. Sleegers, PhD, is professor of Educational Organization and Management at the University of Twente, Enschede, The Netherlands. He has published extensively on leadership, innovation, and educational policy in more than forty refereed journal articles and several edited books. Current research projects include studies on the effects of educational leadership on student motivation for school, longitudinal research on the sustainability of reforms, and design studies of professional learning communities. p.j.c.sleegers@utwente.nl

Jantine L. Spilt, PhD, is a postdoc research fellow at the Department of Developmental Psychology, Free University Amsterdam, The Netherlands. Her research interests address socioemotional and behavioural development in the context of interpersonal relationships including teacher-student relationships. jl.spilt@psy.vu.nl

Jan van Tartwijk, PhD, is a full professor of education at the Faculty of Social and Behavioural Sciences, Utrecht University, The Netherlands. In his research he focuses on teacher-students communication and classroom management, but he is involved in research on other educational topics as well, including coaching and assessment in teacher and medical education, and the development of teacher knowledge over the course of a teaching career. j.vantartwijk@uu.nl

Sibel Telli, PhD, is a post-doc researcher at the DFG-Graduate School Processes in Education at Koblenz-Landau University in Landau, Germany. Her research interest is classroom learning environments, in particular teacher-student interpersonal behaviour as part of these environments. telli@uni-landau.de

Isabell van Ackeren, PhD, is a professor of Educational Sciences at the University of Duisburg-Essen, Germany, and a member of the research group Teaching and Learning of Science. Her main research interest lies in school effectiveness and school improvement research, education systems and policies and comparative education. isabell.van-ackeren@uni-due.de

Helen M.G. Watt, PhD, is associate professor at Monash University, Melbourne, Australia. She previously served on Faculties of the University of Michigan,

University of Western Sydney, University of Sydney, and Macquarie University. Her research has received several national and international awards; her interests include motivation, educational and occupational choices, teacher motivations and self-efficacy development, and research methodology. helen.watt@monash.edu

Kathryn R. Wentzel, PhD, is a professor in the Department of Human Development at the University of Maryland, College Park, USA. Her research interests focus on parents, peers, and teachers as motivators of adolescents' classroom behaviour and academic accomplishments. wentzel@umd.edu

Theo Wubbels, PhD, is professor of Education, and Associate Dean of the Faculty of Social and Behavioural Sciences at Utrecht University, The Netherlands. His main research interests developed from the pedagogy of physics education, via problems and supervision of beginning teachers and teaching and learning in teacher education, to studies of learning environments and especially interpersonal relationships in education. t.wubbels@uu.nl

CPSIA information can be obtained at www.ICGtesting.com
Printed in the USA
BVOW011554270912

301556BV00003B/1/P